IN CONFLICT WITH THE LAW

IN CONFLICT WITH THE LAW

Women and the Canadian
Justice System

EDITED BY

ELLEN ADELBERG and CLAUDIA CURRIE

Press Gang Publishers
Vancouver

The Publisher gratefully acknowledges financial assistance from the Canada Council
and the Cultural Services Branch, Province of British Columbia.

Canadian Cataloguing in Publication Data

Main entry under title:
In conflict with the law

   Includes bibliographic references and index.
   ISBN 0-88974-054-2

   1. Female offenders—Canada. 2. Sex discrimination against women—Canada.
3. Sex discrimination in criminal justice administration—Canada. I. Adelberg, Ellen. II. Currie,
Claudia.
HV6046.I52 1993   364.3'74'0971   C93-091907-6

First Printing 1993
1 2 3 4 5   98 97 96 95 94 93

Edited for the press by Barbara Kuhne and Robin Van Heck
Text and cover design by Valerie Speidel
Printed on acid-free paper by Best Gagné Book Manufacturers Inc.
Printed and bound in Canada

Press Gang Publishers
101–225 East 17th Avenue
Vancouver, B.C. V5V 1A6
Canada

Acknowledgements

We remain indebted to the Canada Council and to the many friends and colleagues who assisted us in the completion of *Too Few to Count,* some chapters of which are reproduced herein. The preparation of this book was further assisted by the word processing expertise of Betty Brown and Sue Scott; the advice of Alison MacPhail, Kim Pate, Sharon McIvor, Margaret Shaw, and Patti MacDonald; and the ongoing support of Jim Davidson and Mark Jodoin. We are grateful for their help, and for the contributing authors' dedication to this project.

For all the women we have met

who have come into conflict

with the law

Contents

Introduction

Ellen Adelberg and Claudia Currie

The publication of *In Conflict with the Law: Women and the Canadian Justice System* offers us a chance to re-examine the issues we first explored in *Too Few to Count: Canadian Women in Conflict with the Law.* When *Too Few to Count* was published, the title reflected the stature we felt was accorded women offenders, both by government and correctional officials, and by most Canadian feminists. Six years later, there has been progress, but it has been largely at the level of policy discussions and in the consciousness of the feminist movement. Daily life for women in conflict with the law, and those at risk of committing offences, seems much the same as it did six years ago.

We believe it is important to document the changes that are occurring, insofar as they reflect a shifting political climate which may allow significant future improvements to the status of women in conflict with the law. Some of these developments are discussed in the new chapters in this volume by Ellen Adelberg and the Native Women's Association of Canada, Sheila Noonan, and Margaret Shaw. There have also been changes which, while forward-looking in appearance, have not successfully translated from policy into practice, as Frances Shaver's new chapter on prostitution documents. Our interest in editing this volume was also to provide the reader with the most recent data available regarding women's crimes and criminogenic conditions. The revised chapters by Holly Johnson and Karen Rodgers, and by Carol LaPrairie meet this end.

We published *Too Few to Count,* and now this volume, because we felt compelled to break the historic silence surrounding women offenders. As social workers a decade ago, while working with convicted women in the community and in Canada's only federal prison for women we witnessed events which left deep imprints on our hearts and minds. The wasted lives and intense pain and anger of those behind prison walls engendered in us a commitment to explore how and why this destructive system was sustained.

We were then both employed as halfway house directors for the Elizabeth Fry Society of Ottawa. In our work, we met dozens of female residents who had committed petty offences such as shoplifting, fraudulent cashing of welfare cheques, or selling small amounts of street drugs (usually as fronts for male marijuana or hashish dealers). Their crimes made us question the economic conditions and life circumstances that surrounded them. The significantly smaller number of women we met who were charged with or convicted of assault, or other forms of violence (which usually took place in abusive domestic situations), made us question the social conditions of women's lives that led to such events.

We entered the correctional system as professional "helpers," but quickly realized that far from needing help, our "clients" needed liberation—both economic and social—from a patriarchal system based on male dominance and male property rights. We also realized that as social workers with community-based social service agencies, we were cogs in the larger wheel of social control the state exercises to protect such rights. Because non-profit organizations are funded by provincial and federal departments of corrections, in essence we were paid by those departments to monitor and enforce sentences handed down to women in the justice system. No matter how good our intentions to help women surmount the system, we were restricted to acting as arms-length law enforcers by relying on the state for funding.

Most of the women we met were young and poor. Very few had finished high school, and still fewer had any training for the job market. However, as a result of coming into conflict with the law, their lives were laid open for inspection and judgement by various people in the justice system, and judges, correctional officials, and we ourselves expected these women to attain respectability by finding employment, paying off fines and debts, and, frequently, learning to be better mothers.

It became obvious that, despite our best intentions and those of women offenders, their chances of finding employment, furthering their education, or regaining custody of their children were virtually nil. Few jobs existed for unskilled, uneducated women, particularly those with criminal records. Those jobs that did exist, such as waitressing or office cleaning, paid poorly and demanded hours incompatible with other duties expected of mothers. Training and academic upgrading programs were scarce and provided such miserly living stipends that it was virtually impossible for anyone to survive financially while enrolled in a program. No amount of good will on our part made up for the appalling lack of resources for poor, uneducated women in this country.

Despite the existence of voluntary social service agencies and state-run probation and parole programs, women offenders' lives did not seem to improve after coming in contact with the criminal justice system. In fact, quite often just the opposite occurred. As a result of trauma experienced in the courtroom and in prison, trauma which often included loss of their children, many women we knew developed physical and mental ailments which compounded difficulties they already faced in the struggle to survive on low incomes. These problems continue to be encountered by women who come into conflict with the law.

It became clear to us that the vast majority of Canadians know little about the actual workings of the justice and correctional systems, and still less about women who enter that system as offenders. Media images of courtrooms, prisons, and criminal acts serve as the source of public knowledge about offenders. Particularly in the case of women, these images are hugely distorted from reality. As documented in Karlene Faith's chapter, women offenders tend to be uniformly portrayed in television shows and movies either as violent individuals and/or predatory lesbians. This book, as was the case with *Too Few to Count,* is intended to provide a more accurate portrayal of women's conflict with the law and their experiences in and outside of prison. It also provides an analysis of the possibilities for reducing women's conflict with the law by altering social institutions, and by reassessing the law itself in cases when it discriminates against women by failing to acknowledge gender-based differences.

In *Too Few To Count,* we commented on the dearth of Canadian writing pertaining to women in conflict with the law, while noting that British and American researchers had made significant contributions to the literature. Recent British contributions to our understanding of women in conflict with the law include Allison Morris's *Women, Crime and Criminal Justice* (1987); Loraine Gelsthorpe and Allison Morris's *Feminist Perspectives in Criminology* (1990); Anne Worrall's *Offending Women: Female Lawbreakers and the Criminal Justice System* (1990); and Carol Smart's *Feminism and the Power of Law* (1989). These texts have contributed substantially to the development of theoretical criminology as it pertains to women. British criminologist Pat Carlen has continued to analyze the practical application of academic concepts to women offenders' lives in *Alternatives to Women's Imprisonment* (1990).

In the United States, recent anthologies have contributed to our understanding of the particular context in that country for women's conflict with the law. Two valuable examples are Ralph Weisheit and Sue Mahan's *Women, Crime and Criminal Justice* (1988) and Jocelyne Pollock-Byrne's *Women, Prison and Crime* (1990).

While books pertaining to women offenders in other jurisdictions have continued to proliferate, only a few specialized topics have been the subject of Canadian publications.[1] Yet, as several of the contributors to this and the previous volume have pointed out, accurate and reliable information is essential to dispel the many myths pervading public understanding of women in conflict with the law. Both information about and analysis of the treatment of women offenders and its results are necessary if we are to improve upon our dismal record of incarceration and failed "rehabilitation" of women who come into conflict with the law.

Since 1987, the most significant research on Canadian women prisoners has been the work of the 1990 Task Force on Federally Sentenced Women.[2] Numerous studies were commissioned by this task force, which produced a wealth of original and comprehensive data. Members of the task force also critically reviewed the underlying philosophy and treatment of women offenders, and developed a feminist framework for new services designed for imprisoned women. Later in this book, Margaret Shaw discusses the problems this rather radical departure from current correctional practices has met during the implementation phase of the task force's recommendations. Whatever the fate of its recommendations, the task force's research reports have made an immense contribution to understanding who federally sentenced women are, their types of criminal behaviour generally, and their needs within the justice system.

In the broader context of Canadian life, since we wrote the introduction to *Too Few to Count,* feminists have continued to work steadily to advance women's place in society. That work began in a concentrated way more than twenty years ago. The publication of the Royal Commission on the Status of Women's report in 1970, with its agenda for action to attain equality for women, is an early landmark in the current period of feminist action.[3]

Throughout the past twenty-five years, feminist thinking about women's oppressed position in society and about ways to eliminate that oppression has evolved considerably. Many white, middle-class feminists began this period believing that women's liberation from patriarchal oppression could be achieved through equality measures such as equal pay for work of equal value, and the elimination of sexist legislation. But even when their efforts bore fruit, the subordinate position of many women, particularly those who were working-class, Aboriginal, or members of racial minority groups, failed to improve. The notion that all Canadian women face the same barriers has been tested and found largely wanting. In recent years, the context of women's lives—that is, the intersection of social, racial, economic, and political factors—has taken more prominence in feminist analysis.[4]

The liberal notion that equality with men in the workplace would be enough to eliminate women's oppression has also proved inadequate. Even those women who have benefited from provisions such as equal pay for work of equal value usually find themselves carrying a disproportionate share of family responsibilities. Most realize that their personal relationships with men are still based on inequality. To counter this oppression, feminists are moving from goals of equality to equity, wherein gender neutrality is replaced with gender sensitivity.[5]

Feminist thinking about ways to improve the lot of women in conflict with the law reflected the move from a notion of equality in the 1970s to that of equity in the late 1980s. In *Too Few to Count,* Lorraine Berzins and Brigid Hayes described the problems they encountered in 1980 when they attempted, as members of a group called "Women for Justice," to obtain equality for federal women offenders. In a move that seemed bold (even though Hayes noted that members were not convinced it would lead to fundamental change in the treatment of female offenders), the group launched a complaint with the Canadian Human Rights Commission.

Hayes described the problems the group faced when asked to substantiate its claims:

> Counting became the name of the game—counting programs, counting institutional options, counting employment opportunities. We recoiled at this process, because none of us believed that the system for male inmates was an ideal to be achieved. The process began to smack of equality meaning sameness, not equal value—in the sense of developing equally useful programs for women in prison which would likely be different from those available to men.[6]

When the Commission came down with a ruling that upheld nine of the group's eleven charges of discriminatory treatment of female offenders, Hayes described the group's reaction:

> We were jubilant!...
>
> Our enthusiasm waned considerably, however, when we entered into the conciliation process that the Commission had ordered....
>
> The CSC [Correctional Service of Canada] conducted interviews with every inmate asking for her needs in education, vocational and counselling programs, but there was little follow-up.... And to bring things into line with the men, the women were told to remove personal possessions from the walls.[7]

Learning from the bitter experience of Women for Justice in their quest for equality with men, members of the Task Force on Federally Sentenced Women made it explicit in their 1990 report that they were using a "woman-centred approach" to analyze the needs of federal female prisoners. In order to accept the report's recommendations, it was necessary to accept the notion that women experienced specific social realities in their lives and meeting their needs was dependent upon understanding and working within those realities.

The publication of this task force report was perhaps the most significant event to occur at the policy level in recent years in regard to women in conflict with the law. Indeed, the very nature of the task force was groundbreaking, with its members' philosophy of developing consensus, and respecting the input of women prisoners, including—but acknowledging their uniqueness—Aboriginal women. The ripples from the task force's work are already being felt in some provinces, where provincial correctional authorities have either commissioned reviews of women's prison facilities under their jurisdiction, or have at least determined that they need to know more about women who come into conflict with the law.[8]

But the task force report was also in keeping with at least a dozen previous reports in its recommendation that the federal Prison for Women in Kingston be closed. Why, then, did only this one lead to a formal government announcement that the prison would indeed close in 1994? Clearly feminists' cumulative efforts for social change was one key factor. While the federal task force members were busy researching and writing their report, another group of influential women were engaged in courtroom struggles to give women's lived realities a voice. The Legal Education and Action Fund (LEAF), a feminist litigation fund created to introduce or intervene in test cases on behalf of women under the Charter of Rights and Freedoms, began working soon after the Charter's equality provisions became law in 1985.[9]

Although the use of human rights concepts and laws carries with it the danger of pitting one individual's or group's rights against another's, it does carry some possibility of advancing women's position. As Sherene Razack eloquently argues in *Canadian Feminism and the Law,* at the very least using rights language enables women to talk to men in a language they understand.[10] Razack's analysis of LEAF's early documents led her to conclude that "they told a story of women stretching rights language to almost unrecognizable lengths in order to introduce into a court of law some of their realities as an oppressed group."[11] Supreme Court decisions on issues related to women's and other groups' rights are often covered prominently by the national news media, reflecting and feeding the respect granted to the courts by our (mainly male) members of government and by the general public. As a tactic to pressure the government for institutional change, arguments made to Canada's highest court are doubtlessly of value. In its final report, the Task Force on Federally Sentenced Women cited the existence of Charter challenges to the federal treatment of female prisoners as one of the important factors in the "broader environment" supporting a change in programs and policies.[12]

Two of LEAF's early cases concerned women in conflict with the law. One was on behalf of inmates serving sentences in the federal Prison for Women, and the other concerned women in Ontario collecting social assistance who were charged with fraud if they were found to be living with a man. The Ontario social assistance regulations were amended before LEAF's case reached the courts (after years of sustained lobbying by anti-poverty and women's groups for its repeal). In the case concerning federal female inmates, LEAF was about to file a statement of claim with the court when the federal government announced that it would implement the rec-ommendations of the task force. LEAF's case was based on the assertion that practices by the Correctional Service of Canada violated women's guaranteed equality rights "[in part] by the failure of the system to provide equal means for women to serve their sentences within a reasonable dis-tance from their homes; to provide equal parole opportunities; to provide equal programming, and to provide equal quality and standards of facili-ties both in comparison to men and in comparison to federally sentenced women serving their sentences in another institution."[13] LEAF's prepara-tion of its case served as notice to the Government of Canada that its treat-ment of female offenders was not only considered inadequate by prisoners' advocates, but might also be found to be unconstitutional.[14]

Another significant factor that led to both the creation of the task force and the decision to close the Prison for Women was the 1988 appointment of Ole Ingstrup as the new Commissioner of the Correctional Service of Canada. The authors of the task force report stated that:

> After his appointment, one of Commissioner Ingstrup's first actions was to call for a rethinking of the Mission of the Correctional Service of Canada.
>
> One of the objectives of the new Mission is to ensure that the needs of fed-erally sentenced women are met. Achievement of this objective is to be built on the broader statements of principle in the Mission Document, namely:
>
> • that the obligation of the Correctional Service of Canada to treat offenders hu-manely goes beyond the legal obligation to ensure their physical needs are met;
>
> • that it is, therefore, essential that every effort be made to respect the spirit of the Charter of Rights and Freedoms;
>
> • that the Correctional Service of Canada must recognize its responsibility for providing the best possible correctional services; and
>
> • that the primary goal of the Correctional Service of Canada is the reintegra-tion of offenders.
>
> These general principles combined with the overall objective to meet the needs of federally sentenced women have contributed to an internal commit-ment to change, based on the concern of the Correctional Service of Canada

that the current programming and accommodation of federally sentenced women are largely inconsistent with these principles.[15]

For those of us who had worked with women in the federal correctional system before Ingstrup's appointment, this sort of commitment from the commissioner represented a radical departure from that of his predecessors—who generally dismissed female offenders as insignificant or beyond rehabilitation. As an illustration, in *Too Few to Count,* Lorraine Berzins recounted her experience as a social worker at the Prison for Women in 1970–1971:

> To the rest of the system and to the community, the female offender was a low priority: those two hundred women were no trouble compared to the ten thousand men serving prison sentences.... It seemed no one cared if we were effective, as long as we kept the lid on.[16]

Berzins wrote of her later experiences in the heart of the federal bureaucracy in Ottawa as the national co-ordinator of female inmate programs (1976–1979):

> When we produced a review of existing programs which did not meet the commissioner of corrections' approval, it was banned from distribution....
>
> Our participation in decision-making was gradually eroded, our contact with senior federal and provincial officials was virtually eliminated and our roles were reduced to an advisory capacity. Underlying all of this was the fact ... that the commissioner of corrections had no interest in seeing any major changes in the treatment of female offenders.[17]

Berzins and her colleague, Sheelagh Cooper, were dismissed by the same commissioner in 1979 for conduct that he had deemed "emotional, irrational and therefore unprofessional."[18] They had written a memo criticizing an outside consultant's report to re-organize female offender programs. Three years later, faced with demands for change in the Prison for Women due to the successful Canadian Human Rights Commission complaint ruling obtained by Women for Justice in 1982, the same commissioner who had fired Berzins and Cooper stated:

> In my view, no one has ever been able to identify anything that some of the

women [at P4W] are in any way interested in doing.... But when you look back over their life history, there's a limit to what we can do and what can be expected of CSC with regards to this residual group. That's 250 women in all of Canada: now to me that's not a very large number.[19]

However, while Ingstrup was far more progressive than his predecessor in his views of women and the role of correctional programs, his tenure as the commissioner of correctional services was brief. In 1992, four years after his appointment, Ingstrup left for another federal post. At the time of writing this introduction, a new permanent commissioner has not been named. In the meantime, as Shaw demonstrates in her chapter on the task force report and consequent action, there appears to be a reluctance on the part of the bureaucracy to translate the report's program recommendations into the actions envisioned by task force members.

For Aboriginal women in conflict with the law, at the very least the past six years have seen a rise in awareness of their particular plight within prison, and a much greater articulation of their needs as distinct from those of non-native women. The inclusion of Aboriginal women on the Task Force on Federally Sentenced Women did much to promote their agenda. From the start of the process, Aboriginal women made it clear that they wanted a significant number of representatives on the Task Force, and room within the report to present and analyze their own conditions and needs for improved treatment. The final product reflects the benefits of those early demands.

> No previous task force nor royal commission on Corrections, whether it was focused on Aboriginal Peoples, women, or prisons generally, has ever recognized the unique position of Aboriginal women. The Aboriginal voice has been relegated to a few pages of these previous reports or to several recommendations which were disconnected philosophically from the thrust of those works.... Heading into the 1990's, we find that this report has not only acknowledged our voice and our experience but, this report respects our historical and founding position as the Original Peoples of Canada. It is our voice that helps to lead this new vision for women in corrections. The Aboriginal women who helped in this report are celebrating because this is a first.... We trust that the message of Aboriginal women is now clear.[20]

In this book, the chapter compiled by Ellen Adelberg and the Native

Women's Association of Canada (NWAC) on Aboriginal women's experience within the federal prison system reveals that at the moment, Aboriginal women stand the best hope of seeing their recommendations from the Task Force on Federally Sentenced Women implemented, because, unlike non-Aboriginal women, they have (at least for now) retained control over the implementation process. No doubt, the larger political gains made by Aboriginal people in the 1992 constitutional discussions, and the federal government's stated commitment to self-government for Aboriginal peoples, have helped Aboriginal women in conflict with the law gain a credibility that was heretofore denied. Sadly, so too have the relentless stories of tragedies on numerous Indian reserves, where young people are killing themselves, and life is being eked out without running water, sewage treatment, adequate housing, or meaningful employment.

So too has the recognition by NWAC that advocacy on behalf of Aboriginal women in conflict with the law is an important activity for the organization. Seven years ago, we were told by NWAC members that they did not view the plight of Aboriginal women in prison as a priority, in view of the massive problems Aboriginal women were facing outside of prison. Their thinking has changed, as reflected by the active role of NWAC members on the federal task force, as advocates for individual women serving sentences, and as leaders in developing the new healing lodge which will house Aboriginal women when the Kingston Prison for Women closes.

In the first section of this book—Federal Imprisonment of Women: Past, Present and Future—Sheelagh Cooper traces the imprisonment of women serving federal sentences since the time incarceration was first used to punish women in Canada. Cooper demonstrates that treatment of federal female prisoners has consisted of a "fascinating mixture of neglect, outright barbarism and well-meaning paternalism," not unlike the history of women's treatment in society at large. According to Cooper, women prisoners as a group were thrown only the crumbs by the predominantly male correctional establishment. This was particularly true with respect to the facilities used for their incarceration. Cooper reveals that the policy of centralized imprisonment for women was ill-advised from its inception sixty-five years ago, but was maintained for bureaucratic reasons, at an exorbitant cost to both the prisoners and the federal government. In providing this base, Cooper lays the foundation for Margaret Shaw's analysis, which follows, of the results of the most recent task force reviewing services for federal female offenders.

As indicated earlier, the Task Force on Federally Sentenced Women released its report in 1990. Unsparingly feminist and condemning in tone, the report demanded a complete overhaul of the treatment of federally sentenced women. In "Reforming Federal Women's Imprisonment," Margaret Shaw outlines the report's recommendations and provides an account of their implementation. By examining the many forces at work in the transformation of services to federally sentenced women, she demonstrates how a creative vision for change can be distorted in the implementation process.

Material prepared by Aboriginal women for the Task Force on Federally Sentenced Women, as well as information about the implementation of the task force's recommendation for a healing lodge for Aboriginal women convicted of offences, is presented in the next chapter, by Ellen Adelberg and the Native Women's Association of Canada. The survey of Aboriginal women commissioned for the task force and carried out by the Native Women's Association of Canada eloquently testifies to the need for a radical rethinking of the role of the justice system in the Aboriginal community.

In the book's second section—Images and Realities: Profiles of Women Offenders—Holly Johnson and Karen Rodgers document that women are charged largely with petty property offences, and comprise fewer than 20 percent of all offenders. Their chapter, "A Statistical Overview of Women and Crime in Canada," presents demographic data that suggest a link between Canadian women's crimes and their generally inferior economic and social position compared to men. Johnson and Rodgers provide as complete a statistical picture of women offenders as possible, given the large gaps in data collection in this area.

Their discussion of the data raises a multitude of questions about women in conflict with the law, some of which are addressed by other contributors. The statistics showing a disproportionately high rate of certain offences by Aboriginal women are addressed by Carol LaPrairie. Sheila Noonan's chapter tells the story behind women's homicide statistics, and points to the circumstances that give rise to these offences.

Without hearing first-hand the voices of women offenders, the theory, data, and history of women in conflict with the law seems less than real. For the chapter that follows Johnson and Rodgers', we interviewed seven women convicted of serious offences and they told us their stories. The women's perceptions concerning significant events in their lives, as well as the larger factors related to the tragedies they experienced and the crimes they committed, are discussed. The women's experiences bring to life the statistics Johnson and Rodgers present, and their stories reveal some of the most brutal examples of the condition of women under patriarchy. Their experiences of physical and sexual assault, child abuse, and powerlessness within the family and the economy are common to many women in Canada. Our view is that there is a strong link between those traumas and the crimes these women committed. For the most part, it is difficult to imagine their offences occurring in a society characterized by economic and sexual equality.

Frances Shaver's chapter then forces us to question the common perception of prostitution as a crime, and as a predominantly female crime. Her data illustrate that although women more often than men are prosecuted for prostitution-related offences, the participation of males (especially once "johns" or clients are counted) may far exceed that of females. Based on data she has collected or reviewed in Canadian and American cities, she suggests that the public image of female prostitutes as young, single, uneducated, poor, and addicted may be inaccurate. She points out that the public generally assumes all prostitutes work on street corners, but in fact a great deal of work in the sex trade is carried out in private. Shaver outlines the sexist character of law enforcement practices related to prostitution offences and also explains the limitations of existing theoretical approaches to understanding prostitution.

In the final chapter in this section, Karlene Faith analyzes the messages behind popular media portrayals of women in prison. She explains how these depictions have generated public misconceptions about female offenders, and how they serve to maintain stereotypic images of criminal women as lesbian, and somehow, by association, masculine and violent.

In the third section of the book—Theoretical Considerations about Women in Conflict with the Law—Shelley Gavigan points out that until fairly recently, criminological theory has portrayed women offenders as deviators from their socially-defined feminine and sexual roles. Gavigan first discredits these traditional theories, then examines the work of a number of theorists who maintain that "women's liberation" is responsible for growing female crime rates. She suggests that these rates may be due instead to a more punitive attitude towards women on the part of those who feel threatened by the women's movement.

Gavigan argues that feminist theory in criminology, which tries to redress the mistakes of earlier approaches, must begin to incorporate historical, economic, and social factors relevant to the subordinate position of women in society in order to fully understand women's relationship to the criminal justice system. The implications of theory are not restricted to the academic world; many sexist views found in the theoretical treatment are replicated in correctional practices. Sheelagh Cooper's exploration of the discriminatory treatment of women in prison earlier in the book testifies to the accuracy of Gavigan's point.

In the following chapter, Carol LaPrairie explores the historical and material conditions which lead to the overrepresentation of Aboriginal women in the criminal justice system. LaPrairie examines the link between the oppression of Aboriginal people by white colonizers and the consequent breakdown of the Aboriginal family structure. She argues that Aboriginal men who have lost traditional roles in this process act out their frustration by turning on themselves, and on women and children in their families. Aboriginal women who attempt to escape this abuse by moving to large urban centres become particularly vulnerable to crime and arrest, due to their lack of job skills and consequent poverty and visibility. Those who commit crimes of violence, she suggests, are often retaliating against men who have violated them.

In the book's final chapter, Sheila Noonan provides an insightful review of the legal position of women who have killed abusive partners. As a lawyer, she is working with the Canadian Association of Elizabeth Fry Societies for the release of women currently incarcerated for these offences. In her chapter, she explores the development of Canadian law regarding permissible defences for killing abusive partners, and assesses strategies that could be employed to secure the release of women who are already imprisoned.

Drawing on recent studies as well as on interviews with sentenced women, Noonan sheds light on the circumstances in which these killings occur, and demonstrates the inequities in case law and sentencing. While many see judicial acceptance of the battered woman syndrome as significant progress for women who have killed a partner as an act of survival, Noonan explains the limitations of using the battered woman syndrome as a defence in court. She argues that further changes in the law are required to appropriately and successfully defend these women.

A theme running throughout the book is how discrimination against women is manifested in our society, from theoretical myth-making to double standards in law enforcement, from violence in the home and community to institutional abuses. Any potential for change in the status and treatment of women in conflict with the law must be viewed within the context of other currents of change that are taking place in Canadian society.

Two years after *Too Few to Count* was published, fourteen women were gunned down by a man in the engineering department of the École Polytechnique in Montreal. In his suicide note, the killer attributed his action to his hatred for "feminists," whom he blamed for ruining his life. The event seared into the Canadian psyche the horrific cost to women of male violence. Within a year, the Canadian government held special hearings on the issue of male violence against women, and following recommendations of numerous women's groups, established the Canadian Panel on Violence. The panel's mandate was to research the depth of the problem, and propose a blueprint for action leading to "zero tolerance of male violence against women." Members of the panel are expected to submit their report in 1993.

Although feminists had been conducting research on male violence against women for at least ten years before the Montreal massacre, the issue was given a far greater public profile than ever before by this single event and women's efforts afterwards to ensure that Canadians would never forget the price paid by the young women at the École Polytechnique. Now, each year on December 6, the anniversary of the massacre, memorial events are held across the country by women, and by men who have started the White Ribbon Campaign against male violence.

At the same time, the larger issue of community safety, not just for women but for children too, in the face of a seemingly endless string of horrific incidents mirroring television dramas, has taken up reams of newsprint in the past few years.[21] In February 1993, the federal government's Standing Committee on Justice and the Solicitor General issued a report on crime prevention in Canada with recommendations for a national strategy.

After committee members heard from more than one hundred witnesses across the country, they wrote a report stressing the failure of the conventional crime control model to "address the underlying factors associated with crime and criminality."[22] The report argued strongly that "our collective response to crime must shift to crime prevention efforts that reduce opportunities for crime and focus increasingly on at-risk young people and on the underlying social and economic factors associated with crime and criminality."[23] It quoted Henry David Thoreau: "There are a thousand hacking at the branches of evil to one who is striking at the roots."

In the report, the links between violence against women and children, and the later criminality of both men and women, were made clear. Carol Hutchings of the Elizabeth Fry Society of Edmonton was cited:

> The progression we see over and over again is sexual abuse, truancy, running away from home, prostitution, drug abuse, and criminal behaviour. The first year I worked with the Elizabeth Fry Society 17 of our clients died. Fourteen of those clients were aboriginal and all were victims of early childhood sexual abuse.[24]

The report also quoted Hugh Baker, of the Native Courtworker and Counselling Association of British Columbia, who "cautioned the committee that any attempt to reduce crime and violence in aboriginal communities will not succeed unless the social and economic deprivation suffered by native people is addressed."

> Crime is greater in the aboriginal community because pimps come to the aboriginal community knowing there are women who are desperate to earn an income. Drug dealers come to the aboriginal community knowing there are people who are desperate to escape, even if only mentally. People come to the aboriginal community knowing there are going to be people who are intoxicated who they can take advantage of, either by beating them or robbing them. People come to the aboriginal community trying to start youth gangs because they know the youth have no future ... and the gang can offer them something better than what they have.[25]

The committee was impressed by a cost-benefit analysis of a Michigan early childhood program developed in 1962 to increase poor children's chances of successful completion of high school and attaining employment. The cost-benefit analysis by the General Accounting Office of the United States Congress showed that for every dollar invested in the one-year program, there was a return of five dollars. The figure was based on the finding that the pre-school participants absorbed fewer public resources because they were more likely than those in a control group to have completed high school and be employed as adults, and less likely to commit criminal offences.[26] Following the release of the Justice Committee's report, Progressive Conservative Robert Horner, who chaired the committee, said:

> Listen, if anybody had told me nine years ago that I'd be studying the social causes of crime, I would have said they were nuts. I'm an ex-member of the RCMP [Royal Canadian Mounted Police] and I'm strictly for law and order. But I can tell you that we can't just continue to build more jails and spend more money on police budgets and have crime increasing the way it is.[27]

The mood of the report, with its suggestion that conventional thinking about law and order simply cannot cope with the current trends towards more crime, and more violent crime, reflects a much larger societal shift. Throughout the 1980s in North America, the ideology prevailed that neo-conservatism would bring about peace, stability, and economic growth. But a deep and prolonged recession in Canada and the United States in the late 1980s, which shows only small signs of lessening in 1993, has caused thinkers, even those who are neo-conservative, to have doubts. Americans went to the polls in November 1992 and ushered in Democrat Bill Clinton, who campaigned on promises of rebuilding America's social infrastructure to meet the needs of the "new world order."

In Canada, where the Progressive Conservatives held power federally from 1984 to 1993, politicians are ever mindful of American public opinion trends, which invariably wend their way north. There is presently talk and some action based on a stated need to reform Canada's fundamental social programs (such as welfare, socialized medical care, and unemployment insurance), which have been in place in large measure throughout the period after World War II. In a paper presented in 1992 to the Organization for Economic Co-operation and Development, Canada's Health and Welfare minister cited his government's concern about Canada's rising national debt and the failure of current social programs to break welfare dependency, or to educate citizens for new jobs requiring greater skills.[28] Unstated in the paper, but underlying it, is the position that social programs are too expensive so the government wants to cut their costs.

During their time in power, the Progressive Conservatives made the reduction of the national deficit a priority, and they significantly cut spending on social programs. In 1992 they abandoned a commitment made in the mid-1980s to a national child care program, and they pledged tough measures for offenders, designed to make Canada's communities safer. The Standing Committee reported that Canada spent $7.7 billion maintaining the criminal justice system in 1989; almost $1 billion was spent on the Correctional Service of Canada for prisons, guards, and parole programs.[29] Yet, the committee's report showed that spending on law and order has not yielded any benefits. Perhaps the biggest challenge now for women in conflict with the law, and those advocating on their behalf, is to show how, dollar for dollar, money spent on preventative programs for children, and educational programs for women with minimal job skills, or counselling for women haunted by past violence in their lives, is in fact Canada's best hope for ultimately reducing the costs of female crime.

It is within this larger context that work to improve the lot of Canadian women in conflict with the law will take place in the next few years.

Ellen Adelberg and Claudia Currie
July 1993

Notes

1 See for example Laurie Bell, *Good Girls/Bad Girls: Sex Trade Workers and Feminists Face to Face* (Toronto: Women's Press, 1987); Anne Kershaw and Mary Lasovich, *Rock-A-Bye Baby: A Death Behind Bars* (Toronto: McClelland and Stewart, 1991); and Marlene Webber, *Street Kids: The Tragedy of Canada's Runaways* (Toronto, University of Toronto Press, 1991). We look forward to an exception to such specialization to be released later in 1993 by Press Gang Publishers, Karlene Faith's *Unruly Women: The Politics of Confinement and Resistance.*

2 The reports generated by this Task Force include: *Creating Choices: The Report of the Task Force on Federally Sentenced Women* (Ottawa: Correctional Service of Canada, 1990); Lee Axon, *Model and Exemplary Programs for Female Inmates: An International Review* (Ottawa: Correctional Service of Canada, 1989); Jan Heney, *Report on Self-Injurious Behaviour in the Kingston Prison for Women* (Ottawa: Correctional Service of Canada, 1990); Margaret Shaw, *The Federal Female Offender: Report on a Preliminary Study* (Ottawa: Correctional Service of Canada, 1990); Margaret Shaw et al., *The Release Study: Survey of Federally Sentenced Women in the Community* (Ottawa: Correctional Service

of Canada, 1990); Margaret Shaw et al., *Paying the Price: Federally Sentenced Women in Context* (Ottawa: Correctional Service of Canada, 1991); Margaret Shaw et al., *Survey of Federally Sentenced Women* (Ottawa: Correctional Service of Canada, 1990); Fran Sugar and Lana Fox, *Survey of Federally Sentenced Aboriginal Women in the Community* (Ottawa: Native Women's Association of Canada, 1990).

3 Canada, *Report of the Royal Commission on the Status of Women* (Ottawa: Supply and Services, 1970).

4 See for example Sherene Razack, *Canadian Feminism and the Law* (Toronto: Second Story Press, 1991), particularly pp. 18–26.

5 See for example Canadian Advisory Council on the Status of Women, *Evaluating Child Support Policy: A Brief to the Federal/Provincial/Territorial Family Law Committee* (Ottawa: 8 December 1992). The Council explains in this brief how seemingly gender neutral language and values in fact discriminate against women. Therefore, to effect positive change, new policies and laws must use language that acknowledges the imbalance between women and men, and aims to redress it.

6 Brigid Hayes in L. Berzins and B. Hayes, "The Diaries of Two Change Agents," in *Too Few to Count: Canadian Women in Conflict with the Law,* ed. Ellen Adelberg and Claudia Currie (Vancouver: Press Gang Publishers, 1987), p. 172.

7 Ibid., p. 173.

8 In a Nova Scotia study of incarcerated women, the authors stated, "The report of the Task Force provided us with a model for research, and a wider context for the study we undertook, as well as the inspiration to seek the truth. We adopted many of the Task Force's principles and methods, and found our work made easier by these pioneers in systemic change." In *Blueprint for Change: Report of the Solicitor General's Special Committee on Provincially Incarcerated Women* (Halifax: Province of Nova Scotia, 1992), p. ii.

9 See Razack, *Canadian Feminism and the Law,* for an insightful review of the possibilities and limitations of LEAF's court interventions.

10 Ibid., p. 50.

11 Ibid., p. 12.

12 Task Force on Federally Sentenced Women, *Creating Choices,* p. 80.

13 Ibid., p. 82.

14 Helena Orton, LEAF litigation director, stated that the Solicitor General's department was well aware of LEAF's preparation of its case regarding women held in the Kingston Prison for Women. Orton believed that LEAF had strong

grounds to argue that women's incarceration at the prison was in contravention to the equality provisions in the Canadian Charter of Rights and Freedoms. Interview with Ellen Adelberg, 29 June 1993.

15 Task Force on Federally Sentenced Women, *Creating Choices*, p. 83.

16 Berzins, in Berzins and Hayes, "The Diaries of Two Change Agents," p. 166.

17 Ibid., p. 168.

18 Ibid., p. 169.

19 Hayes, in Berzins and Hayes, "The Diaries of Two Change Agents," p. 176.

20 Task Force on Federally Sentenced Women, *Creating Choices*, p. 23.

21 The horrific killings in Ontario of Christine Jessop in 1986, and Kristin French and Nina De Villiers in 1991, and the alleged murder of a two-year-old boy by two ten-year-olds in Britain in 1993, are examples of violent crimes against children that have received extensive media coverage.

22 Standing Committee on Justice and the Solicitor General, *Twelfth Report. Crime Prevention in Canada: Toward a National Strategy* (Ottawa: House of Commons, Issue no. 87, 23 February 1993), p. 1.

23 Ibid., p. 2.

24 Ibid., p. 10.

25 Ibid., p. 11.

26 Barry McKillop and Michelle Clarke, *Safer Tomorrow Begins Today* (Ottawa: Canadian Council on Children and Youth, 1989), p. 5.

27 "Justice Committee Targets Poverty," *Globe and Mail*, 27 February 1993.

28 Organization for Economic Co-operation and Development, *Canadian Paper on New Orientations For Social Policy* (Paris, France: OECD, December 1992).

29 Standing Committee on Justice and the Solicitor General, *Twelfth Report*, p. 5.

I

FEDERAL IMPRISONMENT OF WOMEN:

PAST, PRESENT AND FUTURE

The Evolution of the Federal Women's Prison†

Sheelagh Cooper

A look at the treatment and punishment of the female offender in Canada since the earliest days reveals a fascinating mixture of neglect, outright barbarism, and well-meaning paternalism. Because of their small numbers and the insignificance attached to their crimes, women offenders have been housed wherever and in whatever manner suited the needs of the larger male offender population.

Early attempts to understand the female criminal generated a range of theories to explain an apparently bizarre kind of deviation from the socially defined female role.[1] The criminological literature, the perceptions of correctional administrators, and general public opinion have reflected a series of contradictory images and myths over the years. Early socio-biological theories of women's criminality, when coupled with the prevailing protectionist public attitude towards women, clashed sharply with the predominantly punitive correctional practices geared to the male majority. The female offender has been portrayed as "poor and unfortunate" on the one hand, and "lazy and worthless" on the other. She needs protection, yet can be a very destructive and scheming temptress. She has been said to require

† This chapter is reprinted with minor changes from *Too Few to Count: Canadian Women in Conflict with the Law*, ed. Ellen Adelberg and Claudia Currie (Vancouver: Press Gang Publishers, 1987).

special and more delicate care, and yet she has also been considered far more difficult to confine than her male counterparts.[2]

The 1981 ruling by the Canadian Human Rights Commission that found the Correctional Service of Canada guilty of discriminating against women offenders was a turning point in a long history of bureaucratic decision-making based on factors that had more to do with political expediency than with the welfare of the women in their charge. This historical review explores the evolution of this kind of practice and describes the way women have been imprisoned. As well, it provides an account of the controversy surrounding the unsuccessful attempts that spanned over fifty years to close Canada's only federal penitentiary for women, a period which ended with the Solicitor General's 1991 announcement that the prison would close in 1994. This chapter illustrates the forces that have neutralized each other so that until recently, little which has been recommended in the best interests of the female offender has ever been implemented.

The Early Years of Punishment (1640–1912)

The first person to be officially condemned to death in Canada, in 1640, was female. She was a sixteen-year-old French girl convicted of theft. A male criminal being tried at the same time escaped death by acting as her executioner.[3] From that time on, the death penalty was regularly invoked for theft and burglary. By 1810, there were over 100 more offences punishable in Canada by execution.

Corporal punishment, in its various forms, provided the only alternative to the death penalty. For example, in the Eastern Township District of Upper Canada on 24 April 1800, the sentence given the offender Mary Myers was that "you be taken from the place of confinement to the place of punishment and be stript and then tied to a post fixed for that purpose, and that you may be then and there whipped with small rods until your body be bloody."[4] The nature of the charge against Mary Myers is unclear. However, it is reported in the records of the Assize Court in the District of York in Upper Canada in 1804, that Elizabeth Ellis, for "being a nuisance," was pilloried opposite the market house for two hours on two different days.[5] The pillory consisted of a wooden frame into which the ankles and wrists (and sometimes the neck) were imprisoned and held fast for a stated period of time, usually from sun-up to sun-down. It was positioned in the marketplace where anyone with a sadistic turn of character could add to the punishment by spitting, jeering, or pelting the offender with rotten vegetables or eggs (stones were not permitted). The hangman supervised the carrying out of such sentences along with his other punitive duties.

These forms of punishment were gradually replaced by periods of imprisonment in the early part of the nineteenth century. Penitentiaries began to be used in order to reform criminals through seclusion and penitence.[6] After the building of the penitentiary for men in Kingston in 1835, the first two women were sentenced to periods of imprisonment there. Mary Ingram from the Home District (Toronto) was sentenced to one year on a charge of accessory to larceny, and Mary Anne Lane arrived from Midland later in the year to serve a one-year term for grand larceny.[7] These women were kept closely confined in a small temporary location directly above the mess table of the male convicts. In 1836, John McCauley, President of the Penitentiary Board of Inspectors, noted that

It is to be observed that the sentencing of females to the penitentiary causes some inconvenience … and though their labour as seamstresses can always be turned to good account, they cannot be effectually subjected to the peculiar discipline of the prison until the separate place of confinement suggested for them by the plans and report of the recent Commissioner shall have been prepared for their reception.[8]

It was clear from the beginning that, because of their small numbers, women would be confined wherever and in whatever manner best served the administration of the larger male population. McCauley's quote also refers to the primary task of women prisoners in those early days, which was to make and mend the bedding and clothing of the male inmates.

Public concern during the early years of the Provincial Penitentiary at Kingston centred around the brutal treatment of the women and children confined there. The public perception of women and children as victims of a system designed for and appropriate only for men runs through the nineteenth century. Yet women in prison were often considered by correctional administrators to be far more difficult to manage than men, as revealed by one of the first wardens of the Kingston Penitentiary: "A few of the worst of the female convicts are absolutely more turbulent than those of the male sex, and I may with great safety state the 'cats' would make a very wholesome change with some of the worthless of them and not by any means en-danger their health."[9] (The use of these leather, knotted whips, or "cats," on women prisoners was banned in 1848 following a recommendation of the Brown Commission).

A duality of images held of the female offender was quite evident among the correctional staff in the nineteenth century. When both the war-den of the Kingston Penitentiary and the prison matron argued in favour of new facilities for the women, the nature of their pleas reflects the divergent views held of the female offender and of the objectives of her treatment. The warden characterized the women as:

> Poor unfortunate creatures, who are sent here, generally of the unfortunate classes. They are taught the usefulness of labour, and those well disposed, are al-lowed to learn the working of the sewing machine, so that on their release, they may obtain a livelihood.[10]

His plea for larger accommodation was based on a positive characteri-zation of the work that had been accomplished by the women. He wrote:

> A larger number of women have been employed in making articles of wearing apparel for persons living in the city and country, and have given so much satis-faction by their work, that the number of applicants to have work done, has be-come very great.[11]

On the other hand, the prison matron presented a very different image of the women in her charge, and she offered quite another rationale for ad-ditional space requirements.

> There were serious drawbacks for the want of proper cells, where lazy, worth-less characters would be isolated and their day's work extracted from them. Such a system, I believe, would tend much more to subduing and reforming them than the present way I am forced to adopt—putting them in a dark cell on bread and water, where they can sleep all day, and in the night, sing and ham-mer, so as to disturb the whole establishment.[12]

Thus, there was little agreement among prison officials on how best to rehabilitate women prisoners, and the conflicting views tended to neutralize efforts to change the conditions of women offenders' confinement during the nineteenth century.

In 1843, Mary Douglas from Newcastle, convicted of murder, became the first female to receive a life sentence. She joined other women still confined in the original temporary location. The warden, complaining that this location was required for male convicts as part of an addition to the men's dining hall, described the women's unit as "inconvenient."[13] The welfare of the women prisoners was considered secondary to the space requirements of the men and in 1846, cells were temporarily fashioned for the women from rooms in another part of the building. Now numbering twenty-six, the women inmates were confined in cells measuring eight feet four inches long, seven feet six inches high, and thirty inches wide.[14]

Criticism levelled at the Provincial Penitentiary in the 1840s, including a public outcry against the flogging of women, led to the appointment of an investigative royal commission in 1848. The Brown Commission, as this inquiry was popularly named, revealed a range of abuses, many of which related specifically to the treatment of female inmates, and to the lack of accountability enjoyed by their keepers.

The Commission discovered that girls as young as twelve and fourteen were being lashed with rawhide. Twelve-year-old Elizabeth Breen, for example, was lashed six times on six separate occasions during one year.[15] Although the nature of her misconducts is not known, the Commission revealed a wide use of corporal punishment for such behaviours as bad language, refusing to wear shoes, and insulting staff members.

A strong recommendation was made by the Brown Commission to construct a new, separate unit for the women, in part because of the evidence it heard regarding their living conditions.

> The sleeping cells were frightfully over-run with bugs, especially in the spring of 1846; the women used to sweep them out with a broom. It was so very bad, that on one occasion it was suggested to the warden to let the women sleep in the day room and [the matron] would sit up all night with them, and be responsible for them; the warden would not consent. The women suffered very much, their bodies were blistered with the bugs; and they often tore themselves with scratching.[16]

But it was not only these conditions which spurred the recommendation.

The portion of the north wing which the female convicts now occupy, is not adapted in any way to carry out the penitentiary discipline; nor does it seem even to be attempted.... The labour department has been as inefficiently conducted as every other part of the discipline. Female labour can scarcely be expected to prove a source of pecuniary to a penitentiary; but we believe that occupation might easily be found which would be conducive to the maintenance of order in the prison, [and] at the same time repay, in part, the cost of supporting the prisoners. A suitable building must, however, be erected before any reform can be attempted with success.[17]

In general, the recommendations of the Brown Commission provided a central thrust toward change in the decade that followed. Penitentiary legislation in 1851 introduced a number of new features in harmony with the Report, including a reduction and regulation of the severity of punishment, and the removal of mentally ill women to the lunatic asylum of Upper Canada. However, the major recommendation, which proposed a suitable building for the women, was not implemented. This resulted in their persistent re-shuffling from one inadequate location to the next, inside the walls of the men's prison.

The year after Confederation, there were sixty-seven women sentenced to penitentiary. Of these, sixty-three were housed in Kingston, one in St. John's, and three in Halifax.[18] Those at Kingston were still housed in the "temporary" location and in the small cells that were set up in 1846 for a female population numbering less than thirty. By 1868, the increased numbers of women had rendered the location far too cramped.

This prompted the warden to make an impassioned plea to the Superintendent of Penitentiaries, strongly urging "the building of a proper female prison outside the walls of the Provincial Penitentiary."[19] The following year, similar pleas were made by both the warden and the matron, but apparently to no avail.[20]

After the death of the matron in 1870, the atmosphere within the facility appears to have improved. In 1872 the new matron reported:

I am happy to state that everything in connection with the female department is progressing in a most satisfactory manner. The conduct of the female prisoners has been very good during the year. The system of granting remission of sentence and money gratuity for good conduct and industry has had the most beneficial effect. All the female convicts who could neither read nor write when received here, are being taught by myself and assistants, and I am happy to say, are making fair progress.[21]

The warden also observed:

The good order and cheerful industry maintained in the female prison is very creditable to the matron and her assistants, and the zealous and gratuitous labour of those Protestant and Catholic ladies who now visit the prison regularly to impart religious instruction have, I sincerely believe, produced good fruits.[22]

The Winds of Change (1913–1933)

In 1913, after sixty-five years of recommendations for adequate accommodation for the women, the female prison was finally erected in a new location within the penitentiary walls. The prison was now located in the northwest corner of the general enclosure, which was surrounded on two sides by an inner stone wall.

When public pressure again prompted a re-examination of the entire penal system in 1914, another royal commission recommended that the women be housed closer to their homes in provincial jurisdictions. Their report stated that "the interests of all concerned would be best served if these few inmates were transferred [and] ... arrangements ... made with the provincial authority for the custody of all female offenders."[23]

The relinquishing of federal female offenders to provincial jurisdictions was viewed by correctional administrators of the day as a retrogressive step largely because new facilities had just been provided for the women in the men's grounds. The recommendation, however, has plagued correctional planners to this day. Since 1914, scores of government and private sector reports have been published reiterating that recommendation, primarily because of the severe geographic and social displacement suffered by women under the centralized system of federal imprisonment.

In 1921, the Hon. W. F. Nickle was appointed to investigate the state of management of the female prison. This investigation appears to have been prompted by allegations concerning undue sexual familiarity between the male deputy warden of the institution and the female inmates,[24] although these suspicions were not later substantiated in Nickle's report.

Nevertheless, the report represents a landmark in the history of the treatment of women offenders in Canada. To begin with, it was the first inquiry commissioned to look exclusively at the situation of the female offender. Perhaps even more importantly, the kind of insight offered by Nickle, not just about women convicts, but about corrections in general, represents a marked departure from past approaches. Although in some respects his perceptions of women were very much in keeping with the fallacies of the day concerning women criminals, many of his observations and some of his recommendations clearly reflected a desire to improve the status of female prisoners.

Nickle recommended that the women's pay should be increased to provide an incentive for the work they did. He referred to the labour in the laundry as "hard work that does not improve the worker."[25] The laundry equipment was antiquated (two or three stationary tubs, a poor ringer, a broken mangle, and out-of-date drying kilns), and Nickle recommended that these be replaced by modern electric washing equipment.

He objected strongly to the fact that the inmates were forced to do the personal laundry of the staff, and he recorded:

> At times these washings are very foul and it is surprising that self-respecting people would send such soiled clothes to a public place to be cleaned, more particularly when it is known that the women do the washing by hand.[26]

He reported that the women bitterly resented the indignity and considered themselves degraded by what they were compelled to do. Nickle strongly recommended that this practice be stopped. He offered the following:

> It is useless to contend that there is satisfaction with the work that has to be done or the tasks allotted ... behind all is the fault of the system that ignores the principles of human nature; that work must be productive and reward for labour wrought.[27]

In addition, Nickle expressed concern over a range of other problems at the prison, including the cold concrete floor, the walls in need of paint, and the fact that women were being released with only five or ten dollars and in black gowns that were easily identifiable as prison-release garments. He further complained that the women were locked in their cells for too long, that they should have their own library, that they should spend their evenings receiving instructions in reading, and that they should have their own garden plots.

Reverting to a more popular view, Nickle perceived the women prisoners to be sexually aberrant. As Shelley Gavigan notes later in this volume, correctional practices of the day were informed by early criminological theory which emphasized that women who were criminal were sexually maladjusted, and that their deviance originated in their sexuality. Nickle's perceptions are therefore not surprising:

> Without doubt the women, more particularly at certain periods, are thrown into a violent state of sexual excitement by the mere sight of men ... and my attention was called to one instance of this group of cases where a sedative had to be given to soothe desire ... as a matter of fact, today the male staff, from the warden down, view with apprehension the administration of the female prison ... any decent officers are fearful, knowing that a few designing, crafty women might ruin a well-earned reputation.[28]

In spite of such lingering views, conditions in the female section of the penitentiary appear to have improved considerably as a result of Nickle's report. The women were allowed to have their own garden plots; they were referred to by name instead of number; and the conditions within the work areas improved.

Unfortunately, one of the issues Nickle failed to recognize was the value of proximity to one's home community as part of the reintegration process upon release from prison. The 1914 Commission of Inquiry had suggested the return of the women to their home provinces but Nickle chose not to support that suggestion. His recommendation to build a new facility outside the walls of the male penitentiary was historically important since it was on the strength of this recommendation that the present Kingston Prison for Women was built.

A rather uplifting account of conditions in the female unit a few years after the Nickle Report was provided by a Mrs. Vera Cherry.[29] Cherry arrived at the women's unit of the Kingston Penitentiary in 1923 as an "industrial guard housekeeper." As her title suggests, she was employed in virtually every capacity in which staff assistance was required. She assisted the inmates in the preparation of the meals, supervised the work areas, tutored inmates who wished to learn to write, gave out medicine (she was a nurse by profession), and generally saw her role as that of "house mother."

Cherry lived with the other staff in an apartment adjacent to the unit. She would rise at 5:30 in the morning to let the inmate cook into the kitchen to light the stove and prepare breakfast, and her day finished at 9:00 in the evening when the lights were turned out.

Her description of the prison environment suggests an atmosphere more akin to that of a group home than that of a penitentiary in the early 1900s. Cherry reflected, for example, on the preparation for her wedding as being very much a family affair with the prisoners; the female inmates made her entire trousseau for her.

She recalled that during the early twenties, before a final decision was made to construct the new prison outside the walls, some brief discussion centred around the possibility of returning women to provincial jurisdictions so that they could serve their sentences closer to home. Cherry indicated that the only time this possibility was seriously considered was when the matrons requested a raise in pay. It was then they were informed that the unit would be closed and the inmates sent to the provinces if the matrons persisted with their requests for increased wages.

While some positive changes were occurring within the walls, other aspects of women's correctional treatment had not progressed at all. The notes of the then Secretary of the Parole Commission, Alfred E. Lavell, reveal that in the 1920s the approach of the Parole Board towards women still relied heavily on myths concerning deviant women:

> The women prisoners in Ontario are subnormal and immoral ... I might add that the Board would rather deal with men's cases any day than the women's, and only sees women as a matter of duty and justice to them.[30]

The New Prison for Women (1934–Present)

The acceptance of the Nickle Report meant that the 1914 recommendation to return women prisoners to their home provinces would be disregarded. Construction of the new women's penitentiary began in May 1925 and was completed in January 1934. It was located across the road from the male penitentiary, and it was surrounded by a wall sixteen feet high topped with ten feet of woven wire fabric and barbed wire. The only thing that distinguished its appearance from a typical male institution was the absence of guard towers.

The prisoners were all confined in cells, and the cells no longer had outside windows as had been the case in the old prison. There was no recreation ground within the enclosure, no provision for outdoor exercise or recreation of any kind, and no educational facilities for the female prisoners.[31]

Although the women now had their own institution, its operation was not independent. Rather, the inmates retained their "afterthought" status under a system in which the management of the prison continued to be one of the tasks of the warden of the Kingston Penitentiary. The doctor and two chaplains performed their respective duties for the women's prison as well. Both staff and inmates were reluctant to move to the new facility; it was described by one of the matrons who made the move as a "great big barrack ... cold and empty."[32]

Throughout the century that preceded the building of the new prison, women had been housed for periods of time in penitentiaries in Newfoundland, Nova Scotia, New Brunswick, Saskatchewan and Alberta. With the opening of the new prison, all federal female offenders were gathered in Kingston in order to increase the cost-effectiveness of the operation. This meant that a system which had once allowed for a modicum of decentralization was now obsolete.

In 1938, a royal commission investigating the penal system (the Archambault Commission) was appalled at the inferior conditions of the new institution, stating "the Women's Prison presents a marked contrast to any other institution ... visited anywhere in this or any other country, whether for men, women or children."[33]

Although it was only four years after the prison's opening, this royal commission concluded that the prison should be closed. It reiterated the 1914 recommendation that the women be returned to their home provinces:

> Your Commissioners are strongly of the opinion that the number of female prisoners confined in Kingston Penitentiary did not justify the erection of the new women's prison and that further continuance is unjustified, particularly if arrangements can be made with the provincial authorities to provide custody and maintenance for such prisoners in their respective provinces. Enquiries ... lead us to believe that there would be no great difficulty in making such arrangements. This would have the advantage of eliminating the expense of transporting prisoners from eastern and western provinces. At the present the female

prisoners brought from a distance seldom see any relatives during the period of their incarceration. There are no compensating advantages, only the heavy operating expenses already referred to.[34]

As the Commission suggested, the population profile that preceded the decision to build the prison justified neither the size nor the maximum security design. In the fifteen years prior to its construction, the female inmate population fluctuated from twenty in 1910 to twenty-seven in 1925, reaching a low of eight in 1912 and a high of forty in 1919.[35] The average population during that period was twenty-five inmates—a number which did not call for the building of a 100-bed facility.

In terms of their dangerousness, the women were characterized by the Archambault Commission as being "of the occasional or accidental offender class, carried away by the overmastering impulse of the moment, often the outbreak of long pent-up emotion. They are not a custodial problem...."[36] The view that the majority of federal female inmates are not dangerous has been repeated often in studies and reports since the Archambault Commission.

Following the Commission's recommendations for decentralized housing, the Minister of Justice approached the provinces to discuss returning federal women to their jurisdictions. The responses of the provinces, while generally positive, were accompanied by requests for additional financial assistance. It appears that because of what were considered to be rather substantial short-term savings, the decision was made by the federal government to continue to house their women inmates on a centralized basis in the Prison for Women.

In 1956, another government-appointed committee[37] reiterated the Archambault position and recommended the closure of the prison. This prompted the Minister of Justice, that same year, to rekindle discussions with the provinces. The majority of provinces again responded positively, providing funds were made available. And once more it seemed financially more appealing in the short-term to maintain the status quo.

The prison operated at a limited capacity (never more than 75 percent full) until the late 1940s. But the 1950s saw a significant increase in the number of inmates, due to the incarceration of Doukhobor protesters from British Columbia as well as drug offenders entering the system in record numbers. By 1959, the overcrowding had reached such a state that, with a population of 116 inmates, the women were being housed in the matron's quarters.[38] Rather than increasing the push towards decentralization, the over-population problem resulted in the expansion of the institution by fifty beds in 1960.

A review of the records indicates a remarkable similarity between the Archambault recommendations of 1938 for decentralized housing and the renewed series of reports that began to emerge thirty years later. Since 1968, no fewer than sixteen government studies, investigations, and private sector reports have been produced which reiterate that the Prison for Women should be closed and decentralized facilities made available.[39]

One of these, the 1977 *Report to Parliament by the Sub-Committee on the Penitentiary System in Canada,* quoted a witness who described the Kingston Prison for Women as "unfit for bears, much less women."[40] The report continued:

> One area in which women have equality in Canada—without trying—is in the national system of punishment. The nominal equality translates itself into injustice. But, lest the injustice fail to be absolute, the equality ends and reverts to outright discrimination when it comes to providing constructive positives— recreation, programs, basic facilities and space—for women.... In light of today's advanced sociological knowledge, the institution is obsolete in every respect—in design, in programs, and in the handling of the people sent there ... there seems to be remarkable indifference to a casual neglect of women's needs by both region[al] and [national] headquarters.[41]

The Parliamentary Sub-Committee Report joined those numerous voices that had been raised over many years in an effort to improve the status of women offenders. The culmination of all these efforts was the finding in 1981 by the Canadian Human Rights Commission that federal female offenders were discriminated against on the basis of sex, and that in virtually all program and facility areas, the treatment of federal women inmates was inferior to that of men.

Conclusions

The historical record of federal corrections tells us that the small female population has always been housed wherever and in whatever manner best suited the interests of the larger male population. For almost a century (from 1835 to 1934), the majority of women offenders were housed within the walls of the Kingston Penitentiary for Men. During this period, they occupied at least three separate locations within the walls, each of these, until 1913, considered "temporary"; and, in each case, the moves were made because the location was required for the male inmates.

It is evident that a move in 1914 to the decentralized options provided by provincial facilities would, in the long term, have cut the human and fiscal costs considerably. Despite the ensuing sixty years of recommendations that federal female offenders be housed in their home provinces; despite the ruling by the Canadian Human Rights Commission that centralized housing at the Prison for Women constituted discriminatory practice; and despite continued pressure from outside organizations in this direction, the Kingston Prison for Women continues to house the majority of federal women and houses them in conditions inferior to those in the vast majority of institutions for men.

The costs to the federal government of maintaining the status quo are enormous. In 1992, the Correctional Service of Canada reported that the 1991–92 annual cost per federal female inmate was $83,242.00, while for a maximum security male inmate it was $69,288.00.[42] Journalist Brian Johnson has commented on an additional expense incurred in 1980 by the Correctional Service of Canada:

> Erected ... to replace a crumbling limestone wall, the new barrier, two feet higher than the old, cost $1.4 million and took two years to build. Eighteen feet high and almost half a mile long, it consists of 400 slabs of reinforced concrete, each weighing 16 tons, bolted 13 feet into solid bedrock. Its sole purpose is to contain the energies of about 100 women.[43]

A dominant theme throughout the history of the treatment of the female offender is the juxtaposition of neglect and paternalism. Both are the result of politically motivated bureaucratic decision-making based on expediency. The duality of neglect and paternalism has been rationalized using a whole host of uncontested assumptions, stereotypes, and myths about the woman offender's inherent nature.

This historical review shows that public opinion can have a profound effect upon correctional services for women. The bureaucratic response is most often to commission report after report to diffuse public pressure at the outset, which has been a very effective delaying tactic. (It delayed the construction of the Prison for Women for sixty years.) However, history has also shown that at the point at which it becomes more expedient to accede to public demand than to continue to evade it, even an issue as "insignificant" as the imprisonment of a small group of women can command sufficient attention to force substantive change. Dogged, collective, and continuous pressure from a broad political base can be an effective catalyst for change. The key seems to be to see beyond the smokescreen of bureaucratic reports and piecemeal reforms that are intended to divert the intensity or persistence of public pressure.

Notes

1 See Shelley Gavigan's chapter, "Women's Crime: New Perspectives and Old Theories," in this book for a description and discussion of these theories.
2 The co-existence of conflicting images runs through the various Annual Reports published by the Minister of Justice, but is nowhere more cogently expressed than in the Annual Report of 1868 wherein the warden of the Kingston Penitentiary described the women in his charge as "poor ... unfortunate creatures" and the matron described them as "lazy, worthless characters"; *Annual Report of the Directors of Penitentiaries* 1868, p. 22.
3 Christina M. Hill, "Women in the Canadian Economy," in *The Political Economy of Dependency,* ed. Robert Laxer (Toronto: McClelland and Stewart, 1973), p. 43.
4 Alfred E. Lavell, "The History of the Prisons of Upper Canada," Kingston, Queen's University, 1948 (pages not numbered).
5 Ibid.
6 John W. Ekstedt and Curt T. Griffiths, *Corrections in Canada: Policy and Practice* (Toronto: Butterworths, 1984), pp. 29–30.
7 Upper Canada, *Journals of the House of Assembly,* Vol. 1, App. 19, 1836, p. 2.
8 Upper Canada, *Journals of the House of Assembly,* App. 10, 1836–37, p. 4.
9 Canada, *Annual Report of the Superintendent of Penitentiaries,* 1864, p. 7.
10 Canada, *Annual Report of the Directors of Penitentiaries,* 1868, p. 22.
11 Ibid.
12 Ibid.
13 Canada, *Legislative Assembly Journals,* App. GG, 1843 (pages not numbered).
14 Canada, *Legislative Assembly Journals,* App. 2G-AA, 1846 (pages not numbered).

15 *Report of the Royal Commission to Inquire and then Report upon the Conduct, Economy, Discipline and Management of the Provincial Penitentiary* (the Brown Commission Report), 1849, p. 49.

16 Ibid., p. 34.

17 Ibid., p. 74.

18 Canada, *Annual Report of the Directors of Penitentiaries,* 1868, pp. 14, 45, 54.

19 Canada, *Annual Report of the Superintendent of Penitentiaries,* 1867, p. 14.

20 Canada, *Annual Report of the Directors of Penitentiaries,* 1868, p. 22.

21 Canada, *Annual Report of the Directors of Penitentiaries,* 1872, p. 20.

22 Ibid., p. 12.

23 Canada, *Report of the Royal Commission on Penitentiaries,* 1914, p. 8.

24 Memos from 1921 relating to the establishment of the Nickle Commission, National Archives, RG 73, Vol. 105.

25 Canada, *Report on the State and Management of the Female Prison* (the Nickle Report), 1921, p. 6.

26 Ibid.

27 Ibid., p. 7.

28 Ibid., p. 5–6.

29 Interview with Vera Cherry, 1979.

39 Lavell, op. cit.

31 Canada, *Report of the Royal Commission to Investigate the Penal System* (the Archambault Report), 1938, pp. 314–315.

32 Interview with Vera Cherry, 1979.

33 The Archambault Report, p. 314.

34 Ibid., p. 315.

35 Canada, *Annual Report of the Minister of Justice as to Penitentiaries in Canada,* 1910–1913; *Annual Reports of Inspectors of Penitentiaries,* 1914–1918; *Annual Reports of the Superintendent of Penitentiaries,* 1919–1925.

36 The Archambault Report, p. 315.

37 The Committee Appointed to Inquire into the Principles and Procedures Followed in the Remission Service of the Department of Justice of Canada (the Fauteux Committee), 1956.

38 Canada, *Annual Report of the Department of Justice,* 1959.

39 These include: *Brief on the Woman Offender* (Ottawa: Canadian Corrections Association, 1968); *Report of the Canadian Committee on Corrections* (Ottawa: Queen's Printer, 1969); *Report of the Royal Commission on the Status*

of Women (Ottawa: Information Canada, 1970); *Report of the National Advisory Committee on the Female Offender* (Ottawa: Solicitor General Canada, 1976); *Report to Parliament by the Sub-Committee on the Penitentiary System in Canada* (Ottawa: Supply and Services, 1977); "Brief on the Female Offender" (Ottawa: Canadian Association of Elizabeth Fry Societies, 1978); "Brief to the Solicitor General" (Ottawa: Civil Liberties Association of Canada, 1978); *Report of the National Planning Committee on the Female Offender* (Ottawa: Solicitor General Canada, 1978); "Brief on the Woman Offender" (Montreal: Canadian Federation of University Women, 1978); *Report of the Joint Committee to Study Alternatives for the Housing of the Federal Female Offender* (Ottawa: Solicitor General Canada, 1978); *Progress Report on the Federal Female Offender Program* (Ottawa: Canadian Corrections Service, 1978); *Ten Years Later* (Ottawa: Canadian Advisory Council on the Status of Women, 1979); "Brief to the Canadian Human Rights Commission" (Ottawa: Women for Justice, 1980); Canada, *Report of the Standing Committee on Justice and the Solicitor General on its Review of Sentencing, Conditional Release and Related Aspects of Corrections* (the Daubney Report) (Ottawa: Ministry of Supply and Services, 1988); M. Jackson, *Justice Behind the Walls* (Ottawa: Canadian Bar Association, 1988); *Creating Choices: Report of the Task Force on Federally Sentenced Women* (Ottawa: Correctional Service of Canada, 1990).

40 *The Report to Parliament by the Sub-Committee on the Penitentiary System in Canada* (Ottawa: Supply and Services, 1977), p. 135.

41 Ibid., pp. 134–37.

42 *Basic Facts About Corrections in Canada* (Ottawa: Correctional Service of Canada, 1992), p. 58. The average cost per inmate includes those costs associated with the running of the institution only and does not include parole-related costs, staff training, or headquarters costs. The 1984–85 figures provided in the version of this chapter in *Too Few to Count* were: for women, $56,713.00, and for men, $49,792.00.

43 Brian D. Johnson, "Women Behind Bars," *Equinox,* March/April 1984, p. 52.

Reforming Federal Women's Imprisonment

Margaret Shaw

In April 1990 a new and potentially "remarkable" phase in the history of women serving federal sentences in Canada began with the publication of the report of the Task Force on Federally Sentenced Women, *Creating Choices.*

This chapter was written in 1992,[1] midway through implementation of the task force recommendations, at a time when many people were reserving judgement on just how radically Canada's treatment of federal female offenders would be altered as a result of that report. It outlines the unusual character of the task force report, with its implicitly feminist approach,[2] and initial progress on the equally important implementation phase. It discusses some of the problems involved in implementation, and the extent to which principles espoused in the report are likely to be upheld. Finally, it considers the broader implications of attempts to reform women's imprisonment, and the underlying problems, some of which are inherent in the task force report itself.

The government-appointed task force had been established nearly ten years after the last committee specifically set up to "settle" the issue of the federal imprisonment of women had faded into obscurity.[3] The newly appointed Commissioner of Corrections had established the Task Force to examine "the correctional management of federally sentenced women from the commencement of sentence to the date of warrant expiry and to develop a plan which will guide and direct this process in a manner that is responsive to the unique and special needs of women."[4]

The 1990 report called, once again—and its authors hoped finally—for the closure of the penitentiary for federally sentenced women, Prison for Women (P4W), and its replacement by five regional facilities and a healing lodge for Aboriginal women.[5] It also called for the development of a community release strategy which would expand and strengthen programmes and services for federally sentenced women on parole or at the end of their sentences.

But the task force report differed in many ways from its predecessors. Unlike them, it stated unequivocally its basic feminist philosophy and its recognition of Aboriginal women. It called for a fundamental change in the treatment of federally sentenced women, and established a long-term goal of moving towards treating offenders through community-based justice rather than in institutions. The report was written in a very different climate from that of the late 1970s and, in the view of its authors, with a "groundswell of consensus" in favour of fundamental reform.[6]

Pressure for Change

Between 1978 and 1990, many women inside and outside P4W continued to work tirelessly to improve the treatment of women offenders. Following legal challenges by Women for Justice, an ad hoc women's advocacy group, against the Correctional Service of Canada in 1981, some minor programme changes were made at P4W. Nobody, however, was satisfied with piecemeal reform of an archaic prison building which mainly warehoused women serving federal sentences, and left those serving federal sentences in provincial prisons untouched.[7] There continued to be reports stressing the need to change the approach to women in conflict with the law. Two high-profile reports in 1988, one by the Standing Committee on Justice and the Solicitor General, and another by the Canadian Bar Association, renewed calls for the closure of P4W and the development of alternative institutions and community programmes for women.[8]

But perhaps the most crucial changes occurred more broadly in Canadian society, in terms of public attitudes towards issues affecting women. Nearly twenty years of active lobbying by feminists on a range of issues concerning women began to have some effects on the treatment of women in the courts and the workplace. The introduction of sexual assault legislation in 1983 represented the culmination of some fifteen years of lobbying by women against the previous rape law. Recognition of the extent of family violence and domestic abuse meant that these too rose much closer to the top of the political agenda. Violence against women became a primary focus (and one which was intensified after the massacre of women engineering students in Montreal on 6 December 1989).

Feminist analysis of women's position in the criminal justice system also became much more explicit and articulate in the ten years prior to the establishment of the task force. There was a movement away from a liberal feminist position, which stressed the need for equality of provision with men and took men's situations and requirements as the norm. Instead, there was a more explicit articulation of the differences between men and women when they come into conflict with the law, and a rejection of seeing provisions for men as the standard against which women's conditions should be measured. This emphasized not only women's different needs, but their differing experiences, particularly in relation to violence, their lack of control and power over their own lives, and the importance of a woman-centred approach to justice. The Canadian Association of Elizabeth Fry Societies (CAEFS), for example, had explicitly argued from such a perspective for a number of years, taking the experience of women as the starting point for much of its agenda and critique.[9] These changes were underpinned by feminist research focussing much more on experiential and qualitative approaches and rejecting traditional analyses of correctional problems developed on the basis of the much larger male population.[10]

Ten years earlier the particular problems faced by Aboriginal women in prison had received little attention. By the time the task force was established, there had been a considerable increase in the political strength of Aboriginal peoples and their demands for a separate justice system were at last being taken seriously.

Apart from these broader changes in attitudes and priorities, media attention to the issue of suicide among federally sentenced women highlighted the severe difficulties under which many women at the prison lived, and added to the momentum for change.[11]

With continued pressure from non-governmental groups, most notably CAEFS, and the appointment of an innovative new Commissioner of

Corrections,[12] the time was clearly ripe for a new onslaught on an issue which had been shelved on countless occasions.

The Task Force

AN UNUSUAL COMMITTEE

The task force was appointed in March 1989 and asked to report by December 1989. From the beginning, it was unlike any previous government committee, either in Canada or elsewhere.[13] It was established by the Correctional Service of Canada (CSC) in partnership with CAEFS. Both its steering and working groups were jointly chaired by one government and one CAEFS representative.[14] It was composed almost entirely of women (thirty-eight of the forty-two members) and included two women who had themselves served federal sentences. Of the thirty-one members appointed to the steering committee, just over half (seventeen) were from voluntary organizations and women's groups outside government.[15] The working group similarly included more community representatives than government members.[16]

No previous government inquiry into women's imprisonment had included so many voluntary sector representatives, or Aboriginal or minority groups, and certainly no women who had personal experience of prison. And many of those in the voluntary sector reflected the feminist perspectives outlined above.

THE TASK FORCE STRUGGLE

There can have been few committees appointed in recent years which were so passionately committed to so major a change in the conditions and principles under which federal women serve their sentences. The members did not face an easy task. The report was unusual in publicly alluding to its struggles to work with the mandate given and to reach a final consensus which recognized the differing experiences of women within the group.[17]

Task force members expressed "frustration at the enormity of the task," and a deep sense of the pain experienced by the women at P4W. During the life of the task force, the suicides of two Aboriginal women at P4W had a profound effect upon the members, and continued to do so in the subsequent year as a further four Aboriginal women committed suicide.[18]

From the start, the voluntary sector members were under no illusions about the difficulties entailed in being involved. They were concerned about the implications of working too closely with government, and of the dangers of pressure groups being co-opted or "incorporated."[19] The Aboriginal women were also uneasy about the difficulties of following traditional bureaucratic agendas.

The concerns of voluntary sector members centred around a number of issues, including the limitations of working within the existing legislative structure (when they believed in the necessity of moving towards community-based corrections); the difficulties of trying to effect fundamental change in the way women are treated in so short a time-frame; the fear that the process of the task force itself, and the inevitable time-delay before any action was taken, would provide "an excuse" or act as a barrier to immediate change; and the difficulty of ensuring that the voices of Aboriginal women would really be heard.[20]

As a result of these concerns about Aboriginal women, their representation on the task force was increased, the original terms of reference were changed to stress the over-representation of Aboriginal women in the criminal justice system and the significance of their experience, and a separate survey of Aboriginal women in the community was carried out.[21] As the report states:

> the Task Force came to the understanding that it could not be a joint Correctional Service of Canada/Canadian Association of Elizabeth Fry Societies initiative. Rather it must act as a tripartite initiative, if voices of Aboriginal women were to be heard clearly and without distortion.[22]

THE TASK FORCE: THE VOICES OF EXPERIENCE

The task force undertook a great deal of ground-breaking consultation and research.[23] As a result, for the first time it was possible to know how many women serving federal sentences had children, what were their educational and working experiences, what was their experience of violence and abuse, what kinds of facilities and programmes they felt they needed, and what were the conditions of those serving federal sentences in provincial prisons.

The report emphasized the low level of public risk federally sentenced women presented. It underlined the high incidence of both physical and sexual abuse in these women's lives and the interdependence of such abuse with other problems in their lives. This, suggested the authors, indicated the need for an holistic approach to the development of programmes and facilities. It argued that women must be seen within their social context, in a society in which they live in a position of inequality and dependency, and, in the case of Aboriginal and minority women, discrimination.

Second, in considering the experiences of women, and the history of incarceration and its failure to provide the support women felt they needed, the task force argued that fundamental change in the criminal justice system itself was necessary to provide women with that support: "society must move towards the long-term goal of creating and using community-based restorative justice options, and an alternative Aboriginal justice system."[24]

And in the shorter term, the authors argued, substantial and significant changes must be made to the carceral system in terms of how federally sentenced women are treated, and to the environment in which they live. The current correctional system, with its primary emphasis on security considerations, was seen as incapable of responding to women's needs.[25] It assumed that women were a risk to society, and that their needs could be ordered hierarchically, with those at the top requiring most immediate attention. The task force emphasized the importance of assessing each woman's needs individually and of treating those needs as a whole. In essence, the task force rejected the male model of corrections, which classified risk, prioritized needs, and fitted offenders into pre-structured programmes.[26]

THE PRINCIPLES

Perhaps the most original aspect of the report was its establishment of five fundamental principles upon which any future developments must be based. These principles provided the feminist basis of the report. They included (a) empowering women; (b) providing more meaningful choices in programmes and community facilities; (c) treating women with respect and dignity; (d) providing a physically and emotionally supportive environment; and (e) sharing responsibility for their welfare among both correctional workers and members of the community.

Empowerment was seen by the task force as a way to overcome the inequities experienced by women in society in terms of poverty, abuse, and racism, through the development of programmes to raise their self-esteem. Meaningful choices were to replace the few options available to federally sentenced women. A wider range of programmes and community facilities would give them greater choices and, therefore, control over the training and support they felt they needed.

The principle of respect and dignity was based on the assumption that people can only gain a sense of self-respect and respect for others if they are treated well. The notion of a supportive environment encompassed both the physical environment and how people are treated, as well as the supportive nature of programmes. Finally, the principle of shared responsibility stressed the need for a coordinated support system for the women, including government, correctional, voluntary, and other community members.

These principles, with their emphasis on the empowerment of women and on support rather than control, contrast sharply with those of previous reports. Earlier reports tended to assume that women's needs were just an extension of men's, and to refer in vague terms to the "special needs" of women, to their need to be closer to their families, or to the importance of "well designed" programmes and the appropriateness of less secure conditions, since they are not a risk to the public.[27]

The Recommended Plan

In outlining its practical recommendations, the task force stressed that there were two equally important components—new regional facilities, and a strategy for community release with a greatly enhanced network of community facilities—and that it was essential to accept the plan as a whole.

THE REGIONAL FACILITIES

The new regional facilities were to be "developed and operated on a programme philosophy that approximates community norms,"[28] with extensive use of community expertise. They were to be situated in several acres of land, providing natural light, fresh air, colour, space, and privacy, with cottage-style houses accommodating six to ten women each, and including facilities for family visits or for women to live with their children. To ensure that the new facilities were close to the home communities of the majority of women in each region, they were to be situated in or near major cities.[29]

Programmes were to be holistic in nature and sensitive to different cultures. They would include counselling and treatment for sexual and physical abuse, and substance abuse, as well as educational and vocational development, leisure activities, family visits, and spirituality. There would be an emphasis on developing self-sufficiency in daily living activities, and community responsibility. Considerable use was to be made of support services in the local community, such as those related to physical and mental health diagnosis and treatment.

There was also to be an emphasis on dynamic security—a high level of staff-inmate interaction and staff support—rather than the traditional physical barriers or discipline measures. For women who were regarded as high risk, "enhanced" staff support was recommended, although it was acknowledged that increased security might be required for one cottage at each facility.

THE HEALING LODGE

The most original recommendation was for the establishment of a circular healing lodge for Aboriginal women. This was to be located in the Prairie Region, since the majority of Aboriginal women serving federal sentences come from those provinces, and to be linked with a local Native community and an Elder Council. It was to be built in consultation with Aboriginal peoples, and operated by Aboriginal staff in accordance with Native traditions. Aboriginal women would have the right to choose to go to the Lodge or to one of the other regional facilities.

COMMUNITY RELEASE STRATEGY

The second and equally important part of the plan was the development of an integrated system of community resources for women leaving prison. There were to be increased facilities for both accommodation and treatment in the local community, including halfway houses, Aboriginal centres, community-based treatment residences, satellite apartments, and home placements. An individual release strategy was to be developed by community workers and correctional service staff together with each woman.

RECOMMENDATIONS FOR IMPLEMENTATION

The task force attempted to build in safeguards to ensure that the plan was followed through. It developed a strategy for implementation of the plan, including an externally based Implementation Committee to oversee its completion and an Aboriginal Advisory Committee.[30]

Implementation

ACCEPTANCE IN PRINCIPLE

Following the publication of *Creating Choices* in April 1990, the Solicitor General formally announced a few months later that P4W would be closed by 1994 and replaced by five regional facilities for federally sentenced women, including a healing lodge for Aboriginal women, and covering all provinces except British Columbia.[31] He also announced that halfway houses and services for women in the community would be expanded and improved. Implementation was expected to be completed within four years at a cost of $50 million.

However, while the main recommendations of the report were accepted in principle, those relating to their implementation were not. In particular, the original notion of an external committee with strong voluntary sector representation to oversee the implementation phase was rejected by the Correctional Service of Canada. Instead, this role was allocated to an internal National Implementation Committee (NIC), whose primary task was the development of plans for the new facilities and their location.[32] In contrast to the task force, this committee was composed almost entirely of government representatives.[33]

The role of external watchdog was given to an External Advisory Committee (EAC). This committee was to include three former members of the task force steering committee, and possibly federally sentenced women.[34] They were to receive copies of NIC papers and to be consulted on policy issues. Task force recommendations for the implementation of the healing lodge were also rejected, but in this case by Aboriginal women's organizations, who argued that they should have full control over the planning, and not be subordinate to the NIC.[35]

THE "CLOSER TO HOME" PROGRAMME

For those outside the government, the most tangible and public development in the implementation of the task force plan came with the announcement of sites for the new facilities.[36]

In December 1991, the Solicitor General announced the location of two of the new facilities at a cost of $12 million each. The Ontario site, to house seventy women, was to be in Kitchener, and a thirty-bed facility for the Atlantic Region was to be in Truro, Nova Scotia, and not in Halifax, as originally recommended by the task force.

In May 1992, Maple Creek, Saskatchewan was chosen as the site for the healing lodge to accommodate thirty women. Finally, in December 1992, two years into the implementation phase, Edmonton was announced as the Prairie Region site, and Joliette, rather than Montreal, for the Quebec Region. They were to house fifty-five and seventy-five women, respectively.

Innovation or Entrenchment?

CAN DREAMS BE BUILT FROM BRICKS AND MORTAR?

So far the response from those outside the implementation process has been less than enthusiastic. The overall plan for regional centres with an integrated system of community facilities appears to have been lost, and it is unclear how far the principles of the task force are being adhered to.

A good deal of cynicism and scepticism had been expressed by some groups at the start of the task force itself. The women in P4W, for example, were not convinced of the likelihood of real change taking place. In the prison magazine *Tightwire,* above the picture of a spread-eagled squirrel appeared a suggested motto for the task force: "As soon as I can find a good position, I intend to take a firm stand."[37]

The accompanying article suggested that the task force was an exercise in frustration and futility by women with good hearts and well-meaning attitudes, and that they were "fighting an uphill battle" and were on a "virtually rudderless ship." After the publication of *Creating Choices,* many of the federally sentenced women were, understandably, cautiously optimistic but a number of them expressed disbelief that the necessary money to provide new facilities would ever be found:

"I just can't see it happening. It's a dream."

"It's a really nice book, nice proposals, but they're never going to happen because there is no money."[38]

While that cynicism dissipated for a time with the announcement of the acceptance of the recommendations, there was still nervousness and scepticism about how the new regional centres would turn out. Among the women at P4W cynicism about the "fairytale cottages" returned. Some of them expressed fears that they would have less choice in the new facilities:

"... in five regional facilities where instead of having 100 and some odd women, we've got 40, they'll have less money. We have absolutely nothing in here for us that we can get a trade with. Going to a Region, we're going to get even less."[39]

There has always been a divergence of opinion among the women about the closure of P4W. Some feared a move from what had been their home for a number of years, and were afraid that they would lose their collective voice by being split into small regional groups.[40] For the women serving life sentences, such anxieties are particularly acute.

Apart from the women themselves, others outside the implementation process, including members of the task force, Elizabeth Fry societies, and informed observers, had concerns on a number of fronts. The first of these involved the process of implementation itself and the lack of consultation.

While the government did indeed accept the major recommendations of the task force, it did not accept its recommendations on how they were to be implemented. As a result, the External Advisory Committee had almost no power, and much more limited access to information and decision-making than government officials. They felt that they were informed about small issues but not about major decisions or developments, such as site selection or the choice of wardens, who are crucial to the future development of the new facilities.[41] This was in direct contrast to the philosophy of the task force, which emphasized the need to plan new services in concert with community members.

It was perhaps this lack of communication which exacerbated much of the unease. For a number of people, the implementation appeared to be taking place behind closed doors with little public accountability. With the exception of the implementation of the healing lodge, decision-making in relation to the plan was seen to rest almost entirely with the Correctional Service.[42]

A related concern about process was the extent to which a government committee would be able or willing to realize the full implications of the feminist principles outlined in the report. Very few of the people involved in the implementation phase, even among government members, had been members of the task force. More significantly, there were concerns about how much a government organization with its own history, traditions, and priorities would be able to change those traditions.[43] Too great a focus on physical plant and bricks and mortar, as well as ingrained approaches to issues such as staffing or security, might overshadow the essential message of the task force that there must also be a change in philosophy towards support and choice.

The history of other struggles to change conditions for women suggests such fears are well founded. In Australia, for example, there was selective acceptance of the recommendations of the New South Wales Task Force on Women in Prison. Physical changes were accepted by the government, but recommendations which challenged management practices or traditional staffing methods were not.[44]

A related problem is that the focus on building new facilities has drawn attention and resources away from the equally important community release strategy. Money for the development of the community strategy will not come from the original budget of $50 million as some had initially assumed, following the official announcements in September 1990, but will have to be found at the local level. In a tough economic climate it is difficult to see how local community and voluntary organizations will be able to raise the money needed to fund the network of community-based programmes and facilities envisaged by the task force.

Much of this unease with the implementation phase manifested itself with the announcement that the Atlantic facility would be located in Truro rather than Halifax. That decision, which came as a great surprise to many, followed days of angry press reports in the Halifax area about people opposed to the establishment of the prison in their neighbourhood, and a city council ban on several of the suggested sites.[45]

In the view of many, the choice of Truro, a small rural community some ninety kilometres from Halifax, ignored the explicit and most important criteria stipulated in *Creating Choices* and from the NIC itself.[46] Truro did not have an established network of women's support services, it was far from the home communities of many of the women in the Atlantic Region, and it had poor transport facilities.

Numerous public objections to the Truro announcement were made by CAEFS, local Elizabeth Fry Societies, other community organizations, members of the task force, and federally sentenced women themselves.[47] Many charged that women were being marginalized yet again by a decision they felt had more to do with jobs and political votes than with faithful adherence to the spirit of the philosophy of *Creating Choices*. There were calls for the Steering Committee to be reconvened to assess the implementation phase.

The response of one woman serving a federal sentence was a return of deep cynicism at what she saw as political patronage: "my spirit was engulfed in deep shame for having contributed to the work that was intended to assist in positive change for Federally Sentenced Women but was now politically sabotaged."[48]

Six months later, in June 1992, this unease and a continuing sense of lack of communication culminated in the formal withdrawal of CAEFS from the External Advisory Committee. On the recommendation of all its nineteen member societies,[49] and having consulted with federally sentenced women too, CAEFS publicly announced that it could no longer endorse the implementation of the task force recommendations. It argued that the principles of the task force had not been adhered to, that the National Implementation Committee was devoid of representation from federally sentenced women or CAEFS, that apart from the healing lodge, the sites selected thus far for the regional facilities did not meet the criteria outlined in *Creating Choices*, and that no resources had been forthcoming for development of the community plan. In essence, CAEFS did not feel it was working in partnership with the government.

In Quebec, the final decision to locate the facility in Joliette rather than Montreal went in the face of strenuous lobbying by the local Elizabeth Fry Society and numerous organizations representing women and criminal justice in Quebec, who felt it went against the best interests of the women.[50]

Joliette, as Truro and to some extent Kitchener, will entail a costly journey for family and visitors. Furthermore, the many community resources needed for the women are located in Montreal, where most federally sentenced Quebec women are from.[51]

LONG-TERM EFFECTS

There are other, more long-term considerations about the task force plan. The exclusion of British Columbia is one example of the weakening of the overall plan.[52] While the authors of *Creating Choices* unwillingly conceded that a new facility would be built for that region only if programmes at the new Burnaby Correctional Centre proved inadequate,[53] members of Elizabeth Fry Societies and federally sentenced women became increasingly unhappy with that decision as the new facility entered its second year of operation. Both structurally and physically the new Burnaby Correctional Centre does not conform to the task force model: "The building has been built on the old model, all the rooms are actual cells with locked doors. Anyone can be followed [monitored] with a camera."[54]

In addition, there is concern that the traditionally run and staffed prison, with its large numbers of provincially sentenced women, is not providing a supportive and non-punitive regime, nor is it handling crisis situations the way the task force envisaged. No formal mechanism exists for deciding when and if the new Centre should prove inadequate. If British Columbia remains outside the ambit of the overall plan, then some twenty to forty federally sentenced women will be subject to a traditional regime and conditions.

Other considerations have to do with implications of the task force recommendations themselves. Distance from home communities, with the ensuing difficulties of maintaining ties and contact, will still be a problem for many women.[55] The women may be closer to home, but Canada is a vast country and distance is inevitable. Women from Manitoba, for example, will be far from the Prairie Region facility, and the healing lodge is to be located in a remote corner of Saskatchewan.

Even more problematic is the new system's likely effect on the courts. Members of CAEFS, for example, had speculated long before the task force that some judges would not give federal sentences to women because of the hardship of being sent to Kingston.[56] With a nearby regional facility, well equipped with up-to-date facilities and dedicated to helping women who have faced a number of problems in their lives, what is the likelihood that judges will not be more inclined to give women federal rather than provincial sentences "for their own good," whether or not their offence merits such a sentence? In many ways the new facilities will be considerably more humane and women-centred than local provincial prisons.

To this speculation must be added concern by outside observers that the new facilities as presently planned will provide more places than are currently needed for federal women, since the planned capacity is based on current population figures which include women out on day parole.[57] As observers elsewhere have argued, prison capacity tends to dictate prison use.[58]

Unintentionally, therefore, the task force may bring about an increase in the use of federal sentences for women. Such an outcome would be unwelcome both on the grounds of considerations of justice and for all the accompanying misinterpretation that women are becoming more "dangerous" which such an increase is likely to elicit. This possibility was never far from the minds of task force members. Federal and provincial governments need to focus their attention much more on the crucial importance of changing sentencing practices and judicial education.

UNDERLYING PRINCIPLES

On a more fundamental level, there remain for some the issues of whether the principles on which the task force report is based, and the move towards more community involvement in corrections will in the long run result in a system quite different from the existing structure of corrections. There are those who argue that any emphasis on building new facilities makes the prospect of abolishing the use of prison more remote.[59]

Second, as Cohen has argued,[60] increasing the community component of corrections risks increasing society's hold on individuals, without necessarily dealing with the structures of society which contributed to their difficulties in the first place and which are particularly pertinent to the status of women. The move towards a community corrections model, is, as Cohen himself concedes, perhaps the best we can work for, but for all its appeal, it risks increasing the control of the helping professions, the volunteers, and the local community over the lives of individual women.

In this respect there is a real concern about the ability of any institution, however well thought out, where people are retained against their will, to function supportively, since there will always be an imbalance of power.[61] How far will it be possible for federally sentenced women to be "empowered" to make choices? How far is it possible to provide "meaningful" choices, even given sufficient economic resources, if authority over questions of risk or eligibility for programmes or parole lies with one side? Empowerment requires that the women's views about their needs or circumstances be accepted as valid, something organizations and professionals may find difficult. In its discussion of the empowerment of women to overcome the disadvantages of their position in society, the task force emphasizes women's status as victims and their need to develop self-esteem. This risks characterizing all federally sentenced women as dependant victims without any sense of self-direction or self-worth.

With so strong an emphasis on the individual needs of women, and on seeing them as victims—albeit victims of society, as the task force stresses—who lack the ability to make choices, there is a risk of overcontrol, and of not listening to the women themselves. Not all women serving federal sentences see themselves as victims, and not all women who have suffered abuse feel they need specific help to deal with that experience. However supportive the environment of the new facilities proves, our continuing focus on individuals with "problems" means that the effects of the structure of society, or of the institutions and the context in which activities and events take place, are likely to be ignored. In such circumstances any difficulties in terms of breaches of the rules or expected modes of behaviour tend to be "blamed" on the inadequacies or poor responses of those individuals themselves.[62]

The Continuing Struggle

Some of these problems are inevitable given the difficulties of balancing voluntary and government sector interests, as well as the interests of women serving sentences. They are implicit in the tension between reform and managerial needs, between support and control, and in the process of the reform of correctional systems.

The experience of people who worked to reform women's imprisonment in Australia has considerable relevance to the Canadian situation. As Brown and Quinn have suggested, implementation leads to a struggle separate from that for the development of a model for reform:

> It seems trite to point out that reform recommendations, even when strongly and unanimously supported by government are not self-enforcing ... the process of debate, the discourse and the content of such reports are fields of political struggle in themselves and can be evaluated as such independently of the linked but separate struggle over implementation.[63]

Recent experience in relation to other "grass-roots" initiatives in Canada, such as the victims movement and its transformation of women's concerns with family violence into the Justice for Victims of Crime initiative, or the incorporation of the battered wife syndrome by the courts, also demonstrate the inevitability of the transformation of ideas and issues as they move from the pressure group or voluntary sector to the government domain.[64]

As a number of observers have stressed, vigilance is essential at this stage but total cynicism or dismissal is probably unwarranted.[65] The Aboriginal women on the task force have gained recognition of the problems they have faced. Although not all Aboriginal women agree, progress on the healing lodge has appeared to be satisfactory to those immediately involved.

As critics of the New South Wales Task Force on Women in Prison concluded, the involvement of feminists and prison activists in a task force cannot always be dismissed as incorporation or legitimation, since that report clearly came out firmly against the government position. Some of their recommendations have now been followed, and the task force has brought about a shift in the agenda: "The Task Force and the campaign around it has altered the agenda, in a fundamental way...."[66]

And in Canada, despite the seemingly negligible outcome of the Women For Justice challenge in 1981[67] and the earlier struggles described by Berzins and Cooper,[68] these efforts were essential stepping stones to the present task force. Both made major changes to the climate of opinion, although not to the existence of P4W and only in minor ways to the conditions under which federal women served their sentences. The input of the voluntary sector and the feminist basis of the report are also measures of how much the agenda has changed in the past ten years. In turn, the task force report is itself influencing the agenda elsewhere, in relation to provincially sentenced women, for example, and this is an immensely important factor,[69] not least because Canada makes far greater use of short-term imprisonment for women than many other countries.[70]

The task force report was a partnership between the voluntary sector and government, but also a compromise. The implementation phase, almost inevitably because of the way it was structured, was not a partnership. Whatever the final shape of the new facilities and their community support programmes, the advent of the task force itself is a major landmark in the transformation of women's imprisonment in Canada.

There is, as countless previous observers have pointed out, no easy solution to the reform of women's federal imprisonment. Vigilance is essential if it is accepted that—as a number of post-modernist feminists[71] would argue—there is no inevitable progress or amelioration in society, and that change will, in its own way, impose new or different problems.

For the women still at P4W waiting for 1994, there is, as yet, little evidence of real change.

Notes

1 Many people assisted me in the preparation of this chapter, and I owe a debt to all of them, including Jane Miller-Ashton, Bonnie Diamond, Brenda Le Page, and Kim Pate. The errors are my own.

2 The task force report is careful to avoid using the word feminist, and refers instead to a 'woman-centred' approach.

3 An account of that struggle, which has lasted for some 150 years, is given in Sheelagh Cooper's chapter in this book. The last committee (Chinnery) had reported in 1978. There were 13 commissions or committees before the 1990 report which had recommended the closure of P4W.

4 *Creating Choices: Report of the Task Force on Federally Sentenced Women* (Ottawa: Correctional Service of Canada, 1990), p. 1.

5 P4W is the only penitentiary for federally sentenced women in Canada, but since the early 1970s certain women receiving federal sentences have remained in provincial prisons in their own provinces. Approximately one-third of the federal population is housed in provincial prisons, but in conditions not suited to long sentences, and often without access to any substantive programmes.

6 *Creating Choices*, p. 93.

7 See L. Berzins and B. Hayes, "The Diaries of Two Change Agents," in *Too Few To Count*, ed. Ellen Adelberg and Claudia Currie (Vancouver: Press Gang Publishers, 1987). They describe as cosmetic the changes resulting from the ruling by the Human Rights Commission.

8 Canada, *Report of the Standing Committee on Justice and the Solicitor General on its Review of Sentencing, Conditional Release and Related Aspects of Corrections* (Daubney Report) (Ottawa: Ministry of Supply and Services, 1988); M. Jackson, *Justice Behind the Walls* (Ottawa: Canadian Bar Association, 1988).

9 See Renate Mohr, "Sentencing as a Gendered Process: Results of a Consultation," *Canadian Journal of Criminology* 32 (1990): 479–85.

10 See Kathleen Daly and Meda Chesney-Lind, "Feminism and Criminology," *Justice Quarterly* 5, no. 4 (1988), for an outline of the range of feminist theories. For accounts of the development of perspectives on violence against women and of feminist approaches to criminal justice, see Lorenne Clark, "Feminist Perspectives on Violence against Women and Children," *Canadian Journal of Women and the Law* 3 (1989–90): 420–31; Dawn Currie and Marlee Kline, "Challenging Privilege: Women, Knowledge and Feminist Struggles," *Journal of Human Justice* 2, no. 2 (Spring 1991): 1–36; and Sally Simpson, "Feminist Theory, Crime, and Justice," *Criminology* 27, no. 4 (1989): 605–31.

11 For an account of the life and death of Marlene Moore, who committed suicide at P4W in 1988, see A. Kershaw and M. Lasovich, *Rock-a-Bye Baby : A Death Behind Bars* (Toronto: McClelland and Stewart, 1991). Many Aboriginal women with equally horrific lives of abuse have also committed suicide in custody, but have not had the publicity that developed around this case.

12 The new Commissioner of Corrections, Ole Instrup, had recently established a mission statement for the Correctional Service and was committed to changing the direction of the Service towards the reintegration of offenders into the community, establishing better treatment programmes, and improving staff-inmate relations. The Executive Director of CAEFS 1987–91, Bonnie Diamond, played a central role in maintaining pressure on the government to reform the federal system for women.

13 Very few countries have established official committees to examine the position of women in corrections. A few states in the United States and some in Australia (e.g., New South Wales, Queensland, Victoria) have done so, but in most cases, while there has been some voluntary representation, the committees have remained primarily government committees.

14 The Steering Group was chaired by Bonnie Diamond, Executive Director of CAEFS, and Jim Phelps, Deputy Commissioner, CSC; and the Working Group by Jane Miller-Ashton, Director, Native and Female Offender Programmes, CSC, and Felicity Hawthorn, Past President of CAEFS.

15 These included representatives from CAEFS and individual Elizabeth Fry Soci-

eties (six), groups representing Aboriginal women (five), visible minorities (two), and other parts of the community (four). The fourteen government appointees included representatives of headquarters and the five regions of the Correctional Service of Canada, as well as other federal departments.

16 Four members represented Elizabeth Fry Societies; two Aboriginal women's groups; and five represented the Correctional Service of Canada and the Solicitor General.

17 "The process itself was often painful. Throughout the Task Force we struggled to work within a consensus model." *Creating Choices*, p. 2.

18 Pat Bear and Sandy Sayer died in March and October 1989, respectively. The following year two more Aboriginal women committed suicide and a third never regained consciousness after attempting to do so. She eventually died in 1992. A sixth Aboriginal woman committed suicide at the prison in February 1991.

19 CAEFS, for example, had to weigh the advantages of playing a major role in the task force against the disadvantages of going against its abolitionist stance. As Bonnie Diamond, Executive Director of CAEFS, has said; "It really tried our souls to be designing a prison system when we don't believe women should be in prison" (quoted in Kershaw and Lasovich, p. 234).

20 See *Creating Choices*, p. 92 and p. 32.

21 See Fran Sugar and Lana Fox, *Survey of Aboriginal Women in the Community* (Ottawa: Native Women's Association of Canada, 1990).

22 *Creating Choices*, p. 91.

23 These included the survey of Aboriginal women (Sugar and Fox); surveys of the federally sentenced population in prison and on conditional release, Margaret Shaw et al., *Survey of Federally Sentenced Women* (Ottawa: Solicitor General of Canada, 1990) and Margaret Shaw, with Karen Rodgers and Tina Hattem, *The Release Study: Survey of Federally Sentenced Women in the Community* (Ottawa: Solicitor General of Canada, 1991); a review of the literature on women's imprisonment, Margaret Shaw, *The Federal Female Offender: Report on a Preliminary Study* (Ottawa: Solicitor General of Canada, 1991); a survey of existing programmes for women, Maureen Evans, *A Survey of Institutional Programmes Available to Federally Sentenced Women* (Ottawa: Solicitor General of Canada, 1990); and a review of prison programmes for women in the United States, Lee Axon, *Model and Exemplary Programmes for Female Inmates: An International Review* (Ottawa: Solicitor General of Canada, 1990).

24 *Creating Choices*, p. 95.

25 *Creating Choices*, p. 109.

26 See Curt Griffiths and Simon Verdun Jones, *Canadian Criminal Justice* (Toronto: Butterworths, 1989), pp. 408ff, for a discussion of classification. A number of previous reports on federally sentenced women had stressed that women tended to be overclassified in security terms because of the use of classification procedures based on the male population, as well as the existence of only one federal institution (see Shaw, *The Federal Female Offender*). What was new about the task force report was its rejection of classification for women in favour of individual assessment.

27 See, for example, the Clark, Chinnery, and Needham reports (Ottawa: Ministry of the Solicitor General, 1977, 1978, 1978) and Shaw, *The Federal Female Offender*). The Chinnery Report, in its appendix, stands out for its far more detailed discussion of some of these issues.

28 Correctional Service of Canada, news release, July 1990.

29 The report specified Halifax, Montreal, Edmonton, a city in southern or central Ontario, and, if necessary, lower mainland British Columbia. The position of British Columbia was complicated by the completion of a new Exchange of Service Agreement with the province at the start of the task force. This agreement, which has a ten-year life-span, was finalized in April 1990, and established a new basis for the funding of federal places in the province, and greater federal say in programming. The agreement enabled British Columbia to build a new provincial prison for women at Burnaby into which federally sentenced women in the province have since been moved. It should also be noted that federally sentenced women from Newfoundland have largely been the responsibility of the provincial government and have usually remained there, and that separate plans are being made for women from the Territories.

30 Eight short-term recommendations for changes at P4W were also presented separately to the Commissioner of Corrections because of concerns that there might be a considerable delay before the report was implemented.

31 From this point on the possible development of a regional facility in British Columbia was dropped.

32 Jane Miller-Ashton, who played a crucial role in the task force as Director of Female and Native Offender Programmes, took on responsibility for chairing the NIC.

33 The only non-government members of the National Implementation Committee were two Aboriginal representatives. Much of the work of the NIC was carried out by five subcommittees. From time to time external advisors who were experts in a particular field were invited to attend subcommittee meetings.

34 This was to include Bonnie Diamond (and subsequently Kim Pate), Executive Director of CAEFS, Sharon McIvor, Native Women's Association of Canada, and Kay Stanley, of Status of Women, Canada, a government department. However, for the first eighteen months of the implementation phase the EAC did not meet due to lack of funding, time constraints, and changes of personnel, and no federally sentenced women were appointed to the committee as originally planned. In the view of Bonnie Diamond, it would have been almost a full-time task monitoring progress on the implementation. Without financial assistance CAEFS could not afford to undertake that job. She eventually resigned from CAEFS after CSC failed to accept the task force recommendations for external involvement in the implementation phase.

35 The Native Advisory Committee initially had equal representation of government and Aboriginal peoples and was supported by an Elders Circle to give spiritual guidance. Two Aboriginal women subsequently withdrew from the committee.

36 Even before formal criteria for the sites were made public in January 1991, the CSC had received some 250 unsolicited applications from communities across Canada wanting a regional facility in their area.

37 *Tightwire*, July 1989.

38 CBC TV, *The National*, 20 April 1990.

39 *CTV Newsline*, 16 December 1991.

40 See, for example, comments in *CAEFS Newsletter*, Spring 1992 and *Tightwire*, Summer 1992.

41 For example, the EAC was not informed about site selection prior to announcements in the press.

42 "We've had very little problem with Corrections; in fact they've been 100 percent behind our process" (Sharon McIvor, Chair of the Native Advisory Committee, *Globe and Mail*, 20 March 1992).

43 See, for example, Louise Biron, "Les femmes et l'incarcération, le temps n'arrange rien," *Criminologie* 25, no. 1 (1992): 119–34; Kelly Moffat, "Canadian Female Offenders and Correctional Reform," *Social Justice* 18, no. 3 (1991): 184–202; and, more generally, Laureen Snider, "The Potential of the Criminal Justice System to Promote Feminist Concerns," in *The Social Basis of Law: Critical Readings in the Sociology of Law* (2d ed.), ed. E. Comack and S. Brickey (Halifax: Garamond, 1991).

44 See D. Brown and M. Quinn, "Women in Prison: Review of the New South Wales Task Force Report," *Legal Services Bulletin* (December 1985); see also

Pat Carlen's account of the new prison for women in Scotland, *Women's Imprisonment: A Study in Social Control* (London: Routledge & Kegan Paul, 1983) and Shaw, *The Federal Female Offender*.

45 See, for example, such headlines in the local Halifax press as "Buchanan joins list of prison site critics," *The Chronicle Herald*, 26 November 1991, and "Women's jail banned from residential areas," *The Chronicle Herald*, 29 November 1991. This was in marked contrast to most other communities bidding for the facilities, which have been in strong competition to "win" the new facility with its guarantee of secure jobs and income (compare, for example, "New prison for women on Edmonton's wish list," *Edmonton Journal*, 20 December 1991). While Kitchener was a less controversial decision, concern was voiced by CAEFS and others when the Mayor suggested that the facility should be sited in an industrial park away from residential areas (*Kingston Whig Standard*, 23 December 1991).

46 The selection criteria developed by the NIC listed seventeen features which had to be present at a site, including proximity to the home community of the majority of the women in the region, good transport, and well-established women's support and counselling services. The Solicitor General had announced in 1991 that they must also be within 100 kilometres of the target cities of Montreal, Halifax, Edmonton or Calgary, and Toronto. Separate selection criteria were laid down for the healing lodge. These emphasized nearness to home communities, access to a large rural land base and fresh water, and a supportive local Aboriginal community which had not lost its traditional heritage.

47 See, for example, the Elizabeth Fry Society Halifax/Dartmouth press release 16 December 1991; the *Globe and Mail*, 20 March 1992; *CAEFS Newsletter*, Spring 1992; *Canadian Criminal Justice Association Bulletin*, January 1992.

48 See Jo-Ann Mayhew, *CAEFS Newsletter*, Spring 1992.

49 Eighteen member societies voted for withdrawal at the meeting; after the meeting, the nineteenth reiterated its support for the decision.

50 These included l'Association des services de réhabilitation sociale (A.S.R.S.), l'Office des droits des detenus, l'Association des avocats en droit carceral, la Société de criminologie du Québec, and la Fédération des femmes du Québec, among others. (See *Femmes et Justice, bulletin d'information de la Société Élizabeth Fry de Montréal* 8, no. 1 [automne 1992].

51 To ensure francophone services, Quebec has had responsibility under an Exchange of Service Agreement for the majority of its federally sentenced women since 1979. At the time of the 1989 survey, there were twenty-six federal French-speaking women in Quebec and fourteen at P4W, as well as six anglo-

phone women in Quebec. Both the provincial government of Quebec and the Elizabeth Fry Society of Montreal had initially argued that federally sentenced women should not be separated from provincial women with whom they had been housed. This was on the grounds that separation would lead to a fragmentation of programmes and that provincial women should also benefit from the changes in regime (*Femmes et Justice* 7, no. 1 [Septembre 1991] and 7, no. 3 [Mars 1992]).

52 See notes 29 and 31 above.

53 *Creating Choices,* p. 102.

54 Former task force member Sally Wills, quoted in the *Globe and Mail,* 20 March 1992.

55 See, for example, Moffat.

56 This was thought likely to have happened in the Maritime provinces, where there were no Exchange of Service Agreements. Following publication of the task force, the hardship of transfer to Kingston certainly influenced judicial decisions in the case of Carol Daniels, a young Aboriginal mother given a federal life sentence. The Saskatchewan court specifically prohibited her transfer to P4W in 1990 on the grounds that she would be discriminated against if she had to serve her time at P4W.

57 The proposed Ontario facility at Kitchener is to have a capacity of seventy, and that in Quebec, of seventy-five, for example. In 1988, sixty-eight federally sentenced women were from Ontario and seventy-two from Quebec (Shaw, *The Federal Female Offender*). Nevertheless, these figures represent the total "on register" federal population, including women on day parole in halfway houses as well as those temporarily absent. The actual number of women ever in residence (the "daily count") is always considerably smaller than the "on register" population by some fifty to seventy women. It must also be remembered that British Columbia's population is for the most part excluded from further consideration. In the Atlantic Region, it is expected that the provincial government will "buy" fifteen of the thirty beds in the new Truro facility for provincially sentenced women.

58 See, for example, discussion by A. Blumstein, "The Influence of Capacity on Prison Population: A Critical Review of Some Recent Evidence," *Crime and Delinquency* 29 (1983): 1–51; and T. Hattem, "L'histoire se poursuit...," *Femme et Justice* 5, no. 5 (Juin 1990).

59 See, for example, Pat Carlen, *Alternatives to Women's Imprisonment* (Milton Keynes: Open University Press, 1990) and Moffat, "Canadian Female Offenders and Correctional Reform."

60 Stanley Cohen, *Visions of Social Control* (Cambridge, U.K.: Polity Press, 1985), and "Taking Decentralization Seriously: Values, Visions and Policies," in his *Against Criminology* (Oxford: Transaction Books, 1988).

61 See Tina Hattem, "L'histoire se poursuit."

62 Some of these issues are discussed in Cohen, *Visions of Social Control*; by M. Shaw, "Issues of Power and Control: Women in Prison and Their Defenders," *British Journal of Criminology* 32, no. 4 (1992): 438–52; and by Ngaire Naffine, *Female Crime: The Construction of Women in Criminology* (Boston: Allen and Unwin, 1988). Elizabeth Comack and Laureen Snider make similar points in relation to the battered wife syndrome and its pathologizing and individualizing of women's experiences (see Comack, "Legal Recognition of the 'Battered Wife Syndrome': A Victory for Women?" Paper presented to the American Society of Criminology, San Francisco, November 1991; and Snider, "The Potential of the Criminal Justice System").

63 Brown and Quinn, "Women in Prison."

64 See, for example, Paul Rock's account of the transformation of the National Action Committee's notion of family violence, with its specific feminist connotations, into a government initiative concerning victims of crime (*A View from the Shadows* [Oxford: Clarendon Press, 1985]); Dawn Currie and Marlee Kline's discussion of the limits of political change in relation to women's victimization ("Challenging Privilege"); and Elizabeth Comack's account of the redefining of the battered wife syndrome by the legal system and more general discussion of the incorporation of women's concerns by the criminal justice system ("Legal Recognition of the 'Battered Wife Syndrome'").

65 Biron, "Les femmes et l'incarcération."

66 Brown and Quinn, "Women in Prison."

67 Berzins and Hayes, "The Diaries of Two Change Agents."

68 See L. Berzins and S. Cooper, "The Political Economy of Correctional Planning for Women: The Case of the Bankrupt Bureaucracy," *Canadian Journal of Criminology* 24 (October 1982): 394–416.

69 For example, in July 1992 Nova Scotia published its own Task Force Report, *Blueprint for Change*, recommending the abolition of imprisonment for provincially sentenced women and the development of four community residences. The Northwest Territories and Ontario are both considering alternative policies for women offenders. *Creating Choices* has also attracted considerable international attention.

70 In 1987–88 the number of women serving sentences in institutions in Canada and in England and Wales, for example, was similar, but Canada has a popula-

tion half their combined size. The main difference is in the heavy use of short-term sentences in Canada (see Shaw, *The Federal Female Offender*).

71 Post-modernist feminism is concerned with the recognition of a variety of positions and cultural views on the role and position of women in society. See, for example, the discussion in Loraine Gelsthorpe and Allison Morris, *Feminist Perspectives in Criminology* (Milton Keynes: Open University Press, 1990).

Aboriginal Women
and Prison Reform†

Ellen Adelberg and the Native Women's
Association of Canada

When the Task Force on Federally Sentenced Women began its work in
1989, Aboriginal women were quick to state their desire for representation
in adequate numbers so that they could give voice to the unique problems
they faced in prisons, and could propose recommendations for change. As
a result, the number of Aboriginal women sitting on the task force was increased to six. Two of these women, Fran Sugar and Lana Fox, were commissioned to carry out a survey of Aboriginal inmates in the Kingston
Prison for Women (P4W),[1] and in the final report of the task force[2]
Aboriginal women developed a framework for changes to the prison system intended to create a healing, as opposed to punitive, environment.

A substantial part of Sugar and Fox's report, *Survey of Federally Sen-*
tenced Aboriginal Women in the Community, is reprinted in the first section of this chapter. This is followed by a summary of the recommendations
made by Aboriginal women in the final task force report, and a progress re-

---

† This chapter compiles material first prepared by Fran Sugar and Lana Fox for the Task
Force on Federally Sentenced Women, recommendations by Aboriginal women in *Creating*
Choices, the final report of the Task Force on Federally Sentenced Women, material based on
an interview with Sharon McIvor of the Native Women's Association of Canada, and discussions with Kim Pate of the Canadian Association of Elizabeth Fry Societies and others who are
following the progress of the task force's report.

port on the implementation of the recommendations for a healing lodge, based on an interview with Sharon McIvor of the Native Women's Association of Canada and informal discussions with others.

Highlights from "Survey of Federally Sentenced Aboriginal Women in the Community"[3]

At times when I'd burn my medicines, when we had sweetgrass smuggled in to us because sometimes it was seen as contraband, the sweet smell of the earth would create a safe feeling, a feeling of being alive even though the cage represented a coffin, the prison a gravestone, and my sisters walking dead people. These medicines were what connected me as a spirit child. One time when I was close to suicide I was told by Mista Hiya[4] that my spirit was alive and it was housed in my physical shell. And from that hard time I learned that my spirit was more important than my body because my body was controlled by the routine of life in prison. It was then the connectedness to being an Aboriginal woman began. I began feeling good about myself even though I had only a few reasons to feel good. I understood there was a spirit within me that had the will to live.[5]

This is a report about First Nations women in the Canadian federal prison system. It is also a very personal document, one in which it is difficult for us to be impartial. The experiences to which this report speaks are our experiences: we, the researchers, have lived them. When we retell the stories of the 39 Aboriginal women who speak through the pages of our report we are also sharing our own stories, for we too have known the brutality, violence, racism and oppression of which the stories tell.

Our participation in the Task Force has been difficult. We entered the Task Force as prisoners. As prisoners we spoke with grave hesitation. It was our experience that the last 12 task forces, the numerous commissions, working groups, federal department officials, and other organizations that are said to represent women in cages had already conducted study upon study. We felt that another task force would be repeating what is already known and documented somewhere ... in some brown file ... in some room ... covered with dust. We felt that this task force would be as useless as all the other task forces that have been shelved.

In Task Force meetings, faced with theoretical discussions of the condition of women in prison, voiced by people whose responsibility is bureaucratic, we felt repulsed and suffocated. This talk had no connection to the reality we had experienced. When our rage became uncontainable we spoke of prison conditions, of the actual experiences of being Aboriginal women in prison, of real-life brutality. Yet our words were met with tense silences and appear nowhere in the minutes of meetings. Our descriptions of the reality are buried as our sisters are buried in prison.

In the past we have spoken to other task forces, sentencing commissions, reporters, investigators, Correctional Service staff and various other people who listened politely and nodded in apparent understanding. Yet afterwards our conditions, the conditions of our sisters, remained unchanged. The segregation unit continued to hold us hostage without heat in the dead of winter, without toothpaste or a tooth brush. More seriously, medical treatment for crisis situations was so deplorable that we often believed that death was inevitable for Sisters who slashed.[6] In three years the shower in the bathroom on the upper tier of segregation remained unrepaired. Cells in population[7] have had hot water only since 1987, installed after grievances were organized.

To each task force that we met, we outlined typical issues that affected our lives in prison. We described archaic conditions, arbitrary mass punishment, sexism and racial barriers imposed by administration and security classifications that were applied to us because as Native women we were seen as a collective, as a war party that posed a risk to the good order of the institution. We outlined personal accounts of involuntary transfers to Prison for Women [P4W] for people who were supposed to serve provincial sentences. We talked about living under the special handling unit standards of the blanket 230 code. For the simple fact is that maximum security Native women at P4W were prejudged as violent, uncontrollable, and unmanageable because we refused to cooperate with male guards who ordered us to remove our clothes in provincial prisons or population. We told the numerous task forces that medical/psychiatric evaluations were not culturally appropriate. We knew the questions they asked us were questions made for white people, for white men. We vocalized that most of us were survivors of sexual abuse, rape and wife battering and the only option for treatment was at Kingston Prison for Men [KP]. We pointed out that KP is older than P4W and that it housed sex offenders, the perpetrators who symbolized the same men who victimized us. How did they expect us to help ourselves when that was the only treatment available and it was no damn good in the first place? How can anyone expect to heal themselves under those conditions? And because Native women refused to go for treatment, refused to accept drug treatments offered, our parole applications were not supported because we "didn't address our own treatment needs."

As our stories show, Aboriginal women who end up in prison grow up in prison, though the prisons in which they grow up are not the ones to which they are sentenced under law.

When movement passes were introduced at P4W in 1982 or 1983, they echoed another history. Our ancestors were required to obtain passes from the RCMP or from the Indian Agent to travel off reserve. Now we required written permission to go up a flight of stairs or to move three feet from A Range to the hospital. Our ancestors also understood that such laws were made to be broken. All this may seem trivial, but each part of prison existence for Aboriginal women has a context. It is experienced through eyes and feelings that are *female, Aboriginal,* and *imprisoned.* Each of these things makes a great deal of difference to the way prison is experienced.

No amount of tinkering with prisons can heal the before-prison lives of the Aboriginal women who live or have lived within their walls. Prison cannot remedy the problem of the poverty of reserves. It cannot deal with immediate or historical memories of the genocide that Europeans worked upon our people. It cannot remedy violence, alcohol abuse, sexual assault during childhood, rape and other violence Aboriginal women experience at the hands of men. Prison cannot heal the past abuse of foster homes, or the indifference and racism of Canada's justice system in its dealings with Aboriginal people. However, the treatment of Aboriginal women within prisons can begin to recognize that these things *are* the realities of the lives that Aboriginal women prisoners have led. By understanding this, we can begin to make changes that will promote healing instead of rage.

Essential to an understanding of the destructive nature of P4W is the history of violence that most of us share. For our stories show that we have all been the victims of violence. Many of us are not the victims of violence in the way in which victims of a mugging experience violence. Instead, and all too often, we are the victims of long-term and systematic violence. Many of our stories tell about sexual and physical abuse during childhood. Some of this violence occurred in our birth families, in some cases it arose in foster homes and juvenile institutions. Twenty-seven of the 39 women interviewed described experiences of childhood violence: rape, regular sexual abuse, the witnessing of a murder, watching our mothers repeatedly beaten, beatings in juvenile detention centres at the hands of staff and other children. Twenty-one had been raped or sexually assaulted either as children or as adults.

> I didn't like the way the social worker didn't believe us, she said "if you're lying those people won't get foster children ever again, you can wreck their lives if you say they molested you."

> The foster father tried to molest me, plus a sister would cause trouble for me. I pulled a knife on the foster mother. I thought it was the only way out of there.

For many of us this childhood violence became an ongoing feature of life, and continued into childhood and adulthood. However, to these things were added the violence of tricks, rape, and assaults on the streets. In adulthood, 34 of the 39 had been the victims of violence, at the hands of abusive spouses (25), from tricks who had beaten and/or raped them (12 of 39 shared this experience and 9 had been violent towards tricks), or from police or prison guards.

The violence of which we are the victims, and of which our stories tell, is not occasional or temporary. Most of us have experienced sustained abuse extending through much of our lives. Indeed, our stories have much in common with what the criminal statistics on violence say. The violence we have experienced has typically been violence at the hands of men.

There is no accidental relationship between our convictions for violent offenses and our histories as victims. As victims we carry the burden of memories: of pain inflicted on us, of violence done before our eyes to those we loved, of rape, of sexual assaults, of beatings, of death. For us violence has beget violence: our contained hatred and rage concentrated in an explosion that has left us with yet more memories to scar and mark us.

> I saw my father beat my mother. Inside I said that it would never happen to me. My common-law hit me. I shot him.

> I got sick and tired of being beaten up so I stabbed him. I was charged with attempted murder. After that I still stayed with him because he said he would not testify if I did stay with him. I saw it as my only way out of prison.

Our stories tell of all those self-destructive ways through which women who are victims seek escape. Suicide attempts are common. Thirty-one of 39 had abused alcohol, 10 coming from families with serious alcohol problems, and 10 considering their own abuse serious. Twenty-seven considered themselves severely addicted to narcotics, and many were addicted to prescription drugs. Twenty-three tell of addiction *in institutions* to prescription drugs provided by institutional psychiatrists or physicians. Ten of 39 describe slashing themselves: self-mutilations that are not suicide attempts, but the relief of tension and anger, physical pain self-inflicted as escape from what lay inside us.

Our stories also show that the regime of P4W is not one under which these things can be healed.

When I was in Prison for Women I was the youngest one there. I was seventeen. This was 1977. Older women were there for drug trafficking charges ... few murder convictions. There was no security classification. I was released on mandatory supervision. Had no passes. Too young, couldn't be bothered with parole. I lived on the street when I got out.

But to understand why places like P4W cannot help us requires another insight, an insight into who we are. Not only are we women who are both the victims and initiators of violence, but we are also members of the First Nations, the survivors of people now forced to subsist on the margins of the lands where once they lived freely.

Our understandings of law, of courts, of police, of the judicial system, and of prisons are all set by lifetimes defined by racism. Racism is not simply set by the overt experiences of racism, though most of us have known this direct hatred, have been called "dirty Indians" in school, or in foster homes, or by police or guards, or have seen the differences in the way we were treated and have known that this was no accident. Racism is much more extensive than this. Culturally, economically, and as peoples we have been oppressed and pushed aside by whites. We were sent to live on reserves that denied us a livelihood, controlled us with rules that we did not set, and made us dependent on services we could not provide for ourselves.

The Indian Agent[8] and the police are for us administrators of oppressive regimes whose authority we resent and deny. Like other peoples around the world who live under illegitimate political structures, we learn that the rules imposed by this authority exist to be broken, that they are not our ways, that they are only the outside and not the inside measure of the way a person should act. As children we were taught to fear white authority because of the punishments it could enforce. Faced with institutional neglect and overt racism, our feelings about white authority even before we encountered the criminal justice system mixed passive distrust and active hatred.

Our stories tell of this. Most of the women interviewed have histories that have led them to mistrust white authority. Twenty of the 39 described negative relationships with police; many of these descriptions portray this distrust as "inherent," a consequence of the role the police play in the lives of Aboriginal people. Other white authority figures were commonly the source of negative experiences and are seen as abusive, racist or non-supportive. Of 14 women with experiences in foster homes, 12 described negative relationships with foster parents, and only 2 had had positive relationships. Thirty-two of the 39 women report experiencing racism at some time in their lives. Twenty-three had felt discriminated against in school, 15 in halfway houses, 6 in detox centres. These experiences extend to those who are supposed to provide helping services: case officers (13 reported this relationship as negative), parole officers (20), and social workers (9). Relationships with prison guards are reported in extremely negative terms: physical beatings, rape, sexual harassment, and verbal intimidation.

> The boarding school was run by nuns. They used to call us savages. To this day I hate the word "savage."

> Out of all the women involved I was the only one maced, they had me face down on the floor. One of them had their foot on my head. I couldn't move, they were hitting me on the back with billy clubs. To this day I have a scar there, three-and-one-half inches long, then the goon squad dragged me to segregation after they beat me in front of the whole range. Now they sent my sister home in a box!

In many cases, attitudes to white authority formed an important background to the way in which the women received federal sentences. There are several reports in the interviews by women who had neither believed that the court system would treat them justly, nor trusted the lawyer who was supposed to act on their behalf. Since they felt powerless and had no trust in or understanding of the process, some acquiesced. They accepted an unfavourable plea bargain, or remained silent, refusing to offer evidence that either exonerated them or implicated others in the more serious features of the crimes with which they had been charged. They endured being sent to prison in the same silence with which they had greeted past victimization.

> Before trial, after our arrest, we need support. Most of us were raised in residential places like prisons and the judges convict us for that. I believe we are victims being victimized. We get federal sentences for running away from jail and yet that's all we have ever done, run away from institutions. They think it's nice in there, why in the hell would we run away in the first place?

For Aboriginal women, prison is an extension of life on the outside, and because of this, it is impossible for us to heal there. In ways that are different from the world outside, but are nevertheless continuous with it, prisons offer more white authority that is sexist, racist and violent. Prisons are then one more focus for the pain and rage we carry. For us, prison rules have the same illegitimacy as the oppressive rules under which we grew up. Those few "helping" services in prison that are intended to heal are delivered in ways that are culturally inappropriate to us as women and as Aboriginal people. Physicians, psychiatrists, and psychologists are typically white and male. How can we be healed by those who symbolize the worst experiences of our past? We cannot trust these so-called care givers, and all too often in the views of those interviewed, we again experience direct hostility from the very people who are supposedly there to help. This was why Aboriginal women express anger at these care givers. This is why we refuse to become involved, and then are further punished because we fail to seek treatment.

Almost all the healing experiences that Aboriginal women who have been in prison report in our interviews lie outside the conventional prison order. They come through the bonds formed with other women in prison, through the support of people on the outside, and from the activities of Native Sisterhood. There are occasional reports of positive relationships with caseworkers, but these stand out as exceptions to the prevailing pattern. The refusal of Aboriginal women to trust the "helping" services of prison becomes one more strike against them. Many of those interviewed share the experience of being seen as uncooperative. They were kept at high-security classifications and denied passes. They were located far from their families, who could not afford to visit them, and had their parole ap-

plications turned down because they refused treatment or were uncooperative.

> Because of Native Sisterhood I finally knew the meaning of spirituality. I learned
> how to pray in a sweat and with sweetgrass. I learned the meaning of the Eagle
> feather and colours. With that I was even more proud of who I was in my iden-
> tity.

> Slowly I was changing. Feeling better about myself. My mother was quite tradi-
> tional. When I got out I went back to my family. The whole reconnection to my
> people meant my family to me. I wanted life after going to Native Sisterhood, it
> meant everything to me.

Twenty-six of the women are mothers, and all of them reported negative impacts on their relationships with their children. Such an impact is
not surprising, but it is made worse by distance, the impossibility of seeing
their children, and by the orientations of prison officials, who are widely
seen as insensitive to mother-child relationships. Children were placed in
foster care, juvenile detention centres, or moved between family members.
Twenty-five of the mothers had difficulty being mothers, resuming their relationship with their children, on release, and only 17 were reunited with
them.

> I had to learn to be a mother all over again but this time with bigger children. I
> can't relate to them now. I have no patience.

> Too far from home. I was lonely for my children and had no communication
> from them while I was there.

We have often said that the women inside have the understanding to
help ourselves, that all that is required is the right kind of resources, support, and help. The money spent on studies would be much better spent on
family visits, on culturally appropriate help, on reducing our powerlessness to heal ourselves. But the reality is that prison conditions grow worse.
     This project [survey] began when we voiced our concern that the Task
Force had not heard the views of Aboriginal women who have served time
at P4W. We believe that these women have an essential contribution to
make to the work of the Task Force. The life stories we have heard speak

strongly to the special treatment needs of Aboriginal women, needs that differ from those of non-Native women.

The critical difference is racism. We are born to it and spend our lives facing it. Racism lies at the root of our life experiences. The effect is violence, violence against us, and in turn our own violence. The solution is healing: healing through traditional ceremonies, support, understanding and the compassion that will empower Aboriginal women to the betterment of ourselves, our families and our communities.

Existing programs cannot reach us, cannot surmount the barriers of mistrust that racism has built. It is only Aboriginal people who can design and deliver programs that will address our needs and that we can trust. It is only Aboriginal people who can truly know and understand our experience. It is only Aboriginal people who can instill pride and self-esteem lost through the destructive experiences of racism. We cry out for a meaningful healing process that will have real impact on our lives, but the objectives and implementation of this healing process must be premised on our need, the need to heal and walk in balance.

Aboriginal Women's Recommendations to the Task Force

With the detailed knowledge of their own and their sisters' experiences within the Prison for Women as outlined by Sugar and Fox, Aboriginal members of the Task Force on Federally Sentenced Women spelled out their vision for an improved manner of treating Aboriginal prisoners.[9] They prefaced their recommendations with a broader statement:

Our Peoples, as Nations, have never consented to the application of the Euro-Canadian legal systems and the corresponding values. Our participation in the task force should be viewed as *only* a deep felt concern for the many citizens of our many Nations who suffer daily at the hands of the criminal justice system.[10]

In the final task force report, Aboriginal women also stated that:

... as it stands now, an aboriginal woman is more likely to go to prison than she is to go to university. This is a reality we will not accept for our future.

We also do not accept that any real change will occur by focusing our attention solely on the plight of aboriginal *prisoners.* Those individuals on charge or at risk are of no less concern to us than those already federally sentenced. Efforts must therefore focus on "turning off the tap" so aboriginal individuals no longer come into conflict with foreign justice systems, be they child welfare systems, juvenile justice, federal or provincial systems. It is only when we are able to reach this point that we will again be remaining and living true to our traditional philosophies as they were given to us by the Creator.[11]

Despite their ultimate desire for Aboriginal self-government and a complete change in Canada's treatment of Aboriginal people, the Aboriginal women who sat on the task force developed a model for a new correctional facility for federally sentenced women that they hoped would allow those serving sentences to heal. They called the facility a "healing lodge," and based its structure on Native healing principles. The task force members stipulated that the healing lodge must be located on the Prairies, at a location agreed to by Aboriginal communities, "not [only] the Correctional Service of Canada."

The connection of the healing lodge to an aboriginal community will be essential to its survival. The development of the lodge will also require the expertise of aboriginal women.... Overall responsibility for programs for aboriginal women [should] be given to the Elders Council in each region.

The lodge will be premised on principles which promote:

- a safe place for aboriginal women prisoners;
- a caring attitude towards self, family and community;
- a belief in individualized client-specific planning;
- an understanding of the transitory aspects of aboriginal life;
- an appreciation of the healing role of children, who are closer to the spirit world;
- pride in surviving difficult backgrounds and personal experiences.

The Aboriginal women on the task force called for the lodge to be circular in structure and for the design to be complementary to the surrounding natural environment. The focal point for ceremonies, teaching, and workshops with Elders would be a central round meeting room. Teachers, Elders, and healers were to be involved in "key aspects of the lodge's activities," and a daycare centre would provide a chance for women to be with their children. The living areas would contain communal space, family units, and "opportunities to live close to the land."[12]

The authors of the task force report stated clearly that all federally sentenced Aboriginal women should have the option of serving their sentence at the lodge or at a non-Native facility. Once they arrived at the lodge, the women would be assessed, and their needs would be established "in a manner that is relevant to aboriginal women."[13]

Critical to the success of the healing lodge would be the availability of "Elders, other teachers and healers." It was recommended that at least one Elder be on site at all times, and that the position be rotated to "accommodate women from different nations, and the four directions." Some of the spiritual helpers in the healing process were to be women who were themselves serving sentences.[14]

Regarding programs, the task force members called for "a holistic approach to the needs of federally sentenced aboriginal women, including, most importantly, services to address issues associated with "health, with sexual, physical and emotional abuse, with relationships and with substance abuse."[15] They also emphasized the need for outreach services to prepare women for "walking in the new forest" (a term used to describe cities, which for aboriginal people are traditionally unfamiliar, unlike the forest where they have survived for thousands of years). Such services would include education, vocational training, employment and life skills training, and parenting education.[16]

Perhaps most importantly, task force members called for the hiring of Aboriginal staff for the healing lodge. "Non-aboriginal staff may be recruited from time to time in a support role for specific skills and expertise." They recommended that the lodge be administered "to the largest extent possible through a non-hierarchical model." The coordinator would have "certain responsibilities to other Correctional Service of Canada officials. However, this individual [would] also have responsibility to liaise and work co-operatively with the Elders' Council, the aboriginal community and the women." One of the most important criteria for selecting staff, according to the task force members, would be "their life experience and their ability to act as positive role models for the women serving sentences."[17]

Implementing the Recommendations
for a Healing Lodge

As Margaret Shaw documents in her chapter in this book, the federal Solicitor General acted quickly after the Task Force on Federally Sentenced Women submitted its final report. He announced that the Prison for Women would be closed, and that a healing lodge as well as five other regional facilities for non-Aboriginal women would be opened to house women serving federal sentences. The target date for closing the Prison for Women was 1994. According to Sharon McIvor, who chairs the committee overseeing implementation of the task force recommendations regarding Aboriginal women, initial discussions between the Correctional Service of Canada and the Native Women's Association of Canada (NWAC) regarding NWAC's role during the implementation phase led the organization to refuse to participate in the process.

> Originally they asked us to participate in an advisory way. We told them we wanted to be more than advisors, we wanted Aboriginal women to have control over the planning of the healing lodge. After talks with Ole Ingsgtrup [then Commissioner of Corrections] and others, we were invited to have seven Aboriginal women sit on the healing lodge implementation committee, along with four representatives from the Correctional Service. The agreement was that this committee would make the decisions about implementing the healing lodge. These talks occurred in November 1990. By February 1991, the committee started doing the work of implementing the healing lodge.[18]

McIvor said that in the two years following the committee's formation, work had proceeded to establish an operating plan, select a site, and design a building that will house the healing lodge. "We have had absolutely no problem dealing with Corrections. So far our track record is that the Minister [Solicitor General Doug Lewis] has agreed totally with each of our recommendations." McIvor said she believed the committee had been successful so far in its progress "because we've been reasonable in our requests." And she added, "I think we're a fairly minor project in the overall scheme to close P4W and relocate all of the women."

What she didn't add, but what should be noted, is that these events unfolded at the same time that a much larger drama concerning Aboriginal people had taken centre stage in Canadian politics—the quest of the

Assembly of First Nations and other Aboriginal groups for self-government, as part of Canada's constitutional reform process. The likely impact of these larger events on the mind-set of traditionally inward-looking government bureaucrats and federal politicians can only be speculated upon. As well, the Royal Commission on Aboriginal Peoples was holding hearings across the country, resulting in extended media coverage of the abysmal conditions in which many Aboriginal people live. A few years earlier, Canada's reputation as a country that protected its citizens' human rights had been questioned by its own human rights commission in relation to the condition of Aboriginal peoples.[19]

After a lengthy search, the committee McIvor chaired selected a site for the healing lodge in a remote southwestern corner of Saskatchewan, near a town called Maple Creek. McIvor stated:

We had five pages of conditions for an appropriate site, which included things such as clean, unused land with access to spring water—so that it would be pure—growth [trees and grass], and animals. The Elders had advised us that these elements were essential to the healing process.

We also wanted the site to be near transportation and health services, and to be in Saskatchewan, because the majority of Aboriginal women in the prison come from there. And we wanted a site where Native and non-Native communities worked together, so the women would have access to a supportive Native community, as well as non-Native people.

Despite criticism from some that Maple Creek was too remote (for instance, to make it easily accessible to visiting family members and to specialized services for women at the healing lodge), McIvor said she and other Aboriginal members of the committee were pleased with the site.

We were really looking for a submission that recognized the value of the women. The Nic-a-neek submission [the Nic-a-neek live on a reservation near Maple Creek, a non-Native town] was the only one that articulated the need to help these women. As well, it was one of the few places where we could find unused land, spring water, and the opportunity to build a new building which would meet our specifications. There is racism in Maple Creek, but the Natives and non-Natives have a pretty good working relationship.

McIvor said she felt the Nic-a-neek would provide a supportive Aboriginal community for the women in the healing lodge. "The Nic-a-neek have started their own healing process. They do their own sun dances and teachings, and, a point that is important, they acknowledge that other tribes may be present."

Regarding the design of the actual lodge, McIvor recounted with good humour the many discussions between the committee and the Public Works department, which normally carries out site selection and building design supervision for other government departments.

> Public Works kept telling us we couldn't do things the way we wanted. They had a computerized list of specifications for sites and prison building designs they wanted to use. We explained to them that their specifications weren't good enough and we drafted our own. But it took a long time to convince Public Works to accept what we wanted. In the end we were successful, and we ended up hiring an architectural firm to design the building which had a lot of experience designing buildings for Bands in Saskatchewan, and in designing ceremonial rooms.

Although she was optimistic about the future for the healing lodge, McIvor acknowledged that the committee's toughest negotiating was still to come—over the issue of staffing. McIvor said the Aboriginal women wanted the staff to come from the Aboriginal community, and not from the Correctional Service of Canada. She said the committee had developed a job description for a director of the facility, in keeping with the recommendations from the task force. But she was certain that both Correctional Service officials, and the union representing Correctional Service workers, would need some strong persuading before they would accept the committee's desire to hire staff outside of the traditional correctional framework.

While the Canadian Association of Elizabeth Fry Societies has voiced serious concerns about implementation of the community-based services recommended by the task force for the five non-Aboriginal prisons,[20] McIvor did not have similar concerns about those slated for the healing lodge.

> The budget for training and support services is under our control, which is different than is the case for the other prisons. We want to have the majority of the training sessions for women at the healing lodge available to members of the community. People in the community have expressed a need for healing ser-

vices, so this is something we can share with them, once the healing lodge opens.

In describing the committee's plans for the manner in which the healing lodge will operate, McIvor said:

> Our vision for the healing lodge is a place that's safe for the women. If it's not safe, it won't do anything for them to help them heal. So the operational plan is for non-obtrusive security. There won't be any bars or electronic doors. The land will be fenced, but that's to keep the livestock [from surrounding farms] out. We'll have a safe cottage for women having difficulty dealing with life, for example, those dealing with the effects of sexual abuse. When they're out of control, the safe cottage will be a place with non-breakable glass in the windows. But the women will still have a chance to participate in the rest of the healing lodge activities, and there will be space in the cottage for extra Elders to provide the women with extra companionship.

At the time I interviewed McIvor, in January 1993, of all the recommendations in the task force report, the ones concerning the healing lodge were the only ones about which women outside of government were feeling positive. Within the prison, some Aboriginal women were still feeling skeptical about the potential of the healing lodge to create for them a meaningful alternative to the current facilities. For many, the remote location was of great concern.

But as McIvor pointed out, there was no model to follow in creating a healing environment for Aboriginal women who came into conflict with non-Aboriginal law. She and other task force members looked to the United States, Scandinavia, New Zealand, and Australia, and found nothing.

The move towards the healing lodge represents an important innovation for Canadian corrections. If it is allowed to function in the way envisioned by the Aboriginal women who planned it, it may manage to reverse some of the terrible harm that has been done to Aboriginal women who enter the federal prison system. And it may serve as an example in Canada and to the rest of the world of the possibilities when creativity is allowed to triumph over colonial and patriarchal traditions, as represented by the Prison for Women.

Notes

1 Fran Sugar and Lana Fox, *Survey of Federally Sentenced Aboriginal Women in the Community* (Ottawa: Native Women's Association of Canada, 1990).

2 Task Force on Federally Sentenced Women, *Creating Choices* (Ottawa: Correctional Service of Canada, 1990).

3 With thanks to the Native Women's Association of Canada for permission to reprint sections of Sugar and Fox's *Survey*. The interviews which were the basis of their report were done in 1989. This edited version includes a portion of the interview material quoted in the original report.

4 Mista Hiya was a shaman (or holy person) who ministered to Aboriginal women in the Kingston prison.

5 Fran Sugar, writing from within Prison for Women, Kingston, Ontario, 1986.

6 The term "slashing" is used to describe self-infliction of wounds, usually with a sharp object.

7 "Population" was used to refer to the general area of cells where women who were not being segregated were held in the Prison for Women.

8 "Indian agents" are representatives of the federal government who administer the provisions of the Indian Act under which Aboriginal people are entitled to reserve lands and other rights such as tax exemption.

9 Task Force on Federally Sentenced Women, *Creating Choices.*

10 Ibid., p. 20.

11 Ibid., p. 21.

12 Ibid., p. 145.

13 Ibid., p. 146.

14 Ibid.

15 Ibid.

16 Ibid.

17 Ibid.

18 This and following quotations from Sharon McIvor are taken from an interview with Ellen Adelberg at the Native Women's Association of Canada office, Ottawa, 13 January 1993.

19 In 1988, the Canadian Human Rights Commission reported that Aboriginal women were more likely to go to prison than to university. Canadian Human Rights Commission, *Annual Report* (Ottawa, 1988).

20 See Margaret Shaw's chapter in this book regarding the decision by CAEFS to withdraw formally from the implementation process of the task force report due to CAEFS' grave concerns with the Correctional Service's lack of commitment to the community service recommendations.

II

IMAGES AND REALITIES:

PROFILES OF WOMEN OFFENDERS

A Statistical Overview of Women and Crime in Canada[1]

Holly Johnson and Karen Rodgers

Women account for a minority of all persons charged by police in Canada each year, and rarely pose the kind of threat to public safety as do men who commit more numerous and violent offences. Yet the number of women charged with Criminal Code offences actually amounts to tens of thousands each year. There is also statistical evidence to suggest that thousands more may be at risk of becoming involved in illegal activities because of their poor economic and social standing. Only recently in Canada, with such efforts as the Task Force on Federally Sentenced Women and the work of the Ontario Ministry of Correctional Services,[2] has significant energy been directed toward understanding who these women are, why and how they develop criminal lifestyles, what are their needs, and what can be done to assist them.

Statistical profiles of women offenders have been problematic because of inconsistent data collection at various stages of the criminal justice system, from arrest to incarceration and release. National police statistics have been published annually for three decades, and while the gender of persons charged is specified, further details such as age, race, and other socio-demographic characteristics are not. Recent improvements to the national police survey mean that some details about victims, offenders, and the nature of criminal offences could be released in the near future. The improved data will reveal the age and racial origin (Aboriginal and non-

95

(3)

Aboriginal) of victims and offenders, the relationship between victims and offenders, the extent of injury in violent crimes, and the use of weapons. Data on sentencing of adult offenders is limited because during the 1980s Statistics Canada abandoned efforts to collect national court data.[3] We know little about women sentenced to short terms of imprisonment or remanded in prison awaiting sentence or trial. More detailed data are available on the small group of women serving lengthy terms in the federal prison system. These various data collection systems operate independently of one another, and the task of developing a statistical profile of women offenders is difficult indeed.

Nevertheless, important observations can be made from official statistics about crime involving women. This chapter documents what is known about women in Canada who come into contact with the criminal justice system. It discusses the data within the context of women's social and economic status, and suggests directions for future developments in this area which would increase public understanding of women offenders.

The Status of Women in Canada

The achievements of the contemporary women's movement have meant significant gains for many Canadian women. Over the past two decades or so, women have made inroads into traditionally male-dominated areas of education, the labour force, and politics. The benefits of these advancements have not been shared equally, however. Unemployment, underemployment, poverty, and abuse are still the lot of large numbers of women in Canada today. It is estimated, for example, that one in eight women who lives with a man is abused by him,[4] and that one in two females will be the victim of unwanted sexual acts at some point in her life.[5] During the initial year of divorce, a woman's income drops by about one half, while a man's declines about one quarter. When one takes into account family size, however, a woman's income goes down more than 40 percent, and a man's economic well-being increases slightly.[6] In many jurisdictions, a large proportion of fathers fail to meet their child support obligations.[7] Furthermore, while 82 percent of single-parent families are headed by women, the average income of families headed by women is only half the average income of families headed by men.[8] Fully 56 percent of female single parents have incomes below the poverty line, compared to 20 percent of single fathers.[9]

This imbalance can be explained in part by women's poorer standing in the labour market. Women remain concentrated in part-time jobs and low-paying occupations. Eighty-four percent of working women were employed in service industries in 1988; women also made up 80 percent of clerical occupations.[10] The "ghettoization" of much of women's labour has served to maintain their average earnings at 70 percent of the average earnings of men.[11] Even those with university degrees earn an average of only $2,800 per year more than men with high school education; university-educated women also earn only 70 percent of the salaries earned by men with similar education.[12] For the most disadvantaged women, those comprising the majority of women who come into conflict with the law, equal opportunity remains a distant reality.

The lower socio-economic status of Canadian women can be traced to paternalism and gender-based roles through which women's participation in a wide range of economic activities is limited and their advancement curtailed. Overt discrimination and more subtle gender biases, justified on the basis of women's maternal functions and long-standing expectations of their place in society, put them at a distinct disadvantage in all aspects of social and economic life.[13] Women continue to be socialized to expect a limited range of functions in life, which for the most part preclude economic independence and foster low expectations and low self-esteem.[14] An appreciation of these aspects of women's experience is central to understanding female criminality.

Who Is the Woman Offender?

The public image of women offenders has suffered enormously in the absence of comprehensive data and a focused perspective on female crime. In her chapter in this volume, Gavigan explains in some depth how criminally deviant women have been characterized by early theorists as morally deficient, devious, and deceitful, or maladjusted to their "natural" roles as women.[15] In the 1970s, some theorists contended that we were witnessing an historical upsurge in crime by women and pointed to the contemporary women's movement as the root cause.[16] We were warned, in particular, that women's increased willingness to imitate the behaviour of men was closing the gaps in the incidence and types of crimes committed by women and men, and that a new breed of violent female criminal was on the rise.[17]

As with earlier theories, these too suffered from deep-seated sexism, a bias in favour of male-centred perspectives on crime and criminality, and a lack of scientific rigour.

Statistics in this chapter suggest that there is a link between the socio-economic status and the criminality of women. In the experience of correctional workers, women who come into conflict with the criminal justice system tend to be young, poor, under-educated, and unskilled. A disproportionate number are Aboriginal. Many are addicted to alcohol, drugs, or both. A majority have been victims of physical and sexual abuse, and many are emotionally or financially dependent on abusive male partners. This description is remote from the image of a "liberated" woman attempting to imitate the behaviour of men. Detailed empirical information about the lives of women offenders is critical to the development of scholarly theory, government policy, and appropriate programming. However, such information has been sketchy at best and, until very recently, largely anecdotal.

Police statistics indicate that over the past twenty years, the number of charges against women annually in Canada increased steadily from just under 24,000 to just over 95,000 (Table 1). Women offenders doubled, from 8 percent to 16 percent of all persons charged with Criminal Code offences. Non-violent offences account for the bulk of the increase in female crime. In 1970, 55 percent of all charges against women were for property offences; this proportion remained relatively stable at 57 percent in 1980 and 50 percent in 1991. Forty-six percent of all women charged with Criminal Code offences in 1991 were charged with theft or fraud.

Figures 1 and 2 show the relative distribution of charges laid against women and men in 1991. The proportion of women charged with theft and fraud was more than twice the proportion of men charged with the same offences. Men were more likely than women to be charged with violent offences, impaired driving, and breaking and entering. Women's participation in property offences is consistent with their traditional roles as consumers and, increasingly, as low-income, semi-skilled, sole-support providers for their families. In keeping with the rapid increase in female-headed households and the stresses associated with poverty, greater numbers of women are being charged with shoplifting, cheque forgery, and welfare fraud.

Also in keeping with women's social and economic status is the number of young women who turn to prostitution. The 1985 Report of the Special Committee on Pornography and Prostitution concluded that because of the

Table 1
Women[1] Charged with Criminal Code Offences, 1970–1991

	1970		1980		1991	
	Number	Percent	Number	Percent	Number	Percent
Violent Offences						
Murder/Manslaughter	33	0.1	61	0.1	48	0.1
Attempted Murder/Wounding/Assault	1,667	7.0	4,261	6.3	11,989	12.6
Sexual Assault/Other Sexual	31	0.1	65	0.1	222	0.2
Robbery	206	0.9	538	0.8	647	0.7
Total Violent	**1,937**	**8.1**	**4,925**	**7.3**	**12,906**	**13.6**
Property Offences						
Break and Enter	545	2.3	2,031	3.0	1,759	1.9
Theft over $1,000[2]	1,509	6.3	2,746	4.1	1,956	2.1
Theft under $1,000	8,414	35.1	24,707	36.5	30,077	31.6
Possession of Stolen Goods	497	2.1	1,743	2.6	1,991	2.1
Fraud	2,197	9.2	7,426	11.0	11,890	12.5
Total Property	**13,162**	**54.9**	**38,653**	**57.2**	**47,673**	**50.2**
Other Offences						
Prostitution-related	1,427	6.0	960	1.4	5,601	5.9
Impaired Driving	1,916	8.0	9,091	13.4	9,812	10.3
Other CC Traffic[3]	624	2.6	2,101	3.1	1,170	1.2
Other Criminal Code[4]	4,899	20.4	11,870	17.6	17,895	18.8
Total Criminal Code	**23,965**	**100.0**	**67,600**	**100.0**	**95,057**	**100.0**
Liquor Offences	N/A		24,099		15,211	
Drug Offences	1,519		5,933		5,455	

1 Double counting occurs if an individual is charged in more than one incident.
2 Legislative amendments in late 1985 increased the theft categories (over and under) from $200 to $1,000.
3 Includes criminal negligence, failure to stop at the scene of an accident, dangerous driving, driving while disqualified.
4 Includes gaming and betting, offensive weapons, arson, kidnapping and abduction, wilful damage and other Criminal Code offences.

Source: Statistics Canada, Canadian Centre for Justice Statistics, Uniform Crime Reporting Survey.

Figure 1
Criminal Code Offences, 1991

Women Charged

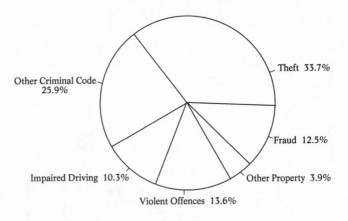

Source: Statistics Canada, Canadian Centre for Justice Statistics, Uniform Crime Reporting Survey.

Figure 2
Criminal Code Offences, 1991

Men Charged

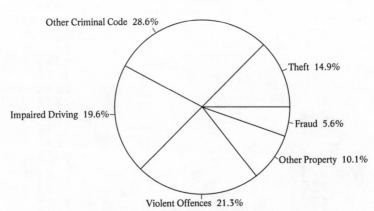

Source: Statistics Canada, Canadian Centre for Justice Statistics, Uniform Crime Reporting Survey.

difficulty of detecting some practices of prostitution, it is impossible to know whether the number of prostitutes in Canada has increased in recent years, but undoubtedly there has been an increase in the number working on the streets.[18] Police records of prostitution-related offences (soliciting, keeping a bawdy house, and procuring for the purpose of prostitution, of which over 90 percent involve soliciting) show dramatic fluctuations over the past two decades (Table 1). These data do not reflect the actual participation of women in prostitution, but are a measure of the impact of prevailing social and legal definitions of this behaviour on police activity. By altering the legal definition of these offences, various court and legislative decisions have had a tremendous impact over the years on the actions of police and, subsequently, on the number of women charged. For example, the offence of soliciting for the purpose of prostitution was severely limited in scope by a Supreme Court of Canada decision in 1978 which held that soliciting was illegal only when "pressing and persistent." In the same case, it was decided that a private vehicle on a public thoroughfare did not constitute a "public place" for the purposes of a conviction. Following this decision, many police forces simply ceased enforcing the law[19] and the number of women charged with soliciting dropped off sharply. Charges for prostitution-related offences quickly surged in 1985 when Bill C-49 was passed. This bill was designed to address the increase in street solicitation by criminalizing the act of "communicating in a public place for the purpose of exchanging money for sex."[20] Between 1985 and 1991 there was a ten-fold increase in the number of prostitution-related charges laid against women (from 566 to 5,601), and an even larger increase in the number of men charged (from 385 to 5,162).

Prostitution thrives in a society which values women more for their sexuality than for their skilled labour, and which puts women in a class of commodity to be bought and sold. Research has shown one of the major causes of prostitution to be the economic plight of women, particularly young, poorly educated women who have limited *legitimate* employment records.[21] Entry into prostitution is also typically characterized by running away from home, often to escape physical and sexual abuse.[22] Rather than providing a refuge from ill-treatment, however, street life puts women at great risk of further violence and abuse, and significantly increases their vulnerability to identification and arrest by police.

One area in particular for which there exists a serious lack of information about women offenders is their role in crimes of violence. The number of charges against women for crimes of violence more than doubled in the 1980s and increased more than five-fold between 1970 and 1991 (Table 1). In 1991, just over 13 percent of women offenders were charged with violent offences, an increase from 7 percent in 1980 and 8 percent in 1970. The percentage of adult male offenders charged with crimes of violence more than doubled over the past decade, from 9 percent in 1980 to 21 percent in 1991 (Table 2). Men's violent offences far outnumber women's; there were 110,000 charges against men for violent offences in 1991, compared to 13,000 against women. Although police statistics hold no clues about the nature of violent acts committed by women, the small body of research in this area suggests that a considerable proportion consists of acts of rebellion or retaliation against men in abusive or exploitative domestic situations. One Canadian study of women imprisoned for violent crimes found the incidents occurred primarily within the family milieu.[23] More recently, the Task Force on Federally Sentenced Women found that 80 percent of women in the federal prison system had been physically and/or sexually abused during their lives, the majority by intimate partners.[24] While homicide by women is relatively rare, 1991 statistics show that 79 percent of the victims in these offences were domestically related to the offenders, and were usually a spouse or common-law partner.[25] The fact that a significant number of women who kill their spouses do so in self-defense has been recognized recently in a legal defense known as "the battered woman syndrome."[26] The increase in non-lethal violence by women over the past twenty years may very well reflect an increase in the incidence of wife battering, in which women ultimately suffer as both victim and offender. Further research and statistical information in this area is critical if we are to understand and respond to the lives of women who are charged with crimes of violence.

The criminality of women may also be understood as symptomatic of a sense of futility with a desperate life situation, such as poverty, homelessness, or abuse. In 1991, approximately 15,000 women were charged with violations of provincial liquor laws such as drinking in a public place or when under age; an additional 9,800 were charged with impaired driving, and 5,400 with drug offences (Table 1). These figures almost certainly understate the number of women who find escape through alcohol or drugs, and who suffer severe health and social consequences as a result.

Hysterical predictions of a female crime wave have been fuelled in recent years by a misrepresentation of police statistics. The worst offenders

Table 2

Men[1] Charged with Criminal Code Offences, 1970–1991

	1970		1980		1991	
	Number	Percent	Number	Percent	Number	Percent
Violent Offences						
Murder/Manslaughter	298	0.1	426	0.1	486	0.1
Attempted Murder/Wounding/Assault	24,822	9.1	36,435	7.1	90,299	17.4
Sexual Assault/Other Sexual	3,768	1.4	4,146	0.8	11,449	2.2
Robbery	3,399	1.2	6,837	1.3	7,950	1.5
Total Violent	**32,287**	**11.8**	**47,844**	**9.4**	**110,184**	**21.2**
Property Offences						
Break and Enter	19,872	7.3	44,557	8.7	37,654	7.3
Theft over $1,000[2]	19,879	7.3	25,829	5.1	16,395	3.2
Theft under $1,000	24,273	8.9	49,825	9.7	60,613	11.7
Possession of Stolen Goods	6,755	2.5	12,959	2.5	14,621	2.8
Fraud	13,952	5.1	23,255	4.5	29,072	5.6
Total Property	**84,731**	**31.0**	**156,425**	**30.6**	**158,355**	**30.6**
Other Offences						
Prostitution-related	452	0.2	569	0.1	5,162	1.0
Impaired Driving	76,178	27.9	148,401	29.0	101,372	19.6
Other CC Traffic[3]	21,436	7.8	43,523	8.5	16,711	3.2
Other Criminal Code[4]	58,079	21.3	114,021	22.3	126,140	24.4
Total Criminal Code	**273,163**	**100.0**	**510,783**	**100.0**	**517,924**	**100.0**
Liquor Offences	N/A		275,292		128,713	
Drug Offences	10,873		53,298		34,764	

1 Double counting occurs if an individual is charged in more than one incident.
2 Legislative amendments in late 1985 increased the theft categories (over and under) from $200 to $1,000.
3 Includes criminal negligence, failure to stop at the scene of an accident, dangerous driving, driving while disqualified.
4 Includes gaming and betting, offensive weapons, arson, kidnapping and abduction, wilful damage and other Criminal Code offences.

Source: Statistics Canada, Canadian Centre for Justice Statistics, Uniform Crime Reporting Survey.

have been the mass media, which also have been the principal source of public information on crime and the criminal justice system.[27] Media reports have often compared percentage increases in Criminal Code charges laid against women and men. But because of the much lower base number of charges against women for any given offence, percentage increases consistently give the false impression of much greater increases in the number of women offenders relative to men. The increase in actual numbers of women, however, is usually much smaller than the increase in the actual number of men under comparison.

For example, a total overall increase of 297 percent in women charged with Criminal Code offences over a period of twenty-one years represents a difference in actual numbers of about 71,000, whereas a percentage change of only 90 percent represents an additional 244,700 men charged over the same period (see Tables 1 and 2). The increase in the actual number of men charged is more than three times the increase in the actual number of women charged.

Similarly, an increase of over 45 percent between 1970 and 1991 in charges against women for homicide offences (murder and manslaughter) reflects a real increase of only 15 women. But an increase of 188 men charged with the same offences amounts to only a 63 percent increase. To claim that crimes by women increased 297 percent and crimes by men increased by only 90 percent, or that the number of homicides by women is sky-rocketing, is an erroneous approach to crime data analysis. Sensational reports of escalating crime by women are simply untrue. If police charges against women follow recent trends, the gradual increase in base numbers in most offence categories will yield increasingly smaller percentage changes, and not the "crime wave" predicted in the 1970s.

"Official" crime statistics are subject to a number of influences independent of the volume of crime that comes to the attention of the police, influences that have considerable bearing on how women are labelled criminal. Although empirical evidence is scarce, it has been argued, for instance, that crimes by women are less likely to be reported to the police than crimes by men, and that criminal justice officials, who are usually male, give preferential treatment to women who come into conflict with the law.[28] Consequently, the argument goes, women offenders are seriously undercounted in police statistics.

There is no consistent empirical support for this argument. Indeed, the reverse has been true where juvenile offenders are concerned. Under the now-defunct Juvenile Delinquents Act,[29] young people could be charged with "status" offences, such as "sexual immorality" and other forms of vice, offences which normally would not result in charges against adults.[30] In practice, these offences were used much more frequently against girls than boys. Although young male offenders outnumbered females by about five to one, girls were traditionally dealt with much more severely by the social welfare and criminal justice systems.[31] Girls were expected to be passive, obedient, and chaste, and when they weren't, the police and courts were quick to classify them as abnormal or disturbed. This practice has been defended under the guise of paternalism and a belief that the virtue of girls is more highly valued and in need of protection than the virtue of boys.[32] Under the Young Offenders Act, introduced in 1984, status offences were eliminated in an attempt to make the treatment of adults and young people more equitable.

It is not possible to determine from police statistics alone the biases individual police officers may have toward laying charges against women offenders or the extent to which fluctuations in the number of charges laid against adult women are the direct result of changes over time in the attitudes of police officers.

The steady increase in recorded crime involving both women and men is occurring in direct proportion to the ability of the police to detect and record crimes. As technology advances, so does the ability of the police to respond quickly, track offenders, and record criminal incidents. The size of the increase in the rate of any one offence is affected by the enforcement practices and priorities of local police, community values and standards, changes in legislation, and legal precedents. For example, fluctuations in the number of drug offences recorded by the police in Canada over the past two decades (drug-related charges against women have more than tripled) do not necessarily reflect the actual occurrence of these offences, but more likely reflect societal tolerance and local political pressures which cause police to target certain offences and offenders for arrest. Legislative changes and legal precedents established with respect to prostitution-related offences, as discussed earlier, have had a profound effect on the level of enforcement of these and other related offence categories and on the number of women charged with criminal offences.

Women in Prison

There are no national court statistics to describe the kinds of sentences received by women in Canada. In 1980, the last year for which court statistics are available, women convicted of criminal offences in British Columbia and Quebec were proportionally less likely than men to receive prison sentences (15 percent compared to 25 percent).[33] The lower incarceration rates for women may be related to the relative seriousness of the crimes in which women become involved, their shorter criminal histories, and the often ancillary role women play to men in serious crimes. The statistics on fines are mixed: in British Columbia women were less likely than men to receive a fine, while in Quebec the reverse was true. Nevertheless, given the social status and economic disadvantage of women, and the growing number of women who are likely to have sole responsibility for young children,[34] the impact of criminal sanctions such as fines and jail sentences are almost certainly felt more acutely by women than by men.

Women who are sentenced to terms of imprisonment may be held in provincial or federal institutions, depending upon the length of sentence they receive. Those serving sentences of two years or more are the responsibility of the federal government, while those sentenced to less than two years, or who are remanded in custody awaiting sentence or trial, come under the jurisdiction of the province or territory in which they are tried. The majority of men and women incarcerated each year serve sentences of less than two years. In 1991, women accounted for 9 percent of all sentenced admissions to provincial institutions, up from 6 percent in 1983. Between 1984 and 1991, women admitted under sentence to all provincial and territorial correctional institutions each year increased from almost 7,000 to 9,855, and women admitted under remand increased from about 1,800 to 8,500.[35] These are only very rough estimates of the actual number of women admitted to jail each year since some are admitted more than once in a year on remand, under sentence, or both, and are counted separately each time.

Apart from their age, little is known from official statistics about women who are remanded in custody: 10 percent of those admitted on remand in 1991 were under twenty years of age, one-half were between twenty and thirty, and the remainder were over thirty.[36] Statistics tell us that less than 10 percent of women admitted under provincial sentence in 1991 had been convicted of a violent offence (Figure 3). More than one in

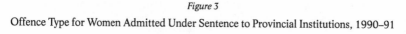

Figure 3

Offence Type for Women Admitted Under Sentence to Provincial Institutions, 1990–91

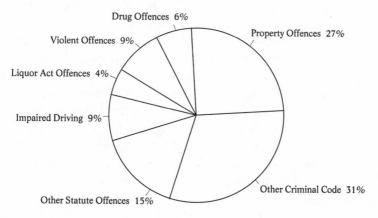

Source: Statistics Canada, Canadian Centre for Justice Statistics, Adult Corrections Survey, unpub.

four women were admitted for property offences, and the remainder for impaired driving, drug offences, violations of provincial liquor acts, and other miscellaneous Criminal Code and other statute offences. Almost 40 percent received sentences of fourteen days or less, and six in ten received sentences of from fifteen days to one month. Almost 30 percent were sentenced to serve between one and six months, while a minority (14 percent) were sentenced to six months or more.[37]

Personal characteristics of these women are also unknown from official records, but the type of offences for which women are typically charged, convicted, and sentenced are predominantly non-violent. For many women, the indirect cause of imprisonment is alcohol abuse. For a substantial proportion of women admitted to provincial jails in Canada each year, their greatest crime is poverty: three in ten were incarcerated for not paying fines.[38] For some, life is a revolving door of theft or alcoholism, and jail.

The large number of non-violent offenders jailed for short periods, often when incarceration was not the intended sentence (as in the case of inability to pay a fine), should be of utmost concern to those interested in the needs of women offenders. The high rate of women being sentenced to jail more than once for minor offences shows the failure of the penal system to deter these women from further criminal involvement, and of society to provide alternatives. Programs that provide women the opportunity to learn marketable work skills and life skills are lacking in most provincial jails, where the majority of women serve less than thirty days. At a minimum, greater emphasis must be placed on programs and services to enable women to serve their sentences in the community, particularly those women unable to meet the requirements of a financial penalty. Programs for women in need of educational training, skills development, addiction counselling, and the like are much more readily implemented and utilized in the community than during a few days or weeks of incarceration.

The smallest group of women offenders in the criminal justice system are those serving prison terms of two years or longer and who come under the jurisdiction of the federal government. The number of women admitted annually to federal penitentiary nearly doubled from 80 in 1981 to 141 in 1991, remaining steady at 2 percent to 3 percent of the total penitentiary population.[39] Longer sentences served by women in federal prison have resulted in an expanding female inmate population. In 1991, there were 71 women in the Canadian prison system serving sentences of ten years or more; of these, 43 were serving minimum twenty-year sentences. Between 1975, when the Correctional Service of Canada began providing detailed statistical information about federal inmates, and 1991, the total number of women imprisoned under federal sentences increased from 173 to 317.

The majority of these women are serving their first federal sentence; for many it is their first contact with the justice system. In 1989, 87 percent of the female federal prison population had never before received a federal prison term, more than 50 percent had never been sentenced to incarceration, and 36 percent had never been convicted of a Criminal Code offence.[40]

Despite the increase in the number of women serving federal sentences, the number incarcerated at any one time remains relatively small, and this adds to the difficulty of identifying their needs and providing adequate programs and services for them. At the heart of much of the controversy over the delivery of services to women is that there are so few correctional facilities. While there are over forty prisons in Canada for men serving sentences of two years or more, until 1990 the Prison for Women in Kingston, Ontario was the only institution operated by the federal government for women offenders. As a result, women have been denied the same opportunities as men for transfer to facilities with a reduced security classification or special program options, or to a preferred geographic location. Particularly where the population of "lifers" is concerned, female inmates have not had these basic options available to them.)

In 1990, a minimum-security institution was opened in Kingston to house 11 federally sentenced women. Located across the road from the Prison for Women, this renovated building offers a less restricted environment for a small number of women but does not bring them any closer to their families.

Beginning in 1973, agreements between the federal government and all provinces except Ontario and Prince Edward Island allowed women under federal sentence to apply to serve their sentences in provincial correctional institutions closer to their homes and families. But the lack of uniform guidelines governing transfers, and the disparity in availability of local facilities, resulted in an unequal opportunity to participate in this option. Of the approximately 315 women on register under federal sentence in 1992, nearly half were serving their sentences in provincial institutions, primarily in Quebec and the western provinces.

Many federally sentenced women are likely to have responsibility for young children. A 1989 survey found that two-thirds of these women had children and nearly half of the women interviewed had children under sixteen. Two-thirds of women with children had been single parents for at least part of their children's lives.[41] Extra hardship is placed on both women and their children when mothers are incarcerated for long periods at great distances from their homes and families.

Aboriginal Women and Crime

Aboriginal people are over-represented among the number of Canadians arrested and incarcerated. The presence of Aboriginal women in the criminal justice system is even more disproportionate than that of Aboriginal men. Although Aboriginal people (status and non-status Indians, Métis, and Inuit) make up an estimated 3 percent of the Canadian population, in 1990–91 they accounted for an average of 19 percent of admissions to provincial and territorial institutions and more than 90 percent of admissions in some areas.[42] This high rate of criminalization of Aboriginal people coincides with their bleak socio-economic profile. That Aboriginal people live in deprived conditions relative to Canadians generally is beyond dispute. The situation is aggravated for Aboriginal women, who suffer racial discrimination, gender discrimination, and, until 1985, when section 12(1)(b) of the *Indian Act* was amended, legislated discrimination that deprived some women of Indian status, forced them off reserves, and denied them rights (see Carol LaPrairie's chapter in this volume, "Aboriginal Women and Crime in Canada").

The 1986 Census reported that single-parent families are twice as common among Aboriginals as among non-Aboriginals, and that families with five or more children are five times more common.[43] In 1986, 40 percent of Aboriginal women had paid jobs, compared to 50 percent of non-Aboriginal women.[44] Nearly two-thirds of Aboriginal women reported incomes under $7,000, compared to just under half of non-Aboriginal women and a quarter of non-Aboriginal men.[45] This reflects low education[46] and the substantially lower rate of full-time, full-year employment among Aboriginal people, and Aboriginal women in particular.

The rate of death caused by injury or poisoning among status Indian women is more than three times the average for Canadian women.[47] Young Indian women aged fifteen to twenty-four have a suicide rate almost six times greater than other Canadian women.[48] It is estimated that over one-half of illnesses and deaths suffered by Indian people are alcohol-related. In addition, Aboriginal people living on reserves have a higher than average incidence of respiratory and infectious diseases—a reflection of poor housing and living conditions, and lack of access to medical facilities.

These statistics offer only a glimpse of the consequences of a near-complete breakdown of the Aboriginal culture and traditional way of life. The number of Aboriginal people who leave their homes for work in cities has been growing. When this occurs, lack of experience in an urban environment, poor support systems, and visibility to police increase Aboriginal peoples' chances of coming into contact with the criminal justice system. However, official statistics on the involvement of Aboriginal people in the justice system are extremely limited. Police statistics do not yet identify the ancestry of persons charged, and details about offenders are available only for those sentenced to prison terms of two years or longer.

Some insight into the conflict between Aboriginal people and the dominant legal system is provided through small local studies. A study of Aboriginal crime in urban centres in Canada found a high incidence of arrest among Aboriginal women. While Aboriginal people comprised between 2 percent and 6 percent of the populations of Calgary, Saskatoon, and Regina, charges against Aboriginal women accounted for 12 percent, 46 percent, and 53 percent, respectively, of all women charged. Charges against Aboriginal men accounted for 8 percent, 34 percent, and 40 percent, respectively, of all men charged.[49] Although these statistics cannot be generalized to other areas of Canada, they raise some important questions about the treatment of Aboriginal people by the justice system, particularly of Aboriginal women in urban communities.

Nearly half the women admitted to provincial facilities in 1991 were Aboriginal.[50] The greatest concentrations of Aboriginal women in female inmate populations occurred in Alberta, Saskatchewan, Manitoba, and Ontario.[51] An earlier study to determine the problems faced by Aboriginal persons incarcerated in Ontario correctional institutions concluded that alcohol abuse, unemployment, and poor living conditions were critical factors in the high incidence of their arrest and incarceration.[52] Women in the sample were eight times more likely to be unemployed than the national average suggested, and any employment they had was usually temporary. Many women were dependent on social assistance.[53] Aboriginal women were twice as likely as Aboriginal men to be incarcerated for liquor-related offences and default of fine payment. The study also reported that Aboriginal inmates are seriously isolated from their culture and their families, and that distance from their communities, the expense of travelling to institutions, and a breakdown in family relationships contribute to this isolation.

Statistics collected by the Correctional Service of Canada indicate that the backgrounds of Aboriginal and non-Aboriginal women sentenced to federal penitentiaries differ in some important respects. In 1991, Aboriginal women comprised one-fifth of the total female inmate population.[54] Aboriginal women admitted to federal terms of incarceration are more likely than non-Aboriginal women to have served a federal sentence previously (35 percent compared to 20 percent), and are more than twice as likely to be incarcerated for crimes of violence (79 percent as compared to 36 percent). Sentences are shorter overall for Aboriginal women owing to the previous minimum mandatory sentences given for the drug offences of importing (more often a white woman's offence) and the greater likelihood of Aboriginal women being convicted of manslaughter, which does not carry a minimum life sentence, compared to murder, which does.

Isolation from family and community support is even more severe for Aboriginal than non-Aboriginal women inmates. Three-quarters of Aboriginal women who receive federal sentences are from the Western provinces and territories, yet in 1991, 60 percent were incarcerated in the Prison for Women in Ontario, a great distance from where they were admitted and presumably from where they will eventually return. This likely has a very negative effect on release plans and on chances for early release. Research has shown that Aboriginal women are less likely to be granted full parole, and those who are released early are more likely to have parole revoked,[55] a situation which may be affected by isolation from families while incarcerated and poor support services available in home communities upon release.

Conclusion

This statistical overview describes the majority of women who come into conflict with the criminal justice system as non-violent offenders who commit petty crimes for economic gain. Their offences are concentrated in the types of property crimes that could well be considered a means of survival in a time when employment options for women with low education and few job skills are becoming increasingly restricted. For some women, sexual or physical abuse as a child marks passage into a life of street prostitution; for others, years of physical or emotional abuse as an adult culminates in a single act of violence. Many women offenders are at the same time victims.

The response of the justice system in many cases has been to impose jail sentences, often for the inability to pay a fine. These women have few options for changing their lifestyles after being convicted of a crime. In fact, a criminal record usually guarantees immobility on the social status ladder and reduced opportunities for success.

The needs of women who come into conflict with the law, or who are at risk of joining the ranks of offenders, extend beyond the criminal justice system. Statistics suggest that to improve the life situations of thousands of women at risk, Canada must offer women greater opportunities for advancement, job re-training, and economic independence. Perhaps most importantly, greater awareness by all who come into contact with women offenders about the devastating effects of violent victimization is essential not only to developing public understanding and academic theory, but to developing correctional policy and programming relevant to the reality of women's lives.

Notes

1 This is an updated version of an article by Holly Johnson, "Getting the Facts Straight: A Statistical Overview," in *Too Few to Count: Canadian Women in Conflict with the Law,* ed. Ellen Adelberg and Claudia Currie (Vancouver: Press Gang Publishers, 1987).

2 See Margaret Shaw's chapter in this volume for a description of the work of the Task Force on Federally Sentenced Women, the surveys it commissioned, and issues related to the Task Force's recommendations. Shaw is also the researcher and author of a recent comprehensive provincial study, *Ontario Women in Conflict with the Law: A Survey of Women in Institutions and Under Community Supervision in Ontario* (Toronto: Ontario Ministry of Correctional Services, 1993).

3 Efforts have been renewed and sentencing data will be released by Statistics Canada within the next few years.

4 Linda MacLeod, *Battered But Not Beaten: Preventing Wife Battering in Canada* (Ottawa: Canadian Advisory Council on the Status of Women, 1987), pp. 2–3.

5 Canada, Committee on Sexual Offences against Children and Youths, *Report of the Committee on Sexual Offences against Children and Youths* (Ottawa: Ministry of Supply and Services, 1984), p. 175.

6 Ross Finnie, "Women, Men, and the Economic Consequences of Divorce: Evidence from Canadian Longitudinal Data," *Canadian Review of Sociology and Anthropology* 30, no. 2 (1993): 205–241.

7 For example, in Manitoba the monthly default rate ranges from 50 percent to 75 percent ("Number of defaulting dads jumps," *Winnipeg Sun,* 19 December 1992).

8 Statistics Canada, *Women in Canada: A Statistical Report* (Ottawa: Ministry of Supply and Services, 1990), p. 106.

9 Statistics Canada, *Survey of Consumer Finances* (Ottawa: Statistics Canada, 1989).

10 Statistics Canada, *Women in Canada,* pp. 73–74.

11 Statistics Canada, *Census of the Population, 1991.*

12 Statistics Canada, *Women in Canada,* pp. 51 and 69.

13 Canada, Royal Commission on the Status of Women in Canada, *Report of the Royal Commission on the Status of Women in Canada* (Ottawa: Ministry of Supply and Services, 1970), p. 11.

14 See Canada, Commission on Equality in Employment, *Report of the Commission on Equality in Employment* (Ottawa: Ministry of Supply and Services, 1985), pp. 133–164.

15 See also Cesare Lombroso, *The Female Offender* (Littleton: Rothman, 1895), p. 151; and Otto Pollak, *The Criminality of Women* (Philadelphia: University of Pennsylvania Press, 1950), p. 3.

16 Freda Adler, *Sisters in Crime: The Rise of the New Female Criminal* (New York: McGraw-Hill, 1975); and Rita Simon, *Women and Crime* (Toronto: Lexington Books, 1975).

17 Adler, p. 14.

18 Canada, Special Committee on Pornography and Prostitution, *Report of the Special Committee on Pornography and Prostitution* (Ottawa: Ministry of Supply and Services, 1985), p. 369.

19 Canada, Department of Justice, *Street Prostitution: Assessing the Impact of the Law* (Ottawa: Ministry of Supply and Services, 1989).

20 Ibid.

21 *Report of the Special Committee on Pornography and Prostitution*, p. 353.

22 *Report of the Committee on Sexual Offences against Children and Youth*, pp. 980–984.

23 Ellen Rosenblatt and Cyril Greenland, "Female Crimes of Violence," *Canadian Journal of Criminology and Corrections* 16 (1974): 173–180.

24 M. Shaw with K. Rodgers, J. Blanchette, T. Hattem, L.S. Thomas, and L. Tamarack, *Survey of Federally Sentenced Women: Report to the Task Force on Federally Sentenced Women*. User Report No. 1991-4 (Ottawa: Ministry of the Solicitor General, 1991), p. 6.

25 Statistics Canada, *Canadian Centre for Justice Statistics, Homicide Survey*, unpublished data, 1991.

26 See Sheila Noonan's chapter in this volume for a thorough analysis of the potential of this defence for accused women.

27 See, for example, "Women Turning to Violent Crime" (*Winnipeg Free Press*, 27 June 1983); "Crimes by Women Increasing" (*Montreal Gazette*, 19 June 1986); and "Crime Rate for Women Up Sharply, Study Shows" (*The Ottawa Citizen*, 15 December 1990).

28 See Pollak, p. 2, and Ralph Weisheit and Sue Mahan, *Women, Crime and Criminal Justice* (Cincinnati: Anderson Publishing Co., 1988), pp. 54–56.

29 *The Young Offenders Act* was passed in 1982 and came into effect in 1984, replacing the *Juvenile Delinquents Act.*

30 Barbara Landau, "The Adolescent Female Offender: Our Dilemma," *Canadian Journal of Criminology and Corrections* 17 (1975): 146–153.

31 Gloria Geller, "Young Women in Conflict with the Law," in *Too Few to Count: Canadian Women in Conflict with the Law,* ed. Ellen Adelberg and Claudia Currie (Vancouver: Press Gang Publishers, 1987), pp. 115–119.

32 Ibid.

33 Statistics Canada, Canadian Centre for Justice Statistics, *Adult Court Survey,* unpublished data, 1980.

34 Statistics Canada, *Women in Canada,* p. 6.

35 Statistics Canada, Canadian Centre for Justice Statistics, *Adult Corrections Survey,* unpublished data, 1991.

36 Ibid.

37 Ibid.

38 Ibid.

39 Canada, Ministry of the Solicitor General, Correctional Service of Canada, *Offender Information System,* unpublished data, 1992.

40 M. Shaw et al., *Survey of Federally Sentenced Women,* p. 6.

41 Ibid.

42 Statistics Canada, Canadian Centre for Justice Statistics, *Adult Corrections Survey,* unpublished data, 1991.

43 According to the 1986 Census, a person fifteen years of age or older is unemployed if during the week prior to enumeration they were without work and had actively looked for work in the past four weeks and were available for work; they had been on lay-off and expected to return to their job; or they had definite arrangements to start a new job in four weeks or less. A person is not considered unemployed if they are without work *and* not looking for work. Forty-nine percent of Aboriginal women compared to 44 percent of non-Aboriginal women were neither employed nor unemployed and looking for work. For Aboriginal men and non-Aboriginal men the percentage is much smaller, 30 percent and 22 percent, respectively.

44 Ibid. Unemployment rates exclude those who have given up looking for work.

45 Ibid.

46 A recent survey indicated that more than two-fifths of Indian women living on reserve had less than grade nine education and only one-fifth had a secondary school diploma (Canada, Indian and Northern Affairs, *Health of Indian Women* (Ottawa: Indian and Northern Affairs, June 1990).

47 Ibid.

48 Ibid.

49 Shelley Trevethan, *Aboriginal Crime in Urban Centres* (Ottawa: Canadian Centre for Justice Statistics, 1992).

50 Statistics Canada, Canadian Centre for Justice Statistics, *Adult Corrections Survey*, unpublished data, 1991.

51 Ibid.

52 Andrew Birkenmayer and Stan Jolly, *The Native Inmate in Ontario* (Toronto: Ministry of Correctional Services and the Ontario Native Council, 1981), p. vi.

53 Ibid., p. vi.

54 Statistics Canada, Canadian Centre for Justice Statistics, *Adult Corrections Survey*, unpublished data, 1991.

55 Robert Hann and William Harman, *Full Parole Release: An Historical Descriptive Analysis* (Ottawa: Ministry of the Solicitor General, 1986).

In Their Own Words:
Seven Women's Stories[†]

Ellen Adelberg and Claudia Currie

This article acquaints the reader with some of the women about whom this book is written. What follows are summarized accounts of the lives of seven women who were convicted of indictable offences, which are those considered most serious in law. While cautioning that these seven stories should not be interpreted as "everywoman's" story of her involvement in crime, our experience as workers with women offenders tells us that they mirror, in many ways, the reality of many women offenders' lives. In an effort to point out how those of us who are feminists can try to understand these dramas, we have added our own commentary in the final pages.

In our own work with convicted women, we became aware of the significance of women's life circumstances, including early childhood experiences, in understanding their involvement with crime. Yet rarely are these factors discussed in the academic or professional literature, particularly from the perspective of women offenders themselves.

The pages that follow reveal the stories of Elaine, a woman charged with three counts of aggravated assault; Barbara, who was convicted of manslaughter; Anne-Marie and Francine, who both served time for armed

† This chapter is reprinted with minor changes from *Too Few to Count: Canadian Women in Conflict with the Law*, ed. Ellen Adelberg and Claudia Currie (Vancouver: Press Gang Publishers, 1987).

robberies; Nicole, convicted of importing narcotics; Cindy, who has an extensive history of drug and fraud convictions; and June, who is serving a life sentence for murder. Their names have been changed to protect their identity because as one woman told us, "we still feel the power that can be used against us, and the reactions of society ... you never stop paying your dues." When contacted, the interviewees were extremely helpful and supportive of our project. It was evident that these women were not often asked their point of view, but felt that they had a lot to share.[1]

The statistics presented earlier in this book provide evidence that the women interviewed represent an approximate cross-section of women serving federal sentences in relation to their age, marital status, and the types of offences committed. The women interviewed are not, however, representative of the ethnic backgrounds of women under federal sentence: only one is an Aboriginal woman, and Aboriginal women have represented up to 30 percent of the federal female prison population. Women who are sentenced to serve any time under two years in prison serve their sentences in provincial jails, usually for less serious offences than those committed by the women we interviewed.

In the stories that follow, poverty, child and wife battering, sexual assault, and women's conditioning to accept positions of submissiveness and dependency upon men are themes that recur frequently among these women. We suggest, as others have elsewhere,[2] that the response to different forms of oppression varies from woman to woman, depending upon the internal and external resources upon which each of them has to draw. The following stories are evidence of seven women's responses to such oppression. In our opinion, the serious crimes committed by these women do not represent bizarre manifestations of "unfeminine" women's instabilities (as traditional criminologists might have us believe), but rather they represent behaviour that makes some sense within the context of each one's life, and within the context of women's status in Canadian society.

Elaine

The first woman you will meet, Elaine, tells a tragic yet far too common story which reveals the depths of depravation that are possible in our patriarchal society. Her story illustrates graphically that women do not have the control they need to ensure their own and their children's safety, and that in certain cases this can lead to devastating consequences.

At the time she was interviewed, Elaine was awaiting trial for three counts of the aggravated assault of her children. Her co-accused was the man with whom she had been living at the time the charges were laid. While she was pleading guilty to lesser charges, he had already pleaded guilty, had been tried and was sentenced to six years in prison for the offences.

Elaine told us that a major event which affected the path of her life was a teenage pregnancy which resulted in her giving the child up for adoption.

I knew I should give [the baby] up because I was still a baby myself, I couldn't handle the responsibility and my parents felt I should give it up, but after I did I always wished I had kept the baby with me. I think I wanted to get married and have more kids right away to make up for having lost my baby.

When she was seventeen, Elaine met the man who eventually became her husband and within a short time they were travelling together across the country. Very quickly, she became pregnant.

At the hospital they wanted to give me an abortion but my husband said no way. He said "that's my child and you're not going to get an abortion or give it up or nothing, we're going to keep it." I was so happy. It was a baby that I could keep and I had somebody who cared.

She was married two months before the baby was born. For a while she had what she described as a "good relationship" with her husband, despite the fact that she discovered that he was wanted by the police for several offences involving fraud. By the time her first child was a year old, the relationship was crumbling. Even so, Elaine stayed with her husband for five more years. When she left him, she was the mother of three small children, ages five, three, and two. She describes the reasons she left him:

He was fooling around with other women, he was on welfare, and going to the race track; he was an alcoholic. I don't know if he took drugs, but I know he was drinking and buying flowers for all his women and sending the bills to our place. And then he hit me once in a while and I couldn't stand it anymore and I just had to get out. I was fed up with having to knock on my neighbours' doors for peanut butter and bread to feed the kids.

Before she left her husband, Elaine had experienced her first conflict with the law. She was convicted of offences related to fraud and sentenced to two years' probation.

I didn't have any money, and I wanted to get stuff for the kids, so I was willing to do almost anything. But I never got caught for drugs or drinking or beating people or anything. That wasn't my style, I wasn't raised that way.

After leaving her husband, Elaine very quickly hooked up with another man, who, as it turned out, had an even more disastrous effect on her life. The new man was to become her co-accused in the child assault charges.

Before those charges occurred, Elaine experienced a very difficult battle with her ex-husband for custody of her children. At one point he abducted and kept one of her daughters for almost two years. She was determined to regain possession of her children and her feelings for them are reflected in this passage, as she recounts the end to the abduction event.

I'll never forget the day I got Cathy back. When I had last seen her she was four and now she was six. She had gotten so big. We both just stared at each other and then she started yelling Mummy, Mummy and she ran right for me and she held me. She sat on my knee all the way home and most of the time we both just cried. I thought finally all three of my children and I were reunited, we could all live together.

Unfortunately though, Elaine's dreams were quickly shattered. Although her new boyfriend bought a house for her and the children to share with him, he offered only violence and intimidation instead of a safe refuge.

At first he started with just hitting and then he started to torture the children, like putting them upside down in hot showers and hitting all of us with a cattle prod. It got worse and worse and I never did nothing about it because I was afraid to. I had just got my children back and I didn't want anybody to take them. He told me if I said anything to anybody he would kill me and the children. I knew he had a gun, a .32.

After all that I had been through I didn't know what to do. I was in a state of mind where I wasn't insane, I knew what I was doing, but I was paralyzed. If I even went out of the house with makeup on John would beat the hell out of me because he thought another man would look at me. It was like I was in jail, I realize now that's what it was.

After charges were laid against her and her co-accused, Elaine experienced a harrowing five months of imprisonment. Even though she maintained throughout that she was not insane, Elaine was sent to a psychiatric hospital for observation and assessment. At the end of the thirty-day psychiatric assessment, Elaine spent four months in prison in "protective custody," to remove her from harassment by other inmates who look down on suspected child abusers. Finally, she was transferred to a community residence for female offenders run by the Elizabeth Fry Society.

The day I got out and got to "Smith" House and I went to the store and bought a pack of cigarettes was like the first day of a new life. John wasn't there to beat me. I could look at someone and smile and they weren't going to beat me up, or think I'm drunk or a dope addict or a pervert, which I'm not. I've been working for ten of the eleven months since I've been here, at an answering service. It's good for me because I can't sit still right now. I'm too hyper. I've got to get up and go. It's a great feeling when you know you're working from nine to five, you come home, have supper, relax, take a shower and go to bed. It feels beautiful. Because at the end of the week you know you're going to do your shopping and it's yours, you don't have to steal for it because you worked for it and nobody can take it away from you.

While facing great uncertainty about her future, one thing has remained clear in Elaine's mind.

I can raise my kids. I can work for them, I know I can do it, I just need that chance. If I don't get that chance then there's no point in me even existing because I won't have my three children. I already lost one when I was young, I don't intend to lose my other three....

That's why I'm working. I can't sleep at night. I have nightmares. I don't eat. If I eat, I feel sick. I will always have to live with having seen my kids beaten in front of me. As far as I'm concerned that is far more punishment than anything they could give me in court. I want the chance to make that up. I do feel guilty of neglect and I have to live with that. I did the best I could at home. What would another woman do in the same situation? Maybe kill the man. Who knows.

She also feels clear about her future relationship with men.

When I get my children back I will never live with another man. Ever. I'm seeing a man now. He's very nice. He knows everything. He's helping me to be strong. He gives me life, he makes me shine and I love him very much for it but I won't live with him. I can't do that to my children. It would go against my rights, my will. Can you imagine what it would do to my children's heads if I lived with another man? They'd say "wow Mummy, you're crazy."… It's going to be hard, but I'll make it.

For Elaine's part in the abuse of her children, she was found guilty of three counts of assault and sentenced to a prison term of four and a half years. The sentencing occurred shortly after our interview with her.

Barbara

Barbara's first offence was manslaughter, committed at the age of thirty. As a child, Barbara lived in northern Ontario. She was exposed to violence early in life.

We moved a lot because my father couldn't pay for the homes we were in. My father's an alcoholic. He beat my mother quite a bit. When my father and mother separated, my brother and I lived in different homes and we were both molested there.

Barbara's natural mother died of cancer, and her father remarried. The abuse continued, at the hands of others as well as her natural parent.

My father used to beat my stepmother all the time and he used to travel out of town quite a bit so we were alone with her. It was never hidden that we weren't wanted. We had to stay in our rooms all the time. She called me a lot of names when I was young, like "stupid," "slut," things like that. She said I was going to go to hell like my real mother.

The first time I was ever raped was by the babysitter's boyfriend and I was eleven at the time. I was always running away from home and of course my father would find me and beat me.

At age fifteen, Barbara moved to Toronto on her own, and hung around "the Village."[3] She then moved to Ottawa, where she worked as a waitress and met her future husband, who was a rock and roll musician.

When I got married I was sixteen and he was twenty-four. It was a horrible marriage.... He was a very possessive, jealous person. He wouldn't allow me to go out alone, to go back to school. I used to go with him where he played but I'd have to sit at a different table because it was bad for his image. He also spent a lot of time calling me "stupid." It got worse and worse and although I wanted to get help, I was just so down. I was used to people treating me that way.

She left the marriage at age twenty, with a two-year-old son. By the time she was twenty-one, she was in another relationship and had another child, who died a few hours after birth.

[The doctor told me] beforehand that the baby was going to die.... I went through a pretty hard time and eventually our relationship ended because of that. Again, I went back to school and again I couldn't make it.... It was always financial reasons that I couldn't get through school.

Barbara started to work part-time to support her child, and moved frequently to find affordable housing. At the age of twenty-eight, she met a man with whom she became pregnant and had a daughter. She moved out west to be with this man, but when he deserted them, she returned to Ottawa.

At that time when I came back, the rent situation was really bad, so for five months we had no place to live. Our name went into emergency housing; we lived in hotels, apartments for a while, at friends' places; there were times when we were separated.

Barbara also suffered two sexual assaults by strangers after returning to Ottawa. She did not report the incidents, and she recounts how she felt at the time:

Along with everything else that had happened in the last few years, that really sent me down. The mistake I've made all through my life is never going for help. I was always afraid to go for help because I thought if they think I can't handle something, maybe I'll lose my kids. I was afraid of authority. I was afraid they were going to tell me I was crazy or something.

Finally Barbara was able to move into a subsidized housing project. Shortly thereafter she began dating a man who was a neighbour. At her interview she described him as being without ambition, a thief and a heavy drinker. Looking back on that relationship, she stated:

I started dating people who didn't really care because it was easier for me ... I felt more a part of them; I never felt comfortable around people who were doing well anymore. I just started living a whole different lifestyle.

Her boyfriend became more physically and verbally abusive as the relationship progressed. One night, he broke into her house and raped her. She did not retaliate until the next day:

We got into a big argument. There was another adult there, my kids and his brother. From what I've been told, I was really hysterical, tried to get him to leave, asked people to call the police, and nobody would do anything. And I walked over to the drawer, took out a knife, and I walked over and stabbed him. I don't remember doing it at all.

He didn't die right away; he died about twelve hours later.... I was charged with second degree murder and I pled guilty to manslaughter.

For the first eight months after the offence, she saw a psychiatrist three times a week, trying to deal with the awful event.

I just couldn't believe that it had happened. And I couldn't believe that I did it. It was not my intention for him to die. And of course I was pretty mad at him too for dying.

In court, Barbara received a two-year federal sentence followed by three years' probation.

The Crown Attorney wanted four years.... I was willing to pay to some degree because I wanted to try to somehow be able to live with it. There's nothing you can do to change it and you really feel like you owe something. I felt I could live with it a little better if I went to jail for it.

But when the first person Barbara dated after the offence also tried to beat her up, she continued to blame herself.

I really started thinking that it must be something I'm doing in my life that this is always happening. Obviously I hadn't learned anything—here somebody was dead and the same things kept happening to me.

Barbara credits the assistance of counsellors in helping her remove herself from the cycle of violence and abuse. She obtained academic upgrading while in prison and is now taking college courses; she participates in a battered women's group and in a group for adult children of alcoholics. Barbara's perspective on her relationships with men has changed and she explained to us why she broke up with her last boyfriend.

He had hit me once and the chances are it would happen again. I just don't want to take that chance. I don't want to go back to the same life at all, or to anybody who abused me. And even though he has done a lot for me, it's not worth the price. I don't owe him. I never asked him to do any of those things. I guess people like making you feel obligated; that's how they keep you.

She has also discovered that she is not alone in her experiences.

I find, well, every halfway house resident, every inmate that I've come across has been abused emotionally or physically throughout their lives. And just about every woman in that federal penitentiary is there because of some guy they believed in while they were on drugs or whatever. Just totally abused. And to see them going back to it really bothers me....
The battered women's group I get really angry with too. I really think the problem there is that nobody seems to realize how fragile life is, the

dangerous games they're involved in. These are serious games, where guys are shoving guns down their throats and machetes at their stomachs and it's only a matter of time before something will happen.

Anne-Marie

Anne-Marie was raised in a small town in Quebec until she was twelve. At that time she moved with her family to the east end of Montreal. She remembers her family life with warmth, describing her folks as "not having a lot of money, but surviving." At a very early age though (seventeen), she married for the first time. From that point on, her relationships with men dominated her life, and that, plus her eventual involvement in drugs, played a monumental role in her later convictions for armed robbery.

After a short and disappointing first marriage to a man who had affairs with other women, Anne-Marie moved back home for a while. She soon met her second husband, the man with whom she eventually committed robberies. Even though her parents disapproved of him from the start, Anne-Marie describes her fatal attraction to him:

We met in a club in North Montreal and because he was big and maybe because he was crude, I don't know, I was attracted to him. I fell in love with him and when I'm in love with somebody, I'll do anything. If you tell me to go slap the person across the street, if I'm really in love I'll go and do it. And that was the problem, I had no judgement at all. So even though I knew it was wrong, I started helping him with his crimes. I thought I was being brave and gutsy.... I certainly wasn't getting a future, or stability or security. But I was always hoping that one day he would change or love me enough that he would go straight....

Her second husband quickly introduced her to hard drugs, and Anne-Marie developed a liking for hashish and cocaine, but she never used heroin. Her husband, however, had a growing heroin habit. She describes the link between their drug usage and the crimes they committed:

It was a vicious circle. We didn't want to work because we couldn't earn enough money to buy the drugs. So we stole the money. If you steal the money, you don't mind using it for drugs because you don't really know the *value of the money. And you want to keep doing the drugs, so you keep stealing so you'll have the money to pay for them. The irony is that I never really got much out of the robberies, maybe a few grams of coke. But most of the money was going to my husband's habit. By then he was using a lot. It could cost $1,000 just in one evening.*

At times, Anne-Marie thought of leaving her husband, but fear of his violence kept her from taking any action.

I was scared. I stayed with him because I was scared of him killing me or doing something bad to me or my family. At the end I was in a love affair that had turned into a scary nightmare. He used to beat me up and that was another reason I liked to take drugs—it made me feel like everything was okay. Even when I was black and blue, if I was on drugs, I felt like it didn't matter.

After a few years of committing robberies with her husband and getting away with it, Anne-Marie got involved in a bank robbery planned by her husband and one of his friends. While her husband waited outside in the getaway car, Anne-Marie and the friend held up the bank. The operation failed though, and both she and the friend were shot by the police and ended up in hospital. Anne-Marie recalls how proud of herself she was at the time for not "ratting" on her husband.

I thought I was such a good person. I thought about how nice it would be if somebody would take my charge for me. I realize now my thinking was totally distorted. When you think like that it doesn't matter if you kill somebody or you're doing life, because you're doing it for Him, but him, he's doing fuck-all for you.

While her husband carried on his life with other women, Anne-Marie spent four years of a six-year sentence in the Prison for Women. She recalls her helpless sense of frustration at the way her husband treated her at the time, and her reaction to this treatment.

When he came [to visit at the prison], there was always a girl in the car with him, waiting while he had his visit with me. Once in a while though he would bring me some hash or some clothes or some money. And that was keeping me from telling him to go to hell. When you're inside, what you miss is the contact with humans. If you don't have lesbian relationships, you're by yourself. It was hard because in those days, I didn't have a relationship with a woman yet. So I depended on my husband and my family for all of my human contact.

When Anne-Marie was released on parole, she moved to a halfway house in Ottawa and attempted to make a fresh start in life. She enrolled in university and received a student loan. Her family was fully supportive.

It was not long though before her husband came looking for her and despite her family's protests, the couple re-united. Within months, she and her husband committed another robbery together. Again, Anne-Marie was caught and charged, while he escaped undetected.

This time, while she was in prison, Anne-Marie decided to separate legally from her husband. She credits the support of her family for helping her to follow through with her decision. Even so, she found the separation hard to accomplish.

I had thought about it before, in fact I even started the proceedings before, but I stopped when I realized that I had no clothes, I had just a pair of shoes, a pair of jeans, a sweater ... after all those years.... This time it's hard too, not just because of losing the relationship, but losing my things. I had a lot of clothes when I lived with him and my books and some other things. We lived together for seven years, and we had lots of furniture and things. Now I've lost everything. I'm starting again at zero at my age. It's not easy.

At the time of the interview, Anne-Marie was feeling positive about her ability to get out and stay out of prison permanently. Her recent conversion to evangelical Christianity was giving her a new focus.

I've really changed the way I think, I've become a Jehovah's Witness. I've already been out on six passes so I could go to the Kingdom Hall here. When I get out I'll be able to do some door-to-door witnessing for the church.

Religion has given me a support group. And I feel healthier, fatter but healthier. I've quit smoking because of the church, and swearing, and I wear a dress whenever I go to the Kingdom Hall. It's really given me a new personality.

This time when I get out, I won't have my husband looking for me and making me go back with him again. I've broken contact with him completely....

Last time when I got out of here, even with a wrong relationship, I stayed out for a year. This time I plan to stay out forever.

Francine

Francine grew up in a large Quebecois family and is the only one of the family's seven children to have been in conflict with the law.

I cannot say my family wasn't a good family. It was really a good family and still is. My dad had a booze problem but he never put us in a bad situation ... we always had three meals, and a roof over our heads, and everything we needed.

At the time of her interview, Francine was twenty-six years old. She had been released from federal penitentiary a year earlier and was serving the mandatory supervision segment of a four-year sentence for armed robbery. She was first charged with a criminal offence at the age of sixteen, although she had been involved in petty drug offences, store thefts, break-ins and acts of fraud since the age of twelve, largely as a consequence of a growing drug addiction.

I started on drugs really early because I didn't like booze and I had started on booze at about twelve years old. I remember I wanted to impress people around me and prove I don't know what, but that's where it started and I got involved with really strange people.

I can say that the gang I was hanging around with were influential, because I was really impressed. They could make a lot of money so easily, have drugs and booze so easily, and big cars. I thought it was great, and I wanted to do the same. Have cars and have money in my pocket all the time and get my own apartment, like I didn't need school anymore.

Francine did quit school at age fourteen and describes her teenage years as "hell."

I got involved so much in drugs slowly but deeply and I got involved in crime and connections and everything.... I also had a kid at fifteen but my boyfriend and I couldn't handle the responsibility. We broke up and I just kept going downhill. I didn't think about the baby, I just thought about myself really, and I thought life wasn't worth it. I didn't want to face any responsibility; just party, get high and get drunk and not care about tomorrow.

Her parents cared for the baby and Francine eventually had to leave her parents' home due to her increasingly aggressive behaviour. As her drug addiction progressed, her property offences became more frequent and serious.

When I started with fraud and things like that it was to support my habit. My little habit at first, but I needed more and more money because I ended up doing coke every day. I never wanted to hurt anybody really, to pull a gun in front of anybody or scare anybody. That was not my nature; but it was the drugs—I needed the drugs. I couldn't think straight and I thought it was the only solution.

Francine was convicted of property offences a few times and was given terms of probation or very short sentences. Her living situation continued to deteriorate, as she describes here:

I got apartments with a girl who had a worse habit than me, and we'd have to leave the apartments because we'd spend the rent on booze and drugs. I was up to my head in debts because of coke.... We ended up in skid row really. No place to go, no place to eat; we'd have to steal and everything. So anyway, I said, "Well, let's go do an armed robbery." I thought we were Bonnie and Clyde.

She and her friend held up a small corner store and were arrested shortly thereafter. She received an eight-month sentence in a provincial prison.

I was always in segregation; I escaped; I was always on everybody's case, fighting and everything, so I did more time than I was supposed to at the beginning. I met some people in there and there were about five of us getting out at the same time. We all went to have a party in the Laurentians. ... That party kept going for about two weeks and we ended up the five of us in jail. For three armed robberies.

Francine was sentenced to two years, four months for those offences. She began serving her sentence in Quebec and escaped five times in five months.

When I was inside I built up more resentment and hate than you could believe. I didn't want nothing to do with anybody. I didn't think the armed robberies were my fault. I thought that people were just putting me in there and leaving me there. Nobody wanted anything to do with me but they wanted me to respect them in return. So I'd say to myself, "When I get out I'll be worse and it'll be your fault."

After her release on parole, Francine's cocaine addiction continued to progress and it wasn't long until she committed another armed robbery, her last.

We walked into the store and I had a gun. There was a little girl in there, and I was high, and it just froze me. I didn't want to hurt nobody. Her mother looked like she was going to have a heart attack and the little girl said, "Just give them the money, that's all they want." It froze me; I got the money and I got out and I felt really cheap. I felt disgusted with myself, like I was not worth a thing.

She and her accomplice were arrested and convicted. Francine was sent to the Prison for Women in Kingston because she was considered a high escape-risk. It was only after arriving at the federal penitentiary that she began to rethink her life.

I made up my mind about it. Like I was going to quit [committing crimes] and that was it. I had lost my family, everyone, anyway; I was all alone. So now it was up to me to do something. I started in school and I'd get good marks, good performance slips and I was really encouraged. My English was improving so people could understand me at least. I took a butchering course and it was great, really great. I was so proud of what I could do, like I never thought I could do any of these things.

It took a longer time for Francine to quit her drug habit and she did overdose once, after her release on parole to a halfway house.

I had a hard time coping with what was going on around me. But after that [the overdose] I had a lot of help at the house. They could have sent me back to Kingston but they didn't. I hated myself for about a month, but I kept going to school and everything, and finally I got back on my feet.

Francine graduated from her college course in meat cutting with excellent marks. She was the only woman in her program and has found a lot of discrimination in the working world. She has not been able to find consistent employment. As Francine described her work experience so far,

I was expecting that there was going to be discrimination, but not as much as I found in that trade.... The first job that I went to I was doing everything but meat cutting, he was using me for clean-up after the butchers were done, and "go-fer" jobs. I didn't think that was really fair.... I told him I was going to look for work where I can practice my trade and he said "Well, you're dreamin'." And, you know, every job I've had so far, that's four jobs, it's been the same thing everywhere.

So now I say, "What the hell, I've got my diploma anyway." I know that I did prove it to myself, that I can go and take courses and I can do it if I really want to. The main thing was to get back my self-confidence.

Francine is also involved in Alcoholics Anonymous and has not used drugs for a year. According to her, she has "turned a chapter" in her life and there is no going back.

Nicole

Nicole was born in Quebec, thirty-one years ago. As a young child, she experienced the harsh conditions of a life of poverty. Nicole describes her later criminal activity as stemming not only from a need for money, but a strong desire for material goods, and a wish to achieve a financial status comparable to those around her.

She recalls the dramatic change in her family's economic situation that occurred when she was seven years old and the eldest of three children.

My father died suddenly. He didn't have insurance and there was no welfare or anything back then. All my mother had left when my father died was a dollar thirty.... We were living four in one room.... We got fed with lots of macaroni, bread and potatoes, things that weren't expensive.

The ensuing years were difficult and painful for Nicole as a child.

We had no money at all; we had to wear second-hand shoes and old socks and stuff. I never had toys unless somebody wanted to get rid of them. It's hard on a kid. I was the only girl, and there was no one to pass me clothes.

Nicole also remembers feeling the injustice of her situation and promising herself a different future.

People were always laughing at us because we didn't have money.... When you're poor, people think you're shit. I was getting angry at everybody and nobody at the same time. Against society, I guess. I would say "Why are we poor? Why are they doing this to us? If my father was here, nobody would do this to us, nobody would say these things to us."

I always said in my childhood, "One day I'll have money, one day everybody will pay me back."

Their financial position did not improve substantially over the next several years. Nicole's mother worked as a cleaning woman and they gradually moved into larger quarters. As a teenager, Nicole babysat for extra money. "But," she says, "I was always thinking: what can I do to make money? I was too chicken to do a robbery or anything, so I never really thought about it too seriously. I just hoped that one day I would have a nice job."

Nicole began working full-time in clerical positions when she was eighteen and remained living at home until she married at the age of twenty. The marriage lasted only a few years, and it was during this time that she first became involved in criminal activity. Both Nicole and her husband began selling marijuana, but were never arrested. Nicole did it for only a brief period because, as she explains:

In three months, I had bought everything I wanted: a sewing machine, a reel-to-reel, a colour TV, and a down payment on a car.... I was making money because I wasn't smoking the stuff myself. I thought that the people who were buying it were really crazy.

After her divorce, Nicole spent time in British Columbia being supported by a wealthy man. She eventually returned to Quebec at age twenty-six. It was after she returned to Quebec that she got involved in a scheme which resulted in her arrest, conviction and sentencing to seven years in prison for a drug importing charge.

I was working for minimum wage, then I was unemployed for a year. Nothing was going on and my unemployment [insurance] had run out. I was offered a trip to Jamaica. This guy was going to pay me $10,000 cash, plus expenses, and all I had to do was stay there for a month, get tanned and bring back some grass.

It was my dream to go down south for a month ... it was just like "Fantasy Island." Instead, for a month in the sun, I got seven years in the shade.

Looking back on her decision to go, Nicole states:

I knew I was taking a risk, but I didn't know the sentence was seven years. I thought it would be a year or something.... Anyway, I couldn't even see jail because the money looked so good. When you see that amount of money, you just do it.... I wanted it badly and fast. I had this nice idea of buying a house that was next to my girlfriend's, and using the $10,000 as a down payment. My intention was to do that one thing and stop.

After her arrest, she was pressured by the authorities to reveal who had sent her on the trip.

The Crown Attorney wanted ten years. They were telling me if I named the guy, I'd be free after a year. I didn't know the criminal law or anything and

they scared me, but I didn't talk. When you're inside they know if you're a
rat. I'd rather do my time and when I come out be free. Now I can go out-
side and not be scared of anyone.

Nicole didn't serve the full seven years in prison, because of early release provisions in Quebec, where she was permitted to serve her time. She
was paroled to a halfway house in Ottawa after approximately one year in
prison and will remain on parole until the expiry of her sentence.

She considers herself lucky to have been released from prison when she
was. The experience of imprisonment was enough to dissuade her from any
further criminal activity.

If someone had told me what it was like in jail, I never would have done it.
I never want to be surrounded by four walls again, or be without my free-
dom. Now, I'm scared to do anything against the law and I get worried
when I see a policeman. The other day, our car had a flash that wasn't
working and I said to my boyfriend, "You better get that fixed right now."

Nicole hasn't lost the desire for more money and a better standard of
living, although she has made a commitment to herself to earn it the "hard
and slow way."

When you try to make easy money, you get the "side effects" as well and
you do get caught some day. Right now, I'm working, it's not a big job or
anything, but at least I get a pay every two weeks [about $400] and I'm out
of trouble because I have my own money. My boyfriend and I would like to
have a child. All I really want is to have a quiet life, you know.

Cindy

Cindy is a twenty-nine-year-old Aboriginal woman who has been in and
out of the prison system for drug-related offences for most of her teen and
adult life. From her earliest memories, loneliness and alienation from her
own culture and the rest of the world were her companions. Her parents
died when she was very young and after that her only family life was in her
grandmother's house on an Indian reserve in British Columbia.

When I turned five I was sent to a residential school. It was run by Catholic nuns and priests and it was super strict. I would say it was even stricter than some of the [correctional] institutions that I've been in. We weren't allowed to speak our own language, or practise our own religion or culture. If we did, we would be struck for it.

Up until I was twelve, I went to the school and I came back to my grandmother's house for holidays. I never felt too protected there. One of my aunts used to beat me brutally and her husband was always trying to molest me. Because I was adopted, I felt a bit like Cinderella. I didn't have nobody to look after me. I didn't belong to anybody. I think I was abused a lot just for amusement and also so that the older ones wouldn't have to do any work. I got to be very tough.

At the age of twelve, Cindy left home and quit school. Since then, she has been on her own. She has had a small amount of contact, none of it very supportive, with members of her family. Her involvement with drugs started early.

By the time I left, my school didn't want nothing to do with me anyway because I was sniffing glue and drinking and smoking and just being a holy terror.... I was nine or ten when I started sniffing and drinking and smoking. It was when I was twelve though that I started doing everything and anything. Mostly chemicals. Just a few months before I turned thirteen, I became a heroin addict.

Cindy's first contact with the legal system came soon after.

By the time I was fourteen I was dealing heroin and hooking, and getting other girls on the streets with me to support my habit.... Sometimes I found sugar daddies who would support my habit for a while, usually I was just finding tricks.... My first charge was for "theft under" [then $200] and I lied about my age. I was using my aunt's I.D. so my grandmother was contacted and they found out I was really a juvenile so they took me to the Juvenile Detention Centre. My grandmother had me charged with "unmanageability."

The Children's Aid system played an ineffectual role in Cindy's life for two years.

... I was made a ward of the Court so I got sent to assessment homes and treatment homes. But I would never stay. I just stayed long enough to pick up my $16 allowance, or sometimes for a month or two so I could get a $200 clothing voucher. I would still continue my life but as soon as I got what I wanted I would leave. By the time I was fifteen I had gone through all of the Children's Aid resources.

The only formal attempt she made to kick her heroin habit when she was a teenager was the result of a decision Cindy made by herself to try a treatment program in Campbell River, B.C.

Me and another guy, this male junkie who I had just met, went on the program. They put us on Methadone, on massive dosages.... Finally, after about six months, I told them I wanted to be detoxed, that I felt like I could handle it. But they wouldn't do it. I told them "Look, if you don't detox me today, I ain't coming tomorrow." They didn't believe me so I went back to Vancouver and started dealing drugs again.

As soon as she turned eighteen, Cindy started doing time in the adult prison system.

The first time I was in I ended up serving about eighteen months altogether in the adult system for various charges of possession, selling to an undercover cop, failing to appear. At one point I escaped and so I lost all of my "good time." After that I was out for a while and then I got arrested for numerous fraud charges. All of the crimes that I've ever done have been related to supporting my habit. When I got out after the eighteen months I went back into dealing heavily, but I wasn't dealing on the street anymore. I was moving up, well, just one step up from the street. I had people middling for me plus other people putting out dope for me, or else I'd put out on my own.

Finally, in 1981, Cindy decided to get off heroin on her own, cold turkey, in a prison cell while she was awaiting sentencing for her most recent round of convictions. Since then, and since spending two years in the federal Prison for Women in Kingston, Cindy has been trying to get her life onto a different track. Her attempts have been frustrated though by her low level of education and skills, her confusion over where she fits in as an

Aboriginal person in a white society, and the failure she has encountered in her attempts to find work. At the time of the interview she was facing new charges for possession of hashish and theft under $1,000.

When I got out of Kingston and moved to the "Y" in Ottawa, I was living on $8 a day. That's what they gave me for food money. Now a woman needs to buy Tampax, Kotex, toiletries and everything and I was not prepared for winter. I was starving. I was about 140 pounds when I got there and I went down to 108. My bones stuck out and I was too proud to ask for help and because of my lack of experience at work, the only skill I have is hairdressing from Kingston, I was not able to find work. I can read, but I still can't add arithmetic. I could not be a cashier or a waitress or anything like that where I got to add quickly, or hand out cash. I don't know any of the school stuff. I don't know algebra, I don't think I know how to do fractions. I really don't remember what I learned in school.

When she thinks about the future, Cindy knows what she wants, and what she does not want, but she voices her own confusion about whether or not her dreams will be possible to attain.

I'm really lonely because I don't want to hang around with street people any more. I don't want none of them in my life. Everybody here seems so cut off and so conservative. I've been through a lot of crowds in this city and I've not been accepted anywhere. I'm too honest and too vulnerable. I have my own code that I learned on the street. It was instilled in me as a child. One thing I know is I'm working hard not to touch heroin again. I don't want to go near it. All those years I didn't feel no pain. I was numb. Now I have to deal with all of the junk that is inside me, all of the resentment I feel. It's hard. It's really hard.

I just want to have a normal life. I'd like to have my own place and maybe my own hairdressing shop. I'd like to take an advanced course in cutting and hairstyling, though I'd concentrate on cutting because I consider myself a cutter. I've applied to take a cosmetician and an esthetician's course. I have a lot of interests, there's a lot of courses I'd like to take.

Being Aboriginal and living in Ottawa, Cindy feels that she has yet to find her way out of a virtual no-woman's land.

The problem is I felt like I didn't belong all the time when I was a kid and I still feel that way today. Like I'm an alien, an outsider. Because nobody's experienced what I've experienced, and I can't erase it or not talk about it. When I tell people the truth, they treat me like I have the plague or I'm a leper. Especially in Ottawa. I'm not white, but I don't feel Indian, and I don't feel accepted by the Indian people here either. I know I'm Indian by race and blood, but I don't know much about my culture. I've been away from it for so long. I'd like to practise my culture, though, I'd like to learn about it.

June

When we interviewed June, she was approaching her thirty-third birthday. Fourteen years earlier, at the age of nineteen, she committed a murder, for which she received a life sentence. June has been on parole for about five years now.

Her early life experience was characterized by intense isolation and alienation, which persisted throughout her teens. June's story is an account of her attempts to deal with those psychologically destructive circumstances.

Born and raised in rural western Canada, June was one of seven children. She describes a home life made painful by her father's character.

I don't think my father liked children, and that was a problem. I was scared and angry with him a lot so I stayed away from him most of the time. When he was home, I lived in my bedroom or I'd be outside to be away from him. And in so doing I isolated myself from the rest of the family.

As an adolescent, June was required to maintain more contact with her father. This caused her a great deal of anxiety, which was not relieved by the existence or support of other relationships.

My mother started working during the week. My dad was drinking a lot and he'd come home at night and we'd all have to suffer his drunkenness. He mostly didn't want us around but because I was taking my mother's place I had to cook for him and do anything he wished to have done, so I couldn't escape him anymore.

My mother and I never really had that much to do with each other. She taught me how to cook so I could take care of the family and to clean and all that kind of thing about being a housewife. We never spoke. We had very little to do with each other.... I wasn't really having contact with anybody in any kind of sense.

June recalls how she dealt with these pressures and the overwhelming loneliness.

I guess to a good degree I didn't care about life itself even at a young age. I was attempting suicide from the age of eight in different ways.... I started drinking when I was about fifteen. I wasn't drinking that bad at that point. It got worse when I was eighteen, nineteen. I was also given valium when I was eighteen years old because I was having a nervous breakdown.

During her teenage years, June's attempts to establish relationships outside of the family were short-lived. "When I was sixteen I started dating and, I don't know, as a consequence or whatever, but I ended up getting raped, and that ended dating." The rape resulted in a pregnancy, a miscarriage, and a further rejection by her parents, who were "disgraced" by June's behaviour. June's parents were unaware that a rape had caused the pregnancy.

I was threatened [by the rapist] that if I told anybody I'd be dead so I didn't tell a soul. So they believed that I just went out with a man and went to bed with him and I just let them believe that. I knew my dad would go after whoever it was and I knew he had a gun in the house at all times and I didn't want him taking after somebody with that so I just kept quiet.

June's reaction to these events within the existing conditions of her life was one of despair.

I started going backward in emotions. I was going back into being a child because I didn't like how I was feeling so I just started leaving reality a lot. I would visit graveyards, picking places like that to be away from people. I guess I quit wanting to make anything of myself at that point because to me I'd ruined my life. All my life had been ruined and there was really no sense anymore to anything.

Her suicide attempts increased in frequency between the ages of sixteen and nineteen. "I started trying to O.D. with pills when I was eighteen. Before that, I was jumping off cliffs, jumping off roofs, I tried to hang myself, that kind of stuff." At the end of these three years and after numerous unsuccessful efforts to kill herself, she committed murder.

June explains that her suicide attempts had been expressions of anger towards others that she had been directing at herself, but she had reached a point where

I couldn't injure myself no matter what I wanted to do.... When I did it [the murder] I felt the same anger that I had when I tried to kill myself....

I was feeling very angry towards the world. It's like they disappointed me. I couldn't get anything out of life; I couldn't relate to people. I felt nobody wanted me around and that made me angry.... I guess a lot of times I felt really rejected by people.

The victim was a four-year-old girl whom she was babysitting. Although it is still extremely difficult for June to talk about the incident, in the interview she shared with us her understanding of why it had taken place.

People ask me why it happened and I can't tell them it's just one thing; it's a whole lot of reasons all mixed up together.... I was on welfare, I had no place to live, I wasn't able to see my family, my therapist wasn't available to see me anymore, I was feeling rejected.

June also recalls more specific factors which influenced her at the time of the murder.

She was always crying. She was a really sad child. I thought nobody deserved to be that sad and that this would make her happier, because the next world must be better than this one.... She also really looked like my younger sister, there were a lot of similarities. I had felt that way before towards my sister, like I had wanted to kill her, although I never did anything to her.

June was sentenced to life imprisonment and spent nine years in federal penitentiary, including one and a half years in a psychiatric institution. Since her release on parole, she has had a difficult time adjusting, and has attempted to overdose with pills on more than one occasion. June currently lives in a halfway house for ex-psychiatric patients and continues to be under psychiatric treatment.

She chose to re-establish herself in an entirely new community upon release from prison and maintains very little contact with her family. Despite the difficulties, she is hopeful.

I'm restricted in jobs at this point; I'm restricted in my lifestyle. I guess being in prison didn't give me a good outlook on life because everyone in there is basically down on life, because life has done them wrong. But when I was able to have some freedom on passes, I could see what life was like outside prison. I could see it in a better light than when I'd gone in. It started making me fight to want to enjoy life, to strive for a good living, a job, just to be happy.

June performs volunteer work in the community and has an active interest in the peace movement.

I guess what I mostly want is to give society myself, to try to give it all the qualities I have to make it better. Like trying to help stop wars and to make an acceptable world. With nuclear arms and stuff lately it gets kind of discouraging you know, because I feel that one day I'm going to feel really great; everything will be going fine and then two presidents will push the button and everyone will be annihilated.... But I try to keep a positive outlook on things.

Conclusions

The stories of these seven women are deeply moving; they are also illustrative of common threads that run through the lives of all women who are oppressed. Early socialization that childbearing and childraising are women's most important tasks, emotional and financial dependency on men, even those who beat and rape women and children, and the inability to earn a decent living due to sex discrimination in the job market are significant factors in several of these stories. They are also key aspects of women's generally inferior social and economic status.

While the women in this article were convicted of serious offences and as such represent only a small minority of women in conflict with the law in Canada, their life circumstances may be shared by hundreds of others who are tried each year for petty offences such as shoplifting, minor thefts, and drug and alcohol infractions. Certainly, of the few hundred women charged with criminal offences with whom we have had personal contact, the majority have been poor, with few job skills to sell on the labour market, and at some point have suffered physical or sexual abuse by men.

Their crimes were vastly different, but Elaine, Barbara, and Anne-Marie all suffered at the hands of men who battered and abused them. Of the three, Elaine's crime of permitting the torture of her children is probably the most difficult for people to accept. How, we might ask, could she allow such brutal events to occur? No doubt that question haunts Elaine, who said during her interview that if she couldn't get her three children back, "then there's no point in me even existing...."

Susan Cole addresses the same question in an article she wrote on "child battery":

> And what about a woman's hellish life within the family? Freedom to choose pregnancy does not entail only choosing when to cope with having a child and terminating the pregnancy when times demand it. Reproductive freedom is real when pregnant women have the self-determination to walk out the door of a battery situation and have the resources to keep their children and rear them. But these circumstances do not occur frequently, and women, whether battered or "just" controlled, find themselves locked into situations which they do not feel they can change.[4]

That sense of being locked in is voiced clearly by Elaine, Barbara, and Anne-Marie. During the time she lived with the man who abused her and her children, Elaine says "I was paralyzed.... It was like I was in jail, I realize now that's what it was." Barbara and Anne-Marie also speak of their inability to help themselves, due to their depression or their fear of reprisals. In each situation, another woman may have been able to cope differently, and leave before she was implicated in any crimes. But as MacLeod demonstrated in her study of battered women in 1980, the psychology of fear and consequent inaction is common to thousands of women abused in this country, who find themselves unable to leave men, even when they are in desperate situations.[5]

Like most North American women in the '50s and '60s, the women we interviewed grew up immersed in the ideology that love, that is, the love of a good man, was the highest goal to which a woman could aspire. Back in 1970, Shulamith Firestone described the way this prevailing ideology defined women's experiences:

> ... a woman needs love, first, for its natural enriching function, and second, for social and economic reasons which have nothing to do with love. To deny her need is to put herself in an extra-vulnerable spot socially and economically, as well as to destroy her emotional equilibrium....[6]

The cases of Anne-Marie, Elaine, and Barbara provide vivid examples of how the struggle by women to attain love, that is, love defined in a man's world, and on men's terms, compromises women's chances to live their own lives, and to live in a state of well-being. Firestone argues that women are socialized to need male love to maintain their psychological stability. Ironically, for these women and for many others who have come into conflict with the law, it was holding onto that ideal which led to their criminal involvement and later emotional breakdowns.

Both Elaine and Barbara spoke of another threat they faced: that if they left their abusive partners, or even if they went for help, child welfare authorities might suspect they were unfit parents and confiscate their children. In Elaine's case, she knew that regaining her children from foster homes was dependent on her ability to provide suitable living accommodation for them elsewhere. Even to this day, she expresses gratitude to the very man who tortured her family because he bought a house for them, and stood by her in confrontation with the Children's Aid Society.

Elaine's and Barbara's stories provide stinging indictments of the Canadian welfare system, which on the one hand sets enforceable standards of proper parenting, and on the other, provides such miserly allowances to single mothers that their ability to provide decent homes for their children is severely reduced. When Elaine attempted to survive on welfare payments with her first husband, she turned to illegal action just to feed and clothe her children because the payments were so low.

It is impossible to know what Elaine might have chosen to do with her life had she not felt, at the age of fifteen, that the most important thing she could do was "get married and have more kids right away to make up for having lost [her] baby." Even in the face of her assault charges, she indicated that her children were the most important thing to her in the world.

Her goals are not surprising given the strong socialization of most young girls and women to believe that childrearing is one of the few things that can give their lives meaning. Again Susan Cole's insights are relevant:

> What the researchers who examine the "breakdown of mothering" fail to note is that many women are in the home via the coercion of social conditioning and that, if this conditioning were not so effective, many women who have no desire to care for children would not be in positions to have them. In other words, sexism's excessive—and false—advertising for the value of the nuclear family and the relative roles within it has a great deal to do with creating the battered child syndrome.[7]

It may be added that the excessive and false advertising for the value of the nuclear family also has a great deal to do with the battered wife syndrome, and the "stand by your man" motto that has landed more than a few women in prison as accomplices in crimes planned by their husbands or lovers. Certainly Anne-Marie stayed with her husband longer than she knew was good for her because she hoped that one day he would love her enough to change his ways.

In her in-depth study of homicide by American women, Ann Jones concluded that their crimes are "a last resort, ... most often occur[ring] when men simply will not quit."[8] Like the majority of women who have been convicted of murder or manslaughter, the person Barbara killed was a man who had abused her. Women who kill are usually victims themselves of rape, battering, or previous child abuse. This direct relationship between a woman's violence and her own victimization has been documented in the United States and Britain.[9] Although Canadian study lags behind, similar observations have often been made by women involved in the criminal justice system here.

Francine's story is one of rebellion at a very early age against the proper roles that were identified for her in her middle-class family. The rebellious streak lasted in Francine throughout her teens and twenties, and combined with her drug abuse, resulted in a rough road through the courts and the prison system. When she finally decided to change the course of her life and become self-sufficient through legitimate means, she entered a nontraditional training program to become a butcher. However, her attempts to work in a predominantly male trade were met with derision from her employers, and at the time of her interview, she was seriously considering learning a more traditional female trade. Like many of the women we interviewed, Francine's overwhelming desire for the future is to have a "quiet, stable life" filled with activities such as "[raising] children, cooking meals and taking Sunday drives with the family." Those role prescriptions still represent social acceptance in our society.

Nicole's crime of importing drugs, for which she received a seven-year sentence, was done for reasons which cannot be condoned, but they are easily understood. Raised in a brutally poor family, yet desirous of the same material goods that are held out to us by the media as necessities of everyday life, Nicole was easily tempted to earn money quickly and illegally by acting as a courier. Like many other women serving sentences for the same offence, Nicole was not the ring-leader of the drug importing operation in which she was involved. That role belonged to a man who was never caught or charged by the police, partly because Nicole refused to implicate him in any way. Even though the state offered her a reduced sentence if she testified against that man, she refused, out of fear for her future.

Between 1980 and 1986, forty-two women were sentenced in Canada to seven-year minimum terms for this crime.[10] Various proposals were made during that time to eliminate the mandatory minimum sentence for drug importation, or to allow for a reduction of sentence length based on the circumstances of the offence. And in June 1987, the Supreme Court of Canada declared that the seven-year sentence applied to every convicted drug importer constituted "cruel and unusual punishment"; therefore, such sentences were prohibited by the Charter of Rights and Freedoms. This finding of unconstitutionality had the effect of reducing the inordinate punishments that were imposed on women who were used as dispensable fronts for drug importers. It also likely alleviated some of their manipulation and intimidation within the criminal justice system.

Cindy, the only Aboriginal woman we interviewed, describes her life as one of alienation and impoverishment. Now living in a large urban centre, far from her roots in Aboriginal society and outside the mainstream of life in the white culture, she does not know where she fits in. As discussed later in this volume by Carol LaPrairie and as illustrated by the data provided in the chapter by Holly Johnson and Karen Rodgers, Cindy's lifestyle is shared by many other Aboriginal women in Canadian cities, particularly in the west.

The poverty and violence that marked Cindy's early life is experienced by many Aboriginal people whose balanced and nurturing lifestyle has been uprooted by the colonization process. It is only too typical that Aboriginal women, who are victims both of white economic oppression and Aboriginal male violence in the face of larger impotence in white society, turn their anger inwards by abusing drugs and alcohol. With an almost total lack of schooling and job-market skills, Cindy and her many Aboriginal sisters who have also been in conflict with the law, have very few options to pursue which will provide economic or social security.

While June's tragic story reveals a number of experiences common to other women in this section, she also tells of her experiences as a psychiatric patient. Phyllis Chesler and others have described the neglect, the sedation, and the sexist treatment of women at the hand of the male-dominated psychiatric profession.[11] They suggest that for many women patients, the problems they are experiencing at the time they first see a counsellor remain unresolved in traditional forms of therapy. June, who was ultimately convicted of murdering a child, was no exception to this; the chemical solutions prescribed for her in the form of valium only compounded her inability to cope with her life circumstances.

As Edwin Schur pointed out in *Labeling Women Deviant,* "the prescribing of drugs is an integral part of the medicalization of women's life situations ... it functions very effectively to 'cool' women out, [and] to support a depoliticizing and pathologizing of their dissatisfactions."[12]

June's offence is one that shocks and disturbs. We do not wish to condone the act or to minimize the tragedy, but we do wish to try to understand it by examining the circumstances within which it occurred. These crimes do not happen in isolation, and in cases such as June's, there are factors specific to women's subordinate status in society which help set the stage for these awful events: factors such as her father's abusive treatment, her sexual assault and subsequent rejection from her family, and the denial by others of her suffering.

These seven women are all very different, yet they are linked through their experiences in the prison system and they are trying, in their individual ways, to pick up and rebuild shattered lives. It is no easy task, as Francine explained during her interview:

A lot of women get out of prison, they feel so guilty and so empty, and they feel rejected. Maybe people should know that they're not a piece of garbage, that they're human. They've been in just a little more trouble than someone else but they shouldn't have the door closed on them. Because if I didn't have the help I had when I got out I would never have made it. People I didn't even know were so good to me; they didn't judge me or judge what I'd done. You know, I'd been judged once and that was enough. I think it was great that I had people telling me, "You don't have to worry about your past, look forward now." Maybe if people were a little bit more openminded it would be easier for other women when they get out.

Their stories lead us to reconsider the definition of crime. Is it a crime to steal food and clothes for one's children as Elaine did—or rather, is it a crime that the welfare system provides such miserly allowances that mothers cannot afford to adequately feed and clothe their children? Is it a crime that a woman kills a man who rapes her? Yes, but is not the causal event the rape, which occurs because society tacitly condones the sexual abuse of women? Is it a crime that a woman takes part in her husband's armed robbery? Of course it is, but it is also a crime that her husband can beat her into obedience and into fearing for her life. Is it a crime that an Aboriginal woman sells drugs on the street? Certainly, but it is also "criminal" that the dominant white culture actively destroys Aboriginal culture and economic self-sufficiency, and causes feelings of such alienation and anger that the drug sub-culture appears as a welcome alternative.

As we listen to these voices, we question not only the morality, but the practicality of maintaining an expensive criminal justice system, when other means of preventing women from committing crime are available. For instance, were our society to provide adequate financial and social support networks for single mothers; or were we to allow women full and safe control of reproduction; or were we to socialize and educate our children to assume equality exists between the sexes; or were we to stop medicalizing female rage and to confront the problems faced by women, our need for criminal justice services would be substantially reduced.

The interviews provided us with far more material than we could incorporate into this section. Several women's comments about their experiences of imprisonment could not be included. We were surprised to find that some women saw their incarceration as a positive experience. We were told by these women that the federal penitentiary was the first place they felt accepted as themselves and were given a chance to work towards personal goals without having to fend for their survival.

The interviews confirmed for us that the problems suffered by women offenders are similar to the problems suffered by many women in our society, only perhaps more acutely. It is this reality, as much as any other, that we hope feminists will note and incorporate into their efforts towards an egalitarian society.

Notes

1 Our interviews took place during the fall/winter of 1985/86. See Appendix 1 for the interview schedule used.

2 See Pat Carlen, ed., *Criminal Women* (Cambridge: Polity Press, 1985).

3 "The Village," now known as Yorkville, in Toronto, was a haven for "hippies" in the late sixties.

4 Susan Cole, "Child Battery," in *No Safe Place,* ed. Margie Wolfe and Connie Guberman (Toronto: The Women's Press, 1985), p. 31.

5 Linda MacLeod, *Wife Battering in Canada: The Vicious Circle* (Ottawa: Canadian Advisory Council on the Status of Women, 1980), p. 39.

6 Shulamith Firestone, *The Dialectic of Sex* (New York: Bantam Books, 1970), p. 145.

7 Cole, p. 30.

8 Ann Jones, *Women Who Kill* (New York: Fawcett Columbine, 1981), p. 298.

9 Jones, *Women Who Kill,* and Carol Smart, *Women, Crime and Criminology: A Feminist Critique* (London: Routledge & Kegan Paul, 1976).

10 Solicitor General Canada, Correctional Services Canada, Offender Information System, 12 December 1986, unpublished data.

11 Phyllis Chesler, *Women and Madness* (New York: Doubleday & Co., 1972); Dorothy Smith and Sara David, eds., *Women Look at Psychiatry* (Vancouver: Press Gang Publishers, 1975); Robert S. Mendelsohn, *Mal(e) Practice: How Doctors Manipulate Women* (Chicago: Contemporary Books, 1982); P. Susan Penfold and Gillian Walker, *Women and the Psychiatric Paradox* (Montreal: Eden Press, 1983).

12 Edwin Shur, *Labeling Women Deviant* (Philadelphia: Temple University Press, 1984), p. 195.

Appendix 1

A. Introduction (to us and to the project).

B. I would like to start off with your early years, so this section of the interview will ask questions about your life at that time.

1 What is your birthdate?

2 What city or town were you born in?

3 What city or town did you spend your childhood in, up to age 12?

4 Who did you grow up with?

— family by birth

— relatives

— foster parents

— friends

— other

5 How many people were in this family or home?

6 Would you say that any of the following problems or pressures existed in the home you grew up in, up to age twelve?

— money problems

— employment problems

— illness or death

— divorce or separation

— psychiatric problems

— personality conflicts among family members

— other, e.g., addictions

7 If so, how would you describe the effect that each had on you, up to age twelve? (For example, having more responsibilities around the home, having fights with family members, avoiding people, being angry or withdrawn, etc.)

8 If not, how would you describe your childhood years? (Happy, fun, average, lots of love and attention, etc.)

9 Who had a big influence on you and on what you did as a child? This could be a positive or negative influence.

10 How would you describe that influence? In what ways did that person (those persons) have an impact on you?

11 Can you remember any events that happened when you were a child (up to age

twelve) that had a big effect on you? These could be really happy events or else very difficult ones.

12 If so, how would you say this (these) event(s) affected you? (Changed your life, made you happy/sad/angry/confused, etc.)

C. Now I'd like to talk about your teenage years. For many people, this is when they started getting into trouble with the law. Whether or not this is true for you, I'd like to ask about the circumstances of your life as a teenager.

13 Where did you live as a teenager, from age twelve to eighteen?

14 With whom did you live? What kind of situation was that for you?

15 Was there anyone who had a big impact on your life at this time? What kind of influence did they have on you (positive, negative, why)?

16 Do you remember any events or things happening at this time of your life that had a big effect on you (deaths, divorce, family problems, romantic relationships, etc.)?

17 If so, how would you describe their impact on you?

18 How would you describe your teenage years overall (happy, sad, difficult, lonely, etc.)? Why?

19 Were you taking drugs as a teenager?

20 Did you ever appear in juvenile court?

21 If yes, for what offence(s)?

22 What sentences did you receive as a juvenile?

23 Did the juvenile court experience have any kind of impact on you? How?

24 What do you think were the reasons you became involved in the juvenile offence(s)? (for instance, the people or events that you mentioned earlier?)

D. This section is concerned with your adult life. I'd like to ask you questions about more recent circumstances and your point of view concerning them.

25 What is the most recent offence for which you have been convicted?

26 What was the sentence you received?

27 What stage are you at in serving the sentence?

28 Did you have any previous convictions to this, as an adult?

29 If yes, what were they?

30 What were the sentences you received?

31 Before your conviction, what was your life like? (in terms of jobs, family, friends, relationships, living situations, finances, drugs and alcohol, etc.)

32 What kind of impact did your sentences have on those situations?

33 What factors do you think contributed to your adult offences? (for example, any of the circumstances you just mentioned, circumstances that you described in your teen or childhood years, other.)

34 What are you doing now? [or] What do you think you will be doing when you get out?

35 What do you see for yourself in the long run?

36 Do you have anything to add that we haven't discussed?

37 Do you have any questions about our research?

Prostitution:
A Female Crime?[1]

Frances M. Shaver

Most public information about women and prostitution is based on police and courtroom statistics. The image generated portrays prostitution as the one type of criminal activity wherein women predominate. This is a major distortion.

The official data, along with film and television representations, distort the picture by grossly over-estimating women's involvement. In addition, their socio-economic background and reasons for being involved are misrepresented. Part of this chapter is therefore devoted to setting straight the facts about who is involved. An analysis of the impact of the current prostitution laws on women's lives will be provided, as will an examination of several theoretical traditions. In the process, some of the charges about the "evils" of sex work will be evaluated.

Data based on Canadian crime statistics[2] are here combined with information from ten field studies conducted for the Department of Justice Canada[3] and my own research[4] in order to provide a more complete and less misleading portrait. The focus is on adult prostitution, since adolescent and child prostitution raise different and additional issues.[5]

*   *   *

Criminal Code Provisions
Pertaining to Prostitution in Canada

Prostitution *per se* (i.e., the buying and selling of sexual services) is not a crime in Canada. Nevertheless, certain activities associated with it are subject to criminal sanction. These activities include: operating or being found in a bawdy-house (s.210(1&2)); knowingly transporting or directing any person to a common bawdy-house (s.211); procuring or attempting "to procure a person to have illicit sexual intercourse with another person" (s.212(1)(a)); living "wholly or in part on the avails of prostitution of another person" (s.212(1)(j)), and communicating in a public place "for the purposes of engaging in prostitution or of obtaining the sexual services of a prostitute" (s.213).[6]

Participants in Prostitution Activities

At first glance, prostitution appears to be a woman's crime. One has only to examine Canadian crime statistics to support this claim. Figure 1 shows the ratio of females to males charged for several types of criminal activity. The height of the bars represents the number of female arrests for each single male arrest. When the bar remains below the value 1 on the x-axis, it means that fewer women than men are charged. When it rises above 1, it shows that more women than men are charged. Prostitution is the only area of criminal activity for which women are charged more often than men and this is the case in three of the four years selected for examination. The ratio, which is particularly startling in 1974 (3.7:1), reverses in 1987, but then reverts back to favour women in 1989 and 1991. The gender differences are much larger with respect to all other offences (violent crime, property crime, and narcotics).

Other data also seem to indicate that prostitution is a woman's crime. Table 1 shows the relative distribution of prostitution charges laid against women and men who come in conflict with the law. For every year represented, the proportion of women charged with prostitution offences is larger than the proportion of men charged.

A breakdown of the prostitution charges by type of offence tells a slightly different story. Table 2 shows the enforcement patterns over sev-

Figure 1
Ratio of Women to Men† Charged by Type of Crime

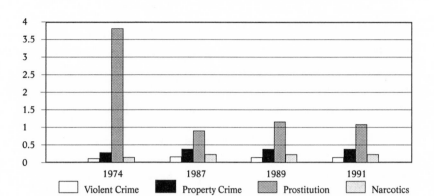

† In each case the rate for men (who are represented invisibly in this figure) is 1.

Source: *Canadian Crime Statistics* (catalogue no. 85–205). (Ottawa: Statistics Canada, Canadian Centre for Justice Statistics).

eral years by gender: not all offences emerge as female crimes. The data indicate that procuring is a male crime: in all years except 1988, more men are charged than women. On the other hand, the bawdy house and other offences (namely soliciting and communicating) clearly show up as female crimes, although the discrepancy between the proportion of charges laid against women and men decreased over the years. In 1975, for example, 87 percent of those charged in the "other" category are women; in 1991 only 52 percent of those charged are women. For only one of the periods considered—1987—are there ever fewer females than males charged.

Overall, these enforcement statistics suggest that women are much more likely than men to be involved in prostitution. In fact, however, women represent only a very small proportion of the individuals implicated. Conservative estimates based on the ratio of female to male street prostitutes in Montreal in 1991 (4:1),[7] and the average number of male clients they service each week (20 and 10, respectively)[8] indicate that only 4 percent of those involved (or at least potentially involved) in communicating for the purpose of prostitution are women. The remainder—a full 96 percent—are men, and of those, the vast majority (99 percent) are clients.

Table 1

Adults Charged with Prostitution-Related Offences† as a Percentage of the Total
Number of Criminal Code Charges in Canada by Gender and Year (1975–1991)

Year	Female		Male	
	Number	%	Number	%
1975	2,372	5.3	696	0.2
1980	960	0.2	569	0.0
1985	566	0.9	385	0.1
1986	3,863	5.9	2,939	0.9
1987	4,938	7.0	5,340	1.6
1988	5,445	7.5	5,179	1.5
1989	5,277	7.3	4,411	1.3
1990	5,523	7.2	4,944	1.4
1991	5,596	6.7	5,075	1.3

† Includes all prostitution-related offences: bawdy-house offences, procuring, living on the avails, transporting, soliciting (up to and including 1985), and communicating (after 1985).

Source: *Canadian Crime Statistics* (catalogue no. 85–205). (Ottawa: Statistics Canada, Canadian Centre for Crime Statistics).

Table 2

Distribution of Charges Against Women for Prostitution-Related Offences in Canada
by Type of Prostitution Charge and Year (1975–1991)

Year	Bawdy House		Procuring		Other†	
	%	(N)	%	(N)	%	(N)
1975	62%	(998)	35%	(95)	87%	(1975)
1980	63%	(668)	23%	(78)	67%	(783)
1985	66%	(714)	22%	(108)	53%	(129)
1986	58%	(756)	38%	(178)	57%	(5868)
1987	52%	(779)	33%	(311)	48%	(9188)
1988	64%	(587)	55%	(292)	50%	(9745)
1989	58%	(600)	14%	(159)	55%	(8929)
1990	65%	(482)	29%	(177)	53%	(9808)
1991	62%	(550)	27%	(216)	52%	(9905)

† Includes soliciting and transporting up to and including 1985, and communicating and transporting after 1985.

Source: *Canadian Crime Statistics* (catalogue no. 85–205). (Ottawa: Statistics Canada, Canadian Centre for Justice Statistics).

Figure 2
Charges for On-Street and Off-Street Prostitution, 1975–1991

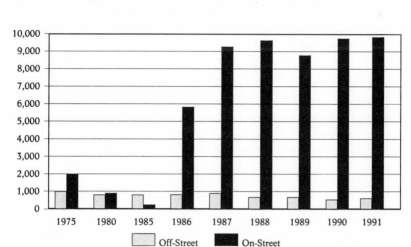

Source: *Canadian Crime Statistics* (catalogue no. 85–205). (Ottawa: Statistics Canada, Canadian Centre for Justice Statistics).

These figures are in stark contrast to those presented in Table 2, which indicate that fewer than 50 percent of those arrested in the last three years were male.

These enforcement patterns focus almost exclusively on the public manifestation of sex work: street prostitution. Less visible forms of prostitution—massage parlours, escort services, brothels, and call-girl operations—rarely result in charges (see Figure 2). In Canada as elsewhere, however, street prostitution represents only a small proportion of the market. According to a study conducted by the Bureau of Municipal Research in 1983, street prostitution in Toronto represented "only 20% of all the prostitution in the city."[9] The estimate provided in 1992 by the Canadian Organization for the Rights of Prostitutes (CORP) is identical.[10] In 1982 in England street prostitution was estimated as representing 30 percent of the total[11] and in 1977 in the United States as 10 to 15 percent of the total.[12] Once again the figures in the police statistics misrepresent the reality of prostitution. The significance of each of these discrepancies will be considered later in this chapter when the impact of current prostitution laws on women's lives is examined.

Prostitute Women: Who Are They?

Police and court-room statistics suggest that most prostitutes are young, single, female, uneducated, poor, and addicted. These impressions are partially corroborated by my own research and by the ten field studies conducted for the Justice Department. Whether female or male, prostitutes are young and begin their careers at an early age: in 1984 the prostitutes interviewed ranged in age from 14 to 56; the mean age varied from 22 to 25, depending upon the region, and the majority began their careers between the ages of 16 and 20.[13] Gender breakdowns, where available, generally show that the males are younger.[14] However, the reverse was true in Montreal in 1991: the mean age for women was 22.4 years and for men it was 24.7. These women also began their careers at a slightly younger age (17.3 years) than did the men (17.7).

According to the field studies, most sex workers are women but the proportion varies between 67 and 90 percent, depending upon the city. In 1989, in Calgary, 82 percent of street prostitutes identified in head counts were female; in Toronto, 75 percent of those counted were female; in Halifax, 67 percent; in Vancouver, 90 percent; and in Montreal, just over 80 percent.[15]

Most have not gone beyond high school: in fact, 43 percent of the women and 50 percent of the men we interviewed in Montreal in 1991 had not completed high school. The other field studies also reported that the level of schooling attained by respondents was relatively low. In all of the studies, however, at least some respondents had undertaken post-secondary studies: 26 percent in Quebec, 15 percent in Vancouver, 11 percent on the Prairies, and 2 percent in the Atlantic Provinces. The 1984 Ontario data are interesting in that they distinguish between various types of prostitutes: the majority of female street prostitutes had begun or completed grade 10 and most male prostitutes had gone as far as grade 12. Generally, it was the call-girls who had begun post-secondary studies.[16]

When asked about their childhood recollections, many mentioned they had been victims of abuse. In the Vancouver study, 67 percent stated they had been victims of physical violence in the family and 33 percent had suffered sexual abuse. In the Maritimes, 40 percent said they were victims of physical abuse and 28 percent of sexual abuse. In Quebec, 44 percent of the persons interviewed said they had been forced to have sexual relations with one or more members of the family and 33 percent had been victims of rape before entering prostitution.[17]

Most of the sex workers interviewed indicated that they came from comfortable, rather than poor or needy, homes. Even so, in 1984 38 percent in Quebec[18] and 16 percent in Vancouver[19] stated their origins were poor. A gender breakdown on our 1991 Montreal data shows that the men were more likely to come from poor homes (30 percent) than the women (17 percent).

Illicit drug use varies by region. It was highest in the Atlantic provinces (50 percent of both women and men admitted to drug abuse)[20] and lowest in Quebec (only 16 percent were heavy users).[21] On the Prairies, 42 percent said they had a problem with illicit drugs.[22] The gender breakdown available with the 1991 Montreal data indicate that use of illicit drugs is extremely low among the women (only 7 percent used hard drugs such as heroin, crack, and other forms of cocaine in the week before the interview), but quite high among the men (50 percent had used such drugs in the same time period). Among the women, alcohol abuse is more common than drug abuse. When it is measured in terms of getting drunk at least once a week, 40 percent of the women and 43 percent of the men in the Montreal sample showed signs of abuse. Nevertheless, only half of the abusers, whether women or men, reported being drunk while at work.

Finally, my research and all but one of the field studies indicate that the majority (80 percent) of prostitutes are white. The one anomaly is the 1984 Prairie sample: half of those interviewed were Native Canadians.[23] That year the sample was drawn in Regina and Winnipeg. In 1989, the sample was drawn in Calgary and very few were of Native background.

These data present a portrait of the women in prostitution which reinforces many of the police and courtroom statistics. It remains to be seen, however, whether these traits are uniquely characteristic of prostitutes. Several factors must be kept in mind. First, neither the educational attainment nor the poverty rates for the prostitutes interviewed necessarily set them apart from the Canadian population at large. Overall, in 1989, 37 percent of adult Canadians had less than a high school diploma. In the Altantic provinces, Quebec, Manitoba, and Saskatchewan, however, the proportions of individuals with less than high school were even higher, ranging from 41 to 48 percent.[24] The poverty rate for Canadian families between 1984 and 1986, when many of our respondents left home, was

14.5 percent; the rate increases to 60 percent for single-parent mothers with children under 18.[25] Since a high proportion of the respondents in the field studies conducted for the Justice Department indicated they grew up in single-parent families, this latter figure is probably the more appropriate statistic to use when comparing family backgrounds. Furthermore, none of the individuals we interviewed was destitute when entering prostitution: 90 percent of the women and 72 percent of the men had other jobs before turning to sex work, for the most part in clerical, sales, or service occupations. Indeed, 50 percent of the prostitutes in Vancouver and 74 percent in Montreal stated in 1984 that they had taken up prostitution voluntarily— "nobody forced them into the business."[26] As with many individuals who take up jobs with unpleasant working conditions (one has only to think of garment workers and poultry processors[27]), pull factors, such as economic problems[28] or knowing someone in the business,[29] may have been involved.

A history of violence and abuse may not be peculiar to those entering prostitution either. Results from a national population survey conducted for the Badgley Committee indicate that 53.5 percent of female respondents and 22.3 percent of male respondents had been the victims of unwanted sexual acts. These figures suggest that sexual abuse is such a common phenomenon in our society that only one woman in two will reach adulthood without being a victim of an unwanted sexual act.[30] The Badgley definition of abuse included a wide variety of sexual acts, some more serious than others. The acts ranged from sexual exhibitionism, to unwanted touching, to forced sexual relations. When prostitutes in the field studies indicated that they had been sexually abused as children, the tendency was to assume they were victims of serious abuse, although this was rarely elaborated upon.[31] It remains to be seen, therefore, whether the level of serious sexual abuse of prostitutes when they were children is higher than the level of serious abuse in the general population.

Finally, most of the interviews for the field studies were conducted with individuals involved in street prostitution. The profile of all female prostitutes is somewhat less bleak. Data from the 1984 Ontario field study suggest that older, higher status, more affluent, more educated, non-addicted prostitutes are less likely to be involved in street prostitution and more apt to like their work.[32] In addition, as you will see below, off-street prostitutes are also much less likely to be arrested.

The actual conditions of work of street prostitutes are also less bleak than the stereotype suggests. Findings from all of the 1984 field studies clearly indicate that many women work for themselves: 62 percent in Vancouver,[33] 50 percent in Toronto,[34] and 69 percent in Montreal[35] claimed that they worked for themselves. The presence and influence of pimps was more extensive in the Maritimes (where fewer than 25 percent of the women worked for themselves)[36] and on the Prairies (where most of the white women but only a few of the Native women worked for themselves).[37] Estimates by CORP in 1992 indicated that 60 percent of street prostitutes in Toronto worked for themselves.[38] Our Montreal data indicate that 50 percent work for themselves.

There is a tendency on the part of many feminists and other concerned citizens, including police officers, to challenge the validity of these figures and the veracity of the women reporting them. However, the consistently disparate patterns we observed in Montreal in 1991 between the women who worked for themselves and those who worked for a pimp are evidence of their basic accuracy. The women working for pimps were younger (19.6 years versus 25.5 years), less likely to have completed high school (33 percent versus 53 percent), and more likely to be cohabiting (80 percent versus 33 percent). They also worked longer hours per day (7.9 versus 6.7), more days per week (6.1 versus 5.5), and charged an average of 15 percent more for the services provided. There is no reason to believe that lying about pimps would occur in a manner which correlates with these differences.

Both female and male prostitutes were found to exercise a great deal of discretion when choosing clients, to practise safe sex, and to have regular check-ups for sexually transmitted diseases and AIDS. Gender differences regarding job hazards and earnings were very evident, however.[39] Women were more at risk on the job than men. They reported more rapes and more assaults, were more likely to be robbed by their clients, and were more likely to be arrested for prostitution-related offences.

On the other hand, they earned more than the men: much more. In Montreal in 1991, estimated gross earnings per week were $1800 to $2000 for women but only $600 to $800 for men.[40] Net earnings are more difficult to estimate and may, in fact, offset the difference: fines are heavy and more likely to fall to the women than the men; half of the women but none of the men "paid off" third parties in order to work (pimps, hotel managers, desk clerks, etc.); and women incur more legal costs than do men. Many women also have dependent children to support: in 1984, in

Vancouver, 29 percent supported children financially;[41] on the Prairies, 68 percent of the women had children;[42] in the Atlantic provinces, 35 percent reported having at least one child.[43] In 1991 in Montreal, we found that 30 percent of the women compared to 10 percent of the men shared in the financial support of a child or another adult (excluding the pimp).

Overall, these data on the demographic characteristics of prostitute women reflect their heterogeneity rather than their homogeneity. There are some similarities among the women and men who practise the trade but one also finds significant individual differences within each group. For some women sexual or physical abuse as a child marks the passage into prostitution; for others prostitution becomes an economic necessity because sex work is the best of a number of limited employment options; for still others it is a voluntarily chosen service occupation.[44] Much more comparative work is necessary before we can provide clear-cut explanations for why some individuals rather than others are drawn into prostitution.

Gendered Justice

A closer look at the laws pertaining to prostitution reveals that their impact on women is profound, in terms of both the definition and the enforcement. For a long period in Canadian history, prostitution actually *was* a female crime by social and legal definition. The earliest prohibitions, which made the status of being a prostitute or street walker an offence, were gender-specific and directed only against women. In Lower Canada in 1839, for example, the police were authorized to apprehend any common prostitute or nightwalker wandering in the fields, public streets, or highways who failed to give a satisfactory account of *herself*.[45]

Dictionary and lay definitions of prostitution during this period were similarly biased. Both focused entirely on the female seller. Even after Confederation in 1867, when statutes were introduced to protect women and children from the wiles of the procurer, pimp, and brothel keeper, it was the *selling* of sexual services that was most likely to be criminalized.[46]

Prostitution is *still* considered to be a female crime. Most dictionaries continue to define prostitute as "a woman who has promiscuous sexual intercourse for payment" and *limit* prostitution to "the act, practice or profession of offering the body for sexual relations for money."[47] Similar attitudes are reflected by the students in my sexuality classes. They are somewhat more open-minded regarding the sex of the prostitute (mentioning both men and women), but of the 200 students polled over the last three years, 58 to 69 percent focused on the seller when defining prostitution.

Gender-neutral legal provisions were introduced into the Criminal Code in the mid-1980s. A definitional amendment in 1983 provided that prostitute meant "a person of either sex engaging in prostitution." The communicating section (s. 213), introduced in 1985 and replacing the soliciting section, was meticulously designed to be non-sexist in nature and to criminalize both prostitutes and customers. Nevertheless, as currently enforced, section 213 focuses in the main on the *selling* of sexual services, and penalizes women more than men. This is clearly evident in several sets of data gathered for the Justice Department during the three years following the enactment of the section.

First, male prostitutes were under-represented in the charge statistics in several cities. In 1989, in Calgary, where 18 percent of street prostitutes identified in head counts were male, only 12 percent of prostitution charges involved males. In Toronto, about 25 percent of the prostitutes counted were male but only 5 percent of the prostitution charges involved males. In Halifax the figures were 33 percent and 11 percent respectively, and in Vancouver they were 10 percent and 8 percent. Montreal was the exception: a slightly higher percentage of males were charged (27 percent) than appeared in the head counts (20 percent).[48]

Second, more prostitutes than customers were charged in nine of the ten Canadian cities studied in 1989. The law was most equally applied in Toronto and London, where about one-half of the charges laid involved customers. In Winnipeg, Niagara Falls, Montreal, and Quebec City, however, only between 30 and 40 percent of charges involved customers, and in Vancouver, Calgary, and Halifax, customers represented 25 percent or fewer of the charges laid.[49]

The researchers in Toronto also analyzed inequities in the use of pre-trial detention since, for many accused persons, "the stay in detention—whether overnight or longer—is the most serious consequence of their involvement in the criminal justice system."[50] They found that very few customers were held overnight for a bail hearing: 97 percent were released on the street with a notice to appear in court to face charges. In comparison, fewer than 75 percent of the prostitutes were released in this manner.

There is also evidence of discrimination against prostitutes in the sentencing patterns. In 1989, their sentences were more severe than those re-

ceived by customers and varied in severity by region.[51] In addition, when
the prior record of the accused was controlled, first offender prostitutes received more severe sentences than first offender customers in Vancouver
and Toronto, although this phenomenon did not appear to take place in
Montreal.[52] Sentences included fines ranging from $100 in Halifax to $379
in Montreal. Incarceration was used primarily for "recidivist" female prostitutes. The average length of sentence was one month.[53]

Overall, these enforcement patterns, as well as those in evidence na-
tionally (see Tables 1 and 2 above), indicate that except for procuring—
which continues to have a low annual conviction rate—prostitution remains a predominately female crime and the control of street prostitution
the most pressing issue for criminal justice agencies. Of all the participants, female prostitutes are the most likely to end up with criminal
records, and are more likely than their male clients to receive severe convictions.

There are a number of other ways in which the prostitution laws impact
negatively on the lives of the women involved. First and foremost, the ille-
gality increases the risks women face by impeding the flow of information
between prostitutes and customers and increasing the prostitutes' dependence on pimps and other profiteers in order to contact clients.[54] Since the
sentences based on operating a bawdy-house are much more serious, more
women work on the street than would like to. The hazards and risks they
endure, regardless of their base of operation, are seen as part of the job. As
a consequence, prostitutes who have been beaten and raped are often told
by the police that they have no right to protection.[55] This tends to add to
their feelings of stigmatization and decrease their feelings of positive self-
worth. Finally, their family ties are highly vulnerable: the adults they live
with face the risk of being charged with living on the earnings of prostitution and their children are likely to be placed in custody once their identity
comes to the attention of the authorities.[56] This is a particular problem for
women because they are more likely to be cohabiting than the men and are
more likely to have children in their care.[57]

Prostitution as portrayed, practised, and enforced in Canada is highly
sexist in character. Female prostitutes are most likely to be the focus of attention and yet they represent only a small fraction of participants in the
trade. Their distribution within this population is lopsided as well: women
dominate the supply side while men dominate the demand side. The women
and men involved are both culpable under the law—as are all persons en-

gaging in any form of prostitution—nevertheless, the enforcement patterns penalize women more often and more severely than men; they penalize prostitutes more than customers, procurers, or pimps; and they penalize on-street prostitution more than off-street prostitution.

Taken together, these data illustrate two important elements in the maintenance and reproduction of prostitution in its current sexist form. One is the double sexual standard: it is the act of selling sex that is denounced, not the act of buying it. Clearly, monogamy continues to be proclaimed as female virtue while promiscuity continues to be accepted and often valued among men. A second element is the socio-economic disparity between women and men: relative to men, women are still poorer and hold less powerful positions. The sale of sexual services becomes an option for women in a society that endorses sexual bargaining and offers women limited, under-valued employment options. The purchase of these services falls to men. They, for the most part, have more economically viable employment options and are in practice granted more sex rights. The laws and their enforcement perpetuate the double sexual standard and reinforce the socio-economic disadvantages of women.

Theoretical Traditions

Theorizing about prostitution is usually conducted within one of three basic traditions: social-psychological, functionalist, or feminist. All three reflect norms or morals which assume that prostitution is wrongful behaviour. As a consequence, all three fail to adequately interpret the data sets examined here.

The most pervasive approach to prostitution is the social-psychological one. Most theorizing done within this tradition traces not the causes of prostitution, but the reasons why women enter the trade. The actor, rather than the act, becomes identified as the legitimate focus of attention. Entry into prostitution is seen as a consequence of family dysfunction, under-socialization, or different socialization. The first two explanations, grounded for the most part in a consensus model, analyze how individual actors come to violate norms and values we are all assumed to share. Specific theories—developed to explain rule-breaking behaviour of this type (anomie, neutralization theory, and control theory)—are evident in several prostitution studies.[58] The latter approach explains entry into prostitution as a consequence of socially learned differences. It is grounded in a pluralist or class-stratified model of society and centres on how certain behaviour comes to be valued or devalued within different groups. For example, it is argued that the poor and under-educated are more likely to be drawn into the supply side of the prostitution trade because they are more likely, given their reference group, to see it as a viable option. Although this approach draws attention to the broader social and economic structures in which prostitution is located, most of the theorizing focuses on the entry patterns of prostitutes, rather than the institution of prostitution.[59]

Until the 1970s, theorizing about the institution of prostitution was primarily developed within a functionalist perspective. Kingsley Davis (1937), for example, traced its existence and persistence to the double standard of social sexual expectations for women and men: "bad girls" are needed in order to facilitate the stronger innate sex drive of men while maintaining the institution of the family.[60] In this context, the deviancy of prostitution serves as a source of social stability. Davis portrayed the male customer on the one hand as a victim of his stronger sex drive, and on the other, as immune from sanctions because of the important social functions he provides.[61] Such a portrayal legitimates the disparate social and legal responses to the female prostitute and the male customer.

Functionalist and social-psychology perspectives on prostitution are both based on differences between male and female sexuality: the former in biology and the latter in socialization. In addition, they both legitimate, rather than question, the inequitable social and legal responses to the female prostitute and the male customer. In the mid 1970s, when feminists began theorizing about prostitution, they directly challenged these allegations. They located gender differences in sexuality in the wider structures of social (i.e., male) power; exposed the double sexual standard; segregated prostitutes from the business of prostitution; and challenged the commonly held view of prostitutes as "bad girls" by providing clear evidence that prostitutes are women struggling to maintain their socio-economic independence in a male-dominated world.[62]

As feminist theorizing about prostitution developed, several strands of thought emerged. These variations are most evident in the assessment of what is problematic about prostitution and how to eliminate it.[63] Feminist approaches can be broadly classified as either liberal-feminist or radical-feminist in origin. The former approach generally subscribes to the view that a woman should have the right to sell sexual services if she so chooses.

It argues that non-coercive, adult prostitution should be considered no more immoral than other forms of service work, and contends that the degradation and danger currently inherent in the working conditions are related to the gender inequities mentioned above rather than the commercialization of sex.[64] Neither prostitutes nor prostitution are identified as deviant.

In contrast, radical feminists argue that all prostitution involves coercion of one kind or another. They claim that bodies—not services—are being sold, and imply that women who choose to sell their bodies are validating the double sexual standard on the one hand and men's right of access to women's bodies on the other. This is often referred to as "affirming the law of male sex-right."[65] As a result, they argue that feminists should—in the short term—be committed to a non-sexist approach to prostitution control and the decriminalization of prostitution activities as a way of improving the working conditions of prostitutes. In the long term, however, they should be committed to the eventual elimination of prostitution. Prostitutes, especially those who choose to become involved, are seen as suspect, and the practice of prostitution is viewed as unacceptable.[66]

Neither school has adequately evaluated its claims. The arguments are supported philosophically, rather than empirically. Nevertheless, I remain willing to side with the liberal feminists who view prostitutes as agents in their own right and who defend both the possibility and practice of non-coercive, adult prostitution. Much of the empirical data that we have begun to collect and which I have presented here undermines the radical version. Not all prostitution involves coercion: the majority of female prostitutes work for themselves and do not necessarily have less education or fewer employment opportunities than other women. Prostitutes do not unequivocally reinforce male sex-right—some carefully choose their clients who must *pay* for the service provided. More importantly, the differences between female and male prostitutes regarding job hazards and earning power suggest that most of the undesirable aspects of prostitution are linked to broader social problems rather than the commercialization of sex.[67] These findings should challenge us to reevaluate our thinking about prostitutes and prostitution. If we hope to improve the working conditions, reduce the injustice related to the service, and provide acceptable alternatives to street prostitution, we must do so with an accurate view of the situation.

Notes

1 Support for the primary research described in this paper was provided through a grant from the Social Sciences and Humanities Research Council of Canada (Women and Work). I would like to thank my assistant Jane LeBrun for her help in compiling the data for the tables and figures.

2 *Canadian Crime Statistics* (catalogue no. 85–205) (Ottawa: Statistics Canada, Canadian Centre for Justice Statistics).

3 The studies conducted in 1984 include: N. Crook, *A Report on Prostitution in the Atlantic Provinces*; J. Fleishman, *A Report on Prostitution in Ontario*; R. Gemme et al., *A Report on Prostitution in Quebec*; M. Lautt, *A Report on Prostitution in the Prairies*; J. Lowman, *Vancouver Field Study of Prostitution: Research Notes*; and D. Sansfaçon, *Prostitution in Canada: A Research Review Report*. The studies conducted in 1989 include: A. Brannigan, L. Knafla, and C. Levy, *Street Prostitution: Assessing the Impact of the Law—Calgary, Regina, Winnipeg*; R. Gemme, N. Payment, and L. Malenfant, *Street Prostitution: Assessing the Impact of the Law—Montreal*; F. Graves, *Street Prostitution: Assessing the Impact of the Law—Halifax*; J. Lowman, *Street Prostitution: Assessing the Impact of the Law—Vancouver*; S. Moyer and P.J. Carrington, *Street Prostitution: Assessing the Impact of the Law—Toronto*; Canada, Department of Justice, *Street Prostitution: Assessing the Impact of the Law—Synthesis Report*. All were published by the Department of Justice Canada, Ottawa.

4 Eighty Montreal street prostitutes were interviewed during the summer of 1991: thirty women, thirty men, and twenty transsexuals and transvestites. This latter group is excluded from the gender analysis done in this paper. The data include information on socio-economic background, job history and future plans, work activity and work hazards, enjoyment of sex on and off the job, relations with others on and off the job, and where they turn to for help with problems. Interviews generally lasted between thrity and ninety minutes but most took an hour. They were conducted off the street over coffee and in some cases in the respondent's home. Information is also drawn from my earlier writings: F.M. Shaver, "Prostitution: A Critical Analysis of Three Policy Approaches," *Canadian Public Policy* 11, no. 3 (1985): 493–503, and F.M. Shaver, "A Critique of the Feminist Charges against Prostitution," *Atlantis* 4, no. 1 (1988): 82–98.

5 Some of the sex workers in adult prostitution are under eighteen. However, in the field studies to which I refer, as well as in my own study, the majority were eighteen or over at the time of the interview. For information on juvenile prostitution see Canada, *Report of the Committee on Sexual Offences Against Chil-*

dren and Youth [the Badgley Report], vol. 1 and 2 (Ottawa: Supply and Services Canada, 1984).

6 The communicating section (s. 213) was introduced in December 1985. In 1988 two subsections were added to the procuring section that increased the sentences related to living on the avails of prostitution of another person under the age of eighteen (s. 212(2)) and of obtaining or attempting to obtain the sexual services of a person under the age of eighteen (s. 212(4)).

7 The Montreal ratio of female to male street prostitutes (4:1) is based on the average street counts over the summer of 1991. Similar figures were reported for the same area in 1989. Ratios for Calgary (5:1); Toronto (4:1), and Halifax (3:1) are similar (Canada, Department of Justice, *Street Prostitution—Synthesis Report*, pp. 42–44). The ratio in Vancouver was noticeably different (10:1), but this does not affect the overall female to male ratio once customers are incorporated.

8 The female and male prostitutes in the Montreal sample actually serviced an average of 28.5 and 14.5 customers per week, respectively. Nevertheless, the averages were reduced to 20 and 10, respectively, in order to allow for the fact that some customers may have returned during the same week to see the same or another prostitute. These estimates are similar to others that have been reported. In 1977, prostitutes working the streets and bars in Vancouver averaged 14 customers a week (G.A. Forbes, *Street Prostitution in Vancouver's West End* [Vancouver: Vancouver Police Department, 1977]). Prostitutes working the streets in Britain in 1982 averaged 20 clients a week (E. McLeod, *Working Women: Prostitutes Now* [London: Cromm Ltd., 1982], p. 12). In the Maritimes in 1984, female prostitutes averaged 5.2 clients a night and males 2.4 per night (Crook, *Prostitution in the Atlantic Provinces*, p. 39).

9 Bureau of Municipal Research, *Civic Affairs: Street Prostitution in our Cities* (Toronto: Author, 1983).

10 Reported by Alexandra Highcrest in "Fighting the Myths about Prostitution," *The Globe and Mail* (24 February 1992), p. A5.

11 McLeod, *Working Women.*

12 J. James et al., *The Politics of Prostitution* (Seattle, WA: Social Research Associates, 1975).

13 Sansfaçon, *Prostitution in Canada*, p. 57.

14 Gemme et al., *Prostitution in Quebec*, p. 117; Gemme, Payment, and Malenfant, *Street Prostitution—Montreal*, p. 156; and Brannigan, Knafla, and Levy, p. 103.

15 Canada, Department of Justice, *Street Prostitution—Synthesis Report*, pp. 42–44.

16 Sansfaçon, *Prostitution in Canada*, p. 59.

17 Ibid., p. 58.

18 Gemme et al., *Prostitution in Quebec*, p. 117.

19 Lowman, *Vancouver Field Study*, p. 700.

10 Crook, *Prostitution in the Atlantic Provinces*, p. 21.

21 Gemme et al., *Prostitution in Quebec*, p. 119.

22 Lautt, *Prostitution in the Prairies*, p. 89.

23 Sansfaçon, *Prostitution in Canada*, p. 80.

24 *General Social Survey Analysis Series* (1989; Statistics Canada Catalogue 11–612E, No. 7), p. 28.

25 National Council of Welfare, *Poverty Profile Update for 1991* (Ottawa: National Council of Welfare, Winter 1993), pp. 7–8.

26 Lowman, *Vancouver Field Study*, p. 235; Gemme et al., *Prostitution in Quebec*, p. 118.

27 For discussions of the working conditions of women garment workers and poultry processors see Charlene Gannagé, *Double Day Double Bind* (Toronto: The Women's Press, 1986) and C.D. Bryant and K.B. Perkins, "Containing Work Disaffection: The Poultry Processing Worker," in *Varieties of Work*, ed. P.L. Stewart and M.G. Cantor (Beverly Hills: Sage Publications, 1982; pp. 199–212).

28 Sansfaçon, *Prostitution in Canada*, p. 63.

29 Paul Fraser et al., *Pornography and Prostitution in Canada: Report of the Special Committee on Pornography and Prostitution*, vol. 2 (Ottawa: Minister of Supply and Services Canada, 1985), p. 377.

30 Reported in Fraser et al., *Pornography and Prostitution*, p. 373.

31 Fraser et al., *Pornography and Prostitution*, p. 374.

32 Fleishman, *Prostitution in Ontario*, pp. 7–10.

33 Lowman, *Vancouver Field Study*, p. 134.

34 Fleishman, *Prostitution in Ontario*, p. 54.

35 Gemme et al., *Prostitution in Quebec*, p. 127.

36 Crook, *Prostitution in the Atlantic Provinces*, p. 74.

37 Lautt, *Prostitution in the Prairies*, pp. 95ff.

38 Reported in Highcrest, "Fighting the Myths," p. A2.

39 I am exploring these and other gender differences in a paper currently in progress (F.M. Shaver, "The Regulation of Prostitution: Avoiding the Morality Traps," *Canadian Journal of Law and Society*, forthcoming).

40 These estimates are based on the average number of customers per week and the price attached to the type of services usually provided. On the average, the

women charged $48 for oral sex, $95 for coitus, and $130 for a combination of both. About half the clients serviced simply wanted oral sex; the rest were divided between the other two services.

41 Lowman, *Vancouver Field Study*, p. 193.

42 Lautt, *Prostitution in the Prairies*, p. 43.

43 Crook, *Prostitution in the Atlantic Provinces*, p. 16.

44 For discussions of prostitution as voluntary work see V. Jennes, "From Sex as Sin to Sex as Work," *Social Problems* 37, no. 3 (1990): 403–20; G. Pheterson, *A Vindication of the Rights of Whores* (Seattle, WA: The Seal Press, 1989); and *Good Girls/Bad Girls: Sex Trade Workers and Feminists Face to Face*, ed. L. Bell (Toronto: The Women's Press, 1987).

45 Connie Backhouse, "Canadian Prostitution Law 1939–1972," in *Prostitution in Canada* (Ottawa: Canadian Advisory Council on the Status of Women, 1984), p. 7.

46 J.P.S. McLaren, "Chasing the Social Evil: Moral Fervour and the Evolution of Canada's Prostitution Laws, 1867–1917," *Canadian Journal of Law and Society* 1 (1986): 125–65. See also N. Larsen, "Canadian Prostitution Control between 1914 and 1970: An Exercise in Chauvinist Reasoning," *Canadian Journal of Law and Society* 7, no. 2 (1992): 137–56, and C. Backhouse, "Nineteenth Century Canadian Prostitution Law: Reflection of a Discriminatory Society," *Social History* 53 (1985): 387–423.

47 These definitions were taken from the 1972 *Larousse Illustrated International Dictionary*. The revised and updated 1987 version provides the same two definitions.

48 Canada, Department of Justice, *Street Prostitution—Synthesis Report*, pp. 42–44.

49 Ibid., pp. 41–42.

50 P.J. Carrington and S. Moyer, "A Comparison of the Treatment of Prostitutes and Their Customers by the Police and Courts in Toronto, 1986–87," paper presented at the Canadian Sociology and Anthropology Association Annual Meeting, June 1991; p. 10 and Table 1.

51 Canada, Department of Justice, *Street Prostitution—Synthesis Report*, p. 60.

52 Ibid., p. 61.

53 Ibid., pp. 58–59.

54 Shaver, "Prostitution: A Critical Analysis," p. 496.

55 Ibid., p. 496.

56 Pheterson, *A Vindication of the Rights of Whores*, p. 195.

57 In our sample in Montreal in 1991, 57 percent of the women were cohabiting or

married compared to 7 percent of the men. A third of the sample reported having at least one child.

58 For studies dealing with the dysfunctional family, see D. Drew and J. Drake,
Boys for Sale (New York: Brown, 1969); R. Lloyd, *For Money or Love: Boy
Prostitution in America* (New York: Ballantine, 1972). For a perspective focus-
ing on anomie, see J. James, "Prostitutes and Prostitution," in *Deviants: Volun-
tary Actors in a Hostile World,* ed. E. Sagarin and F. Montanio (New York: Gen-
eral Learning Press, 1977), and for those focusing on social control see T.
Hirshi, "The Professional Prostitute," *Berkeley Journal of Sociology* 7 (1969):
37–41; H. Greenwald, *The Elegant Prostitute* (New York: Ballantine, 1970); P.
Alder, "On Becoming a Prostitute," in *Criminal Life,* ed. D. Peterson and M.
Truzzi (Englewood Cliffs, N.J.: Prentice-Hall, 1972); and D. Gray, "Turning
Out: A Study of Teenage Prostitution," *Urban Life and Culture* 1, no. 4 (1973):
401–26.

59 Labelling theory and the group conflict theories are the most common examples
of this tradition and traces of these theories are evident in studies by R. and V.
Winslow, *Deviant Reality* (Boston: Allyn and Bacon, 1974) and R. Akers, *Deviant Behavior: A Social Learning Approach* (Belmont, CA.: Wadsworth, 1977).

60 Davis, "The Sociology of Prostitution," *American Sociological Review* 2, no. 5
(1937): 744–55.

61 J. Lowman, "Street Prostitution," in *Deviance: Conformity and Control in
Canadian Society,* ed. V.F. Sacco (Scarborough, Ont.: Prentice-Hall, 1992), p.
59.

62 See Canada, House of Commons, "Minutes of Proceedings and Evidence of the
Standing Committee on Justice and Legal Affairs," nos. 86, 90, and 91 (1982);
Canadian Advisory Committee on the Status of Women, "On Pornography and
Prostitution: A Brief Presented to the Special Committee on Pornography and
Prostitution" (Ottawa: Author, 1984); National Action Committee on the Sta-
tus of Women, "Prostitution: A Brief Presented to the Special Committee on
Pornography and Prostitution" (Ottawa: Author, 1984); and Fraser et al., *Porn-
ography and Prostitution.*

63 See D. Brock, "Feminist Perspectives on Prostitution: Addressing the Canadian
Dilemma," unpublished Master's thesis, Sociology and Anthropology, Carleton
University, Ottawa, 1984; and C. Overall, "What's Wrong with Prostitution?
Evaluating Sex Work," *Signs: Journal of Women in Culture and Society* 17, no.
4 (1992): 705–24.

64 See Shaver, "A Critique of the Feminist Charges," and G. Rubin, "Thinking Sex:
Notes for a Radical Theory of the Politics of Sexuality," in *Pleasure and Danger:*

Exploring Female Sexuality, ed. C.S. Vance (Boston: Routledge & Kegan Paul, 1984).

65 See C. Pateman, *The Sexual Contract* (Stanford: Stanford University Press, 1988).

66 See C.A. MacKinnon, *Toward a Feminist Theory of the State* (Cambridge: Harvard University Press, 1989) and Pateman, *The Sexual Contract.*

67 For a more detailed evaluation of prostitution and radical feminism, see F.M. Shaver, "The Regulation of Prostitution: Avoiding the Morality Traps," *Canadian Journal of Law and Society,* forthcoming.

Media, Myths
and Masculinization:
Images of Women in Prison[1]

Karlene Faith[†]

This chapter focuses on the distorted and destructive images of women in prison presented in film and television. The media perpetrate mythical and masculinized images of criminal women. These images are rooted in nineteenth-century criminological models and in the tendency of both scholars and media producers to assume female prisoners and prisons are like their male counterparts. As an exploratory discussion, this chapter considers images of the female offender in the contexts of the media, traditional academic theories and the actual prison environment.

Media Fabrication

Most women who are sent to prison are not "career" criminals; that is, they

† This chapter is reprinted with minor changes from *Too Few to Count: Canadian Women in Conflict with the Law*, ed. Ellen Adelberg and Claudia Currie (Vancouver: Press Gang Publishers, 1987). It was adapted from a longer unpublished paper by Karlene Faith, copyright 1987. From 1972 to 1982 Faith taught and co-ordinated programs for women in prison in California.[2] In 1982 she returned to Canada, her home country, where she has continued to teach and do research in this area. This chapter draws on her work and research in women's prisons in Canada and the U.S.[3]

have not purposefully developed devious skills so as to support themselves through intentionally illegal activity. On the contrary, one can generalize that most women are at first traumatized by the experience of being labeled a criminal. They often hold to conventional stereotypes about "criminal" women and they are discomfited by the stigma associated with this label. Those who enter prison generally come to recognize their commonalities with other prisoners—not only in terms of their present circumstances, but also often in terms of shared background factors (such as poverty, racism, single-parenthood, abusive spouses, alcoholism and so on) which may have contributed to their illegal behaviours.

It is difficult in prison to sustain individuality; as "criminal women" they share an institutional identity yet commonly resist being labeled or categorized. To illustrate this point, the following is an excerpt from my journal notes, describing an informal conversation that took place in prison among women who were critical of research for which they had been interviewed:

Today a group lingered after class to talk about sex. We didn't actually talk about sex; we talked about people who talk about sex.

It's not that these women aren't interested in sex. They say that they just don't want to be categorized as "butches" and "femmes" by sociologists who write about prison role-playing as an adaptive form of behaviour, and they don't want to be subjects for deprivation theories.

The women were saying that men who have come to the prison to interview them have been obsessed with sex. Bobbie said, "These research guys would bring us in, one at a time, and ask us, 'How do you do it? How often? With how many different women?'" ... and then she added, "Isn't that sick? Isn't that lewd and perverted?"

They were irked by social scientists who objectify them with negative sex-related characterizations, and also by Hollywood images of women in prison which play on these themes. To continue with my journal excerpt:

They protest that their lives are mocked by B-grade movies about women's prisons which feature male-oriented sex-and-violence plots complete with predatory characters who prey on young, innocent types who somehow got to prison by mistake. These movies almost invariably include stock char-

acters: a cold, "masculine" female warden; sadistic lackey guards who
stalk vulnerable prisoners; tough-broad convicts who inflict torture on
their prison mates; and goody-goody snitches who get everybody in trou-
ble. The violence in these movies typically connects with sex, and the at-
tackers are portrayed as sleazy and very masculine lesbians. These films
give the impression that women's prisons are inhabited by brutal dykes
who rape and corrupt the normal criminals; female prisoners are then
stereotyped in the public eye on the basis of these fictionalized movie/TV
characters.

These women were critical not just of the slander against their identity, but also of the political implications. As one woman put it: "It's this kind of media jive that helps politicians convince voters that more money is needed to build more prisons to protect society from criminal beasts." In a discussion of female imagery in the media, Lisa Steele raises the problem as follows: "For women concerned with the images of women, the question becomes, How do we rescue our images from their virtual control by the mass media?... How can we replace the homogenized stereotypes with our own individual and group portraits?"[4]

As will be discussed in this paper, Hollywood filmmakers have indeed been guilty of generating monstrous images of women in prison, beginning in the 1950s when construction of segregated women's institutions accelerated. One such film that made an impression on me as a teenager was *So Young, So Bad* (1950), starring Anne Francis as the pretty blonde who didn't deserve to be there (unlike the other grotesque women with whom she was imprisoned) and who was tormented by masculine female guards and convicts. In one particularly memorable scene, the women were knocked to the floor with the force of a powerful water hose, all of them screaming in agony while the sadistic guard watched with glee.

Such films are as insulting to the women who work in prisons as to those who are locked in them. Guards are almost invariably portrayed as the enemy. And whereas many prison guards are indeed contemptuous and cruel toward those over whom they wield physical (and often psychological) control, I have also known and observed many guards who are humane and even respectful toward women in their charge, and prisoners commonly credit caring staff members with providing them with needed encouragement and practical support. Given the institutional context, the punitive function of prisons, and the status differential between prisoners and guards, it is reasonable to assume an adversarial climate of distrust, but it is no more realistic to portray guards as predators than it is to portray prisoners in this light.[5]

The Films

This chapter focuses on women's prison films as distinct from films based on the lives of notorious individuals who are in big trouble with the law. The latter films tend to glorify or study the character of the anomalous offending woman, who is portrayed in sharp relief against blurred backgrounds. She isn't intended to represent criminal women, only herself. Examples of this genre would include *I Want to Live* (1958), starring Susan Hayward, who received an Academy Award for her portrayal of Barbara Graham, who was executed in the California gas chamber. *The Badlands* (1973), with Martin Sheen and Sissy Spacek, was based on the story of Caril Ann Fugate, who, at age fourteen, went on a killing spree with Charles Starkweather, her nineteen-year-old boyfriend. Bonnie Parker and Clyde Barrow, 1930s outlaws, were portrayed in the 1937 *You Only Live Once,* produced by Fritz Lang, with Sylvia Sidney and Henry Fonda; another version of this story was produced in 1967, *Bonnie and Clyde,* with Faye Dunaway and Warren Beatty.

More recently there have been films such as the television docu-drama *The Burning Bed,* starring Farrah Fawcett in the story of a battered woman who kills her husband. Such films are of interest in that they offer vivid indicators of social attitudes toward women who commit crimes of violence, but with rare exception, they individualize these women out of context.

Also very different from the women in prison genre are those films with fictional characters whose crimes are fun and amusing: for example, Jane Fonda's role in *Fun with Dick and Jane* (1977) or Whoopi Goldberg in *Burglar* (1986). These films, and others of this genre, are refreshing in that they don't denigrate the female protagonist; they do not, however, accurately represent women who come into conflict with the law.

Two recent films do take seriously the conditions of ordinary women's lives: the Dutch film *A Question of Silence* (1983), directed by Marleen Gorris, is a fictionalized story of three unacquainted women who spontaneously murder a store proprietor (male) who caught one of them shoplifting; their crime is not at all realistic, but the background for their action surely is. The film *Working Girls* (1986), produced by Lizzie Borden in New York, is a graphically accurate and even matter-of-fact portrayal of bawdy house prostitution. This is an important film but, again, it steers away from depicting the lives of the vast majority of prostitutes.

All of these films offer substantially more texture, dimension and human quality than the typical B-grade movies about women in prison, but they do not (nor are they intended to) convey a realistic understanding of the motivations or social conditions behind conventional female crime.

Following are summaries of two women's prison films, the first of which is a Hollywood classic, titled *Caged*, which was produced in 1950 featuring two respected actors—Eleanor Parker and Agnes Moorehead. This film was a prototype of the genre—it established the stereotypes. The second is *Turning to Stone*, a 1986 television feature movie produced in Canada by John Kastner in a departure from his work as a documentary filmmaker. To my knowledge, this was the first Canadian fictionalized film about women in prison, and it is much more reflective of the U.S. women's prison film genre than it is of the actual experience of women in prison in either Canada or the U.S.

"CAGED"

The theme of the sympathetic character whose crime is not her fault, which sets her apart from "real" criminal women, perhaps first occurred with the 1945 film *I'll Be Seeing You*, starring Ginger Rogers as a woman doing a prison sentence for killing a man in defence of her honour. The story, however, takes place not in the prison but during a good-behaviour furlough with her relatives. It wasn't until 1950, with the release of *Caged*, that the prototype of the good-girl-unjustly-imprisoned was fully developed, as follows:

Marie Allen, age nineteen, was waiting in the car while her young unemployed husband robbed a gas station of $40 to buy food for his pregnant wife. He was killed in the act and Marie was convicted, with no prior record, on an accessory charge. Her father is dead and her poor, sick mother is not in a position to help her.

Marie (played by Eleanor Parker) has terror on her very pretty face as the police van approaches the gothic structure of the institution, with the words PRISON FOR WOMEN carved in granite at the portal. Inside, Marie timidly asks for a comb to straighten her hair before her mug shot is taken.

(The viewer is given to understand that she is a very feminine woman who cares about her appearance.)

The warden of the prison (played by Agnes Moorehead) calls Marie into her office to help orient her to the institution. She is like the wardens of most later films in this genre in that she has a "masculine" demeanour. However, she is a kind person—very efficient and reassuring as she tells Marie, "I'd like to be your friend ... you weren't sent here to be punished; just being here is punishment enough." (This film was produced at the outset of the construction of treatment facilities based on the medical model— in which rehabilitation and not punishment is the purported purpose of the institution.) The corrupt matron (Hope Emerson), whose masculinity is overbearing, attempts to gain Marie's attentions by offering her candy or even drugs: "I like to do a good turn for my girls ... maybe you got a little habit...? I could get you whatever you needed."

We quickly learn that it is not the good warden but rather the evil matron who is in charge. Having rebuffed her overtures, Marie is assigned to floor duty—that is, she scrubs floors all day over her protestations that the doctor has warned her against strenuous physical exercise. The matron slaps her hard, shoves her to the floor, and she goes to work. Meanwhile we are introduced to the other women, for whom violence is part of the daily routine. A snitch is held by one woman while others beat her up. Not all of the women are violent: some are simply insane. Kitty, an older prisoner who recruits "new fish" for her crime ring, takes a liking to Marie, and instructs her: "You see, kid, in this cage you get tough or you get killed."

Marie does have one good friend but one day she discovers this woman dead in her cell by hanging. Soon afterward Marie delivers her premature baby. Since she doesn't have any blood relatives who can take care of it, the baby is taken away by the state and placed for adoption. Marie's innocence begins to erode into cynicism as she suffers this heartbreak. She continues to evade the matron's overtures and the angry matron confronts the warden with the need for greater discipline; she says that in the old days if women didn't behave they were hosed down, their heads were shaven and they were treated like "animals in a cage—like they should be."

At her parole hearing, after one year, Marie pleads with the three men on the panel to release her—assuring them that if they'll let her out she'll get a job. "What could you do?" they ask her. She says, "I could be a salesgirl, or wait tables, or do laundry..." but they turn her down because, they say, she's still too young to take care of herself. Her bitterness shows but she continues on bravely, and adopts a contraband kitten. When the evil matron attempts to take it from her she refuses to relinquish it and the other (violent) women assist her by starting a riot. Marie's punishment is that she is taken by the matron into a private room where she is tied up and her head is shaven, her screams stifled with a towel. She is then thrown into dark solitary confinement where, after pleading unsuccessfully with God to release her, she finally becomes hardened like her prison-mates. In a subsequent riot in the feeding unit, a tough older prisoner plunges a fork into the matron's chest while Marie chants "Kill her, kill her...."

When Marie is finally released on parole she is no longer innocent, and she tells the still-kindly warden: "From now on what's in it for me is all that matters." For the $40 her husband attempted to steal, she says, "I got myself an education." As she exits, the warden's assistant inquires, "What shall I do with her file?" "Keep it active," says the warden; "she'll be back."[6]

When this film was produced, not long after the Great Depression in North America, it was not a dishonour to be poor because so many people were, and audiences could identify with the plight faced by Marie and her husband. The primary message, however, with the warden and the matron representing the polar views, is that custody-oriented prisons have exacerbated prisoners' violent and criminal tendencies and have corrupted people who work in them; prisons, instead, should be for the purpose of rehabilitation. In effect, the film advocated the actual trend in the 1950s, when the field of psychology was taking hold, from prisons and penitentiaries to "correctional facilities."

The more insidious message of *Caged* is that most women in prison are hideous, scary or pathetic and decidedly unfeminine. Marie's appeal, as The Innocent, is in her comforting femininity—at a post-war time when women were being strongly encouraged to resume full-time domestic-dependency functions. Even though Marie would have to be employed to survive, following her release, she appropriately anticipates a female occupation: "be a salesgirl, or wait tables, or do laundry...." She abides by society's gender imperatives in demeanour, appearance, attitudes and values; she's self-effacing, pretty and eager to please—until she is finally hardened by the evil surrounding her.

"TURNING TO STONE"

In the tradition established by *Caged,* Hollywood continued to produce low-budget pictures which exploited the theme of the innocent central character who is corrupted by the prison and the criminal monsters with whom she is imprisoned.[7] None of these films, however, surpassed the misogynist imagery which is presented in the 1986 drama *Turning to Stone,* produced by John Kastner for Canadian national television (aired on CBC 25 February 1986) and written by a (female) playwright who had never been inside a prison.[8]

Allison is a middle-class "girl" in her early twenties who, on return from a holiday, is set up by her boyfriend at the airport; he gives her his drug stash to hold while he gets away and the customs officials arrest her. En route to the prison in the van she is treated kindly by Dunk, a large black woman who is being returned to prison and who, we are given to believe, has ulterior motives in her overtures of friendship.

At first Allison remains hopeful that she will obtain a successful appeal and when her worried father visits (her mother is dead) she reassures him that being in prison is "just like boarding school." He advises her that she should "do your own time," and not get mixed up with the other women. His point is well taken, since the other prisoners soon take every opportunity to slap her around until two of them—Dunk and her rival, Lena—begin to vie for her attentions. Both of them are characterized as masculine lesbians (though Lena is apparently latent); Dunk's prison girlfriend begins casting threatening jealous glances in Allison's direction. Allison, however, is a mature young woman and she spurns offered protections by insisting "I gotta do it my own way."

The woman who occupies the cell next to Allison is apparently crazy, but more pathetic than frightening. Like Allison, she is a target of hostile, violent energy, and, in one of the film's turning points, Allison unwittingly colludes with the monsters by distracting the guard while this woman is fiercely beaten up by a mob in a shower stall. Subsequently this same woman violently attacks herself, slashing her arms with a razor blade; the camera zooms in on her bloodied arm dangling through the bars of her cell.

Allison is stalked in a prison tunnel by Dunk, who keeps pornographic pictures of women on her cell walls. Lena, the prison's illicit drug-dealer who is Dunk's rival for Allison's loyalties, threatens Allison with violence if her good but naive father refuses to bring drugs into the prison. During a tense visit with her father, Allison warns him that if he doesn't cooperate she will be badly harmed. Despite her pleas, he insists that the authorities wouldn't allow such a thing to happen. (The authorities in this film are simply not present: we never see the warden, and the guards are innocuous and in the background.)

Having been terrorized throughout the film by masculine women who hit her, or threaten her with much worse, Allison's comeuppance finally occurs full force when she is stripped naked and raped, with a (phallic) knife at her throat, by Dunk's vicious, jealous girlfriend at Lena's bidding and with the collusion of Lena's violent gang of lackeys. This scene is horrifying beyond words, graphically depicting the sadistic violation of the only human symbol of innocence in the film. As the film ends, Allison has snitched and is being escorted to solitary confinement, for protection.

The horror of this film was exacerbated by the advance publicity which suggested that the film would be true to the reality of life at the Prison for Women (P4W), and the exterior shots of the prison erroneously implied that it was filmed within the institution. Having gained the impression prior to viewing the film that it would be an accurate representation, I had encouraged students to watch it. To my chagrin, a number of male students thought it was "really good," "very realistic," or "just what you'd expect." The female students, however, did not find it believable. Women then locked in the prison were predictably distressed over the hideousness of the drama and concerned that their friends and families across Canada would assume that such terrifying brutality was a normal part of the prison routine.[9]

Unlike the typical Hollywood version of women in prison, the guards and the warden were not implicated in the violence in *Turning to Stone*. Instead, they were portrayed as simply passive and apparently unaware of, or unable to do anything about, the atrocities occurring all around them. The onus here was strictly on the prisoners, characterized as animalistic subhumans in keeping with the Hollywood formula and consistent with nineteenth-century criminological mythology. (This film is discussed further in later sections of this chapter.)

Academic Myth-Makers

Many of the fictional media stereotypes of female criminals which have been perpetrated by movies and television are reflective of the assumptions of positivist criminologists, beginning with Cesare Lombroso in the nineteenth century. Together with William Ferrero, his son-in-law, he characterized the female offender as follows:

... we may assert that if female born criminals are fewer in number than males, they are often much more ferocious.... What is the explanation? We have seen that the normal woman is naturally less sensitive to pain than a man, and compassion is the offspring of sensitiveness. If the one be wanting, so will the other be.... women have many traits in common with children; ... their moral sense is deficient;[10] ... they are revengeful, jealous, inclined to vengeances of a refined cruelty.... when a morbid activity of the physical centres intensifies the bad qualities of women, and induces them to seek relief in evil deeds; when piety and maternal sentiments are wanting, and in their place are strong passions and intensely erotic tendencies, much muscular strength and a superior intelligence for the conception and execution of evil, it is clear that the innocuous semi-criminal present in the normal woman must be transformed into a born criminal more terrible than any man.

... women are big children; their evil tendencies are more numerous and more varied than men's, but generally remain latent. When they are awakened and excited they produce results proportionately greater.... the born female criminal is, so to speak, doubly exceptional, as a woman and as a criminal.... As a double exception, the criminal woman is consequently a monster.[11]

Variations on Lombroso's theories are found in the work of most scholars who wrote on the female offender prior to the 1960s, for example, Freud, Kingsley Davis, the Gluecks, and Otto Pollak et al.[12] (For a critique of some of the major theorists, see Gavigan in this volume.) And whereas Lombroso's theme of biological determinism is modified by the sociological orientation of most subsequent scholarship on the female offender, misogynist speculations on women's hidden capacity for evil and cunning prevailed in the literature. Most notably, the 1975 work of Freda Adler[13] was based on her prediction that the women's liberation movement would have the effect of masculinizing female crime. This was a daring theory, contradicting the evidence. Wolfgang and Ferracutti, for example, had noted in 1967 that the overall homicide rate had declined steadily between the 1920s and the 1960s, during which time the status differential between the sexes had also declined. Observing "an increasing feminization of the culture," they comment: "Instead of females becoming more like males, males have increasingly taken on some of the roles and attributes formerly assigned to females."[14]

From a feminist perspective one would conclude that liberation could not be equated with the imitation of "masculine" crime[15] and that some women engage in crime precisely because they lack the social and private conditions for liberation. Adler, however, argues that the new "liberated" criminal woman (a contradiction in terms) would imitate criminal men and would therefore exhibit the same aggressive and violent behaviours as her male counterpart. Her anti-feminist theory, and the sensationalized headlines it evoked, revived fears that if women were liberated the world would be overrun by Amazon terrorists inflicting violent mayhem on innocent people. The concern that women will become "masculine" has been an argument against the emancipation of women in every historical period, so we should perhaps not be surprised at its reappearance in the 1970s: the perplexity, in this case, is that the prediction is offered by a contemporary "career woman."[16]

One positive result of Adler's work was the challenge it offered to feminist scholars to disprove the basic tenets of her analysis. In the past decade a plethora of books and articles have appeared in the United Kingdom and in North America which bring a feminist analysis to bear on the study of the female offender.[17] As stated by Steffensmeier, "the new female criminal is more a social invention than an empirical reality and ... the proposed relationship between the women's movement and crime is, indeed, tenuous and even vacuous."[18] Indeed, since Adler's alarmist predictions, the low rate of violent crime committed by females has remained relatively stable in both Canada and the U.S.[19] Moreover, women who are sent to prison for violent crime include a significant percentage who have killed an abusive spouse as an expression of delayed revenge or self-defence, or as a way to be safe from his violence at any cost.[20] Such women are not generally characterized as violent, and prison authorities have observed them to be among their most cooperative prisoners.[21]

The essential point is that women's prisons differ markedly from men's institutions. The majority of the population does not have a history of inflicting violence and rarely does a woman become violent as a consequence of imprisonment, as will be further discussed. Also, contrary to Adler's predictions, women entering prison seldom bring with them a history of involvement with the women's movement.[22]

The Lesbian as Villain

Reality to the contrary, women's prison movies are blatant imitations of movies about men's prisons, insofar as violence is the pervasive theme. Consistent with this paradigm, the typical rape victim in movies about men's prisons is a young, vulnerable man who has "feminine" qualities, and the rapists are burly, savage brutes.[23] Substitute for these roles the young, pretty, feminine woman and the "masculine" and unattractive butch-lesbian and you have a mirror image of the male prison in which genders are simply switched with a scriptwriter's sleight of hand. To the uninformed viewer, there is reason to believe that women in prison would be just as terrifying as the men depicted in prison films. From the images presented one could easily draw the following conclusions:
• criminal women are masculine;
• criminal women are violent;
• criminal women are lesbians;
• lesbians are masculine and violent.

In reality, criminal women represent a full range of conventional female types. Some are extremely "feminine" and delicate, others are strong and athletic. Many of the women are mothers whose worst punishment is the suffering of their children while they are incarcerated. Some women are creative, others seem to lack imagination. Some women are healthy and others are chronically ill. Some exhibit a lively sense of humour, others are depressed, withdrawn or bitter. And so on. Very few call themselves lesbians and those who do are as likely to be nurturing and supportive as any other woman. For the most part, women in prison are an ordinary range of women who have been exceptionally desperate, foolish or unlucky. Their lawbreaking is a futile response to the continuum of private and/or social abuse to which females are commonly subjected.[24]

The misrepresentations that accrue from formula plots based on myths of female masculinization denigrate males as well as females when masculinity is equated with violence and aggression.[25] And whereas it is well-documented that far more men than women engage in violence,[26] many men do not engage in or even value violence. Thus, as a conventional social construct, "masculinity" could more properly refer to strength, capability, self-control and assertiveness, qualities which may also be attributed to women.[27] Gender characteristics and values are culturally defined and socially variable concepts,[28] and when the media portray women as clichéd dependent "feminine" types, they play into the narrowest kind of sex-role stereotyping. When the media switch those roles, presenting female criminals as parodies of the worst possible stereotyped male criminals, the message is that females are decent only insofar as they are feminine, and a feminine woman, in this view, would not be a criminal any more than she would be a lesbian.

Since there are no physical characteristics by which one can distinguish a lesbian from other women, and since many lesbians are "closeted," there is no fully accurate means of gauging the numbers of lesbians who commit crime or who are incarcerated, and Canadian agencies do not attempt estimates. Officials at the California Institution for Women estimated that 19 percent of their prisoners were lesbian, based on self-report and speculation by the intake officer.[29] Of the women in my sample, approximately 10 percent were self-defined as lesbians, which was somewhat closer to the Kinsey estimate for the U.S. female population.[30] Most of the women, approximately 80 percent, had experienced some consensual physical intimacy with a "best friend" at some time during incarceration, but the majority did not regard themselves as lesbians and expected to return to heterosexual relationships upon release.[31] Conversely, a number of lesbians who participated in the study avoided any physical involvement with other women for the duration of their imprisonment. The penalties for women discovered in a "P.C." (Physical Contact) were stringent, including solitary confinement. Women who entered the prison with an "H on their jacket," identified as homosexual in their prison file, were subject to particular scrutiny in this regard.[32] In any case, there was not a single instance in the prison of a lesbian (or any woman) metamorphosing into the kind of demented, sex-crazed person shown on our movie and television screens.[33]

There is no correlation between lesbianism and violence[34] and lesbians in the California prison felt grossly maligned by any suggestion that they would want to behave that way. The following quotes from incarcerated women make the point:[35]

Kathryn: I'm one of those with an H on my jacket, so I'm really considered a detriment to the prison society, even though I live very quietly in here.... They told me if I was ever caught in my room with a woman I'd go to rack (solitary). It would go with me to the board and hold up my (release). I'm not in here for being a lesbian, but you'd think I was because of the way they carried on about it when I went to the board for my time. They didn't talk to me at all about my crime (fraud). They talked to me about my homosexuality.

I really don't think they understand about love ... two people just loving each other. It has to be something nasty, and it has to be physical. All love isn't physical.

Norma: The institutional policy on homosexuality is "Don't Get Caught." Otherwise you get a write-up and disciplinary action. They can't officially condone it even though it's no longer against the law on the outside.

There's no such thing as rape in here, the way they play it up in books and movies. "Homosexuality in Prison." They make it sound like prison invented it. If a woman cuts her hair, they figure she's turned gay. Sex is always the headliner.

Susan: I never felt threatened by it, nor did anyone ever express to me that they did. There were none of the horror stories you hear of or see in the movies. Stories of being raped, having brooms stuck up them, held down, forced to do it. I never, never saw any intimidation to be involved sexually. I never saw or experienced it ever happening except between two consenting adult women who both wanted to become sexually close with another woman.

... Everybody knows what a relationship is, and sex is not the primary part of any relationship, and it isn't in prison either. Sex is a very important part of a relationship—when all the barriers are gone, and you're really exposed to another person. But what is more primary is the friendship, how you share dealing with the world.... Women are able to comfort each other emotionally and physically. To hold each other, to touch and be gentle and listen and care. To love each other. In a prison situation—that is a very beautiful thing.

Good Women/Bad Women

Females do have an aptitude for violence; we know this. The question is why filmmakers grossly exaggerate the level of violence that women commit and, in the process, reinforce myths of increasing violence by women— women who are categorically portrayed as the antithesis of the feminine woman. Why would filmmakers be so cavalier in bypassing the ordinary prisoner, the woman who is altogether female in her appearance, attitudes and concerns?

The answer, in a word, is profit. Sensationalistic drama is perceived as more interesting and, therefore, more lucrative than ordinary human experience—and stereotypes are more easily sensationalized than ordinary people. But along with the apparent dollar value, the insidious message of the prison-monster films is that women who are segregated from men go completely out of control and start attacking one another.

That sex-role propaganda in movies such as *Turning to Stone* could be delivered so blatantly in the 1980s is reason to believe that the idea of women's liberation was still, perhaps more than ever, seen as a threat to the male-dominant status quo. This is also indicated by the rash of violent pornography that surfaced with the second-wave of the women's movement.[36] Indeed, *Turning to Stone* could be appropriately termed pornography, in that violent images of women in connection with sexuality and vulnerability are central to the story.[37] The pornographic "eroticization" of violence against women is compounded rather than diminished by the ploy of casting females as both perpetrators and victims. By virtue of their absence, men are shown as bearing no responsibility at all. The film suggests that if there are no men around to do it to them, women will do it to one another.

Turning to Stone is disturbing because, while females do have the capability for violence, the reality is that women are far more often victims. The reasons attributed to women's low violence rates relate to the low rank of females on the power scale, fear of the generally greater physical strength of men, a desire for social approval, and habits from years of strict gender training. In other words, female passivity is learned primarily through socialization, rather than biologically inherited.[38] Women may be idealized as having innate gentleness due to the childbearing function, but mothers have certainly, in most cultures, felt free to physically punish their children—ostensibly for the children's own good. Women, no less than men, in socially approved circumstances, have justified violence as necessary to achieve some desired end.[39] There is, nevertheless, a close association between maleness and legal or illegal violence. It is generally men who are expected to go to war;[40] it is men who rape.[41] Indeed, in Canada alone, according to frequency calculations by the Canadian Advisory Council on the Status of Women, a woman is forcibly raped (by a man) every seventeen minutes.[42]

Women in most Anglo, western cultures have been expected to suffer from passivity, irrationality, lack of objectivity and heavy emotionalism. In women's prison films, socially acceptable "feminine" tears are replaced with "masculine" expressions of anger and, whereas anger is an appropriate response to an unjust circumstance, the anger expressed by the film characters is unfocused, displaced or depicted as an obsessive rage. Some of these loathsome and terrifying characters are so extraordinarily aggressive that everyone succumbs to their wishes from sheer fear: their prisonmates serve them as if they were their slaves; their outside connections smuggle drugs to them or assist with other criminal activities; even guards are intimidated into colluding with their schemes. The idea that prison social organization is governed not by the warden and staff but by powerful prisoners is also taken from a media cliché about male prisons. In male prison films these leaders are cool and detached; in women's prison films, on the other hand, the Queen Bee is a seething cauldron of female hysteria, forever on the verge of exploding with a reign of terror.

Although the reality is very different, the duplicity of the media and misogynist scholars has entrenched these stock characterizations of women in prison in the public mind. It is assumed these fearsome fictional women reflect actual criminal women, and it is further assumed that whatever ill treatment they receive in prison is justified and deserved.

One significant contrast between the film *Caged,* which was produced in 1950, and the 1986 film *Turning to Stone* is that sexuality is now a much more explicit theme. Sexuality is depicted in connection with pain, humiliation and power, with rape and the threat of death the ultimate terror. By attributing to criminal women evils more realistically associated with the worst of male behaviours, filmmakers confirm society's satisfied conviction that normal women and criminal women are very different from one another; only very bad, that is, sexually deviant, women would behave that way. In this view, which is as anti-male as it is misogynist, women in prison are isolated for good reasons, including public safety: good, normal women don't break the law unless they've been duped by some bad man; evil, abnormal women have an insatiable lust for "masculine" violence and sexual aggression.

Popular culture exploits the dichotomous good vs. evil view of the world. To simplify the distinction, the contemporary "good" woman is stereotypically white, well-mannered and middle-class. Bad women, by contrast, are drawn from stereotypes of the poor and minority and other groups which fail to conform to the dominant culture. Certainly there is a correlation in real life between class position and vulnerability to imprisonment. No such correlation has been determined, however, between lawbreaking and class; that is, crime is committed by all classes but it is primarily the working or unemployed poor who are incarcerated.[43]

And just as the criminal justice system and sentencing judgements may be biased in favour of the middle-class offender, so do the media reflect that bias in fictional characterizations of offenders. Allison, as the woman who goes to prison by mistake as a consequence of involvement with a criminal man, is perceived as "innocent" because good girls from good middle-class families wouldn't instigate crime. The class bias of filmmakers shows through in such films, projecting assumptions drawn from a middle-class world view and capitalizing on structural class antagonisms.

The good woman in prison, according to the movies, endeavours to isolate herself from the other prisoners, with a sense of being very different from them, and much better. Those who offer to "protect" her from others paradoxically contribute to her "difference" by cultivating her dependency on themselves.

It is consistent with the stereotypes in *Turning to Stone* that the most "masculine" characters would offer protection to the most "feminine" character, based on a traditional heterosexual model in which "helpless" women seek out strong men to protect them (from other men). The incongruity of prison movies is that these "men" are not men, but rather masculinated women. And also, just as in real life, there is danger in relying on a protector because protection can be withdrawn or the protector may turn out to be the greatest threat of all. Allison's misfortunes all stemmed from her inability to depend on those upon whom she was nevertheless dependent. Finally her attempt at isolation resulted only in a complete lack of autonomy, the ultimate price one might pay for femininity.

Actual Violence in Women's Prisons

A man in prison once said to me that the worst humiliation he suffered through imprisonment was being "treated like a woman," meaning that he was expected to be submissive to any institutional demand. Women in prison, similarly, complain that they are treated "like children," because they are expected to respond with unquestioning obedience to those who have power over them. Predictably, discipline problems in women's prisons are much less serious than those in men's institutions since women's rebellions are rarely as threatening as those of their male counterparts. The frustrations inherent to prison life may be no less serious for female than for male prisoners, but the means of expressing those frustrations are reflective of gender socialization; men are expected to direct rage into physical expressions, and women are expected to either not experience rage at all (it is "natural," after all, for women to passively acquiesce) or to direct their anger toward themselves.

A number of women in prison have remarked to me variations on the statement that "prison is the one place where I don't have to worry about getting raped or beaten up." The atmosphere in women's institutions may be deadly boring and depressing, and institutional violations of what society perceives to be human rights are commonplace,[44] but physical danger is not a common concern among imprisoned women, as scriptwriters would have us believe.

As noted in one study, "Women don't riot; thus media attention is minimal."[45] The authors of another study of the effects of incarceration observe: "Factors such as racial conflict and violence, normative violence, and predatory sexual aggression, typically associated with male institutions ... are rarely manifested within the female prisoner community."[46] There has not yet been any study focused on comparative violence levels between male and female institutions, but male prison literature confirms that violence is a significant problem among men whereas the subject doesn't even arise in most women's prison studies.[47] (In this regard, one California female prisoner remarked, "At least in the movies [as compared to academic studies] we seem interesting!") Indeed, the ill effects of programs such as *Turning to Stone* on public perception of women's prisons are exacerbated by the fact that so little authentic attention is given by the media to women's institutions. It would seem that, apart from real or more "interesting" fabricated violence, the media are not interested in prisons at all.

Certainly there are mean-spirited women (and men) whose aggressive attitudes and threatening behaviours are intimidating. When women do commit assault (inside or outside) their victim is most often another woman,[48] although these assaults rarely result in serious injury; conversely, in cases of homicide women's victims are 98 percent adult male.[49] Most often, however, and consistent with "importation" theories of prison social organization, women in prison do not bring with them a cultural habit of violent behaviour. The absence of routine violence in women's prisons is consistent with the absence of violence between women generally. When violence does occur in women's prisons, there is no evidence that the perpetrators are the same women who have been incarcerated on a violent charge. If this were to be the case, it could be speculated that prison violence among women would occur in Canada more frequently than in the U.S. since a proportionately greater number of (federal) Canadian female prisoners have been convicted of a violent offence; that is, U.S. courts show a significantly greater propensity for incarcerating women for lesser offences. In any case, it is reasonable to assume that women in Canadian and U.S. prisons do not behave differently from one another, regardless of offence distribution patterns.

Focusing on a three-year period for which I kept a journal account of unusual occurrences at the California prison, there were approximately a dozen incidents of prisoner-initiated violence, the most serious of which (resulting in solitary confinement) were as follows:

- a prisoner punched a staff member who refused to mail a letter for her, knocking her to the floor;
- a normally calm woman, who was denied her expected parole, shoved her fist through a window in the administrative building;
- two women (unsuccessfully) attempted suicide.[50]

Other women complained of pushing and shoving, and women who became "unmanageable" sometimes got involved in physical scuffles with staff en route to the hospital or solitary confinement. These situations were distressing to everyone, prisoners and staff alike, and their infrequent occurrence was in stark contrast to the commonplace violence at the Soledad men's prison where I had worked previously. (On one particularly dramatic occasion at Soledad, an administrator was stabbed to death in his office adjacent to the room where I was teaching.)

The rationale offered to me by both staff and prisoners when I remarked on the relatively small number of violent disturbances at CIW was that those women who had a history of violence upon entering the institution, or those who showed signs of tension which caused others uneasiness, were invariably assigned to a strict medication regime—generally thorazine or one of the other strong tranquillizers. Tranquillizers and sedatives were also dispensed to most women who requested them, including those who had a history of drug abuse, and medication would surely be a factor in the low occurrence of violence.

Women in the much smaller Prison for Women in Kingston also have access to behaviour-modifying drugs, although my impression from conversations with staff and ex-prisoners is that there is less drugging in

Canada than in the California institution and that drugs are dispensed upon request with much less frequency. A woman experiencing serious adjustment problems can request a transfer to the treatment centre inside the walls of the Kingston men's penitentiary, located a very short distance from P4W, where five beds are reserved for women. It is observed that, in some cases, this change of milieu assists in improving a woman's outlook and better enables her to complete her sentence. In selected cases, when a woman experiences certifiable mental health problems, she may be transferred to the mental hospital in St. Thomas, on the recommendation of the psychiatrist for assessment and medication-centred treatment. Other women who show violent tendencies may be placed in administrative segregation, although this cautionary measure is applied as readily to those perceived as a potential target of violence as to those perceived as potential inflicters of violence against others or themselves. The women themselves sometimes request placement in the segregation unit.

In 1977 the Sub-Committee on the Penitentiary System in Canada reported that 75 percent of the crimes of women at P4W did not involve violence, and they comment as follows: "Most of the women are in reality medium or minimum security inmates in that their character and behaviour conform to the criteria set out for these lesser degrees of custody. Certainly a very small number require maximum security custody [but most] ... do not require equality in punishment because most of them are not true 'crims' who commit offences against others."[51]

A number of women who have served time at provincial jails in Canada have reported to me that there are more "incidents" in these institutions than at the Prison for Women. When asked for an explanation of this variance, it was explained by one woman as follows:

> Rowdies come in for overnights or weekends and they bring all that heavy street energy with them—they yell and carry on. Maybe they don't actually attack anybody but they create an atmosphere. Women who have to put in a lot of time there—like up to two years less a day—or the exchange women—they like to get into a quiet routine. It's the transients who cause these problems.

In a 1987 book by a woman serving a life sentence at P4W for murder, the author acknowledges that there are women at the institution who have "bad attitudes." She carefully avoids, however, the common exaggerations about violence. As she describes it:

Life here is pleasant enough really—for a prison, I mean. Short-termers are usually the ones who get into fights and find themselves locked up in the segregation unit.[52]

There are a few 'toughs' but they generally turn out to be big softies.... When I first came here I thought, "Oh my God, I'm going to be among murderers!" I suppose I expected to be with huge, butch broads, with scars, tattoos, wicked grins and knives in their jeans. Television fosters such misconceptions! ... The media has misrepresented us so much that even outside professionals have misconceptions about us [but] very few ... are actually violent [and the] warden will tell you that the lifers are the most agreeable, stable and well-behaved group in the prison.[53]

Other women who have served time at P4W[54] believe that there is more minor violence at the institution than is ever reported and that it is the "young broads," as one woman put it, who try to push other people around. There are rumours of women getting punched and both staff and ex-prisoners report that occasionally there is an attempted stabbing of one woman by another, purportedly with cutlery stolen from the cafeteria. None of those reporting such incidents to me has been witness to one but that such incidents do occur to some extent I have no reason to doubt. It seems, however, that violence of this kind is neither common nor random nor even remotely of the serious consequence portrayed in the film *Turning to Stone*. The most compelling basis for my belief that the rumours of physical violence are exaggerated is that none of the prisoners or ex-prisoners with whom I have spoken on this subject had ever experienced themselves as being in danger of physical harm by any other prisoner.

A P4W administrator reports, in an informal conversation, that there are few actual assaults but that from 1986 through 1987, over a period of a year and a half, there was one knifing attack (which did not result in serious injury) and there was one serious incident in which a prisoner scalded another with boiling water. There have also been minor physical altercations, not involving weapons, over various personal disputes between two women. He cautioned against being non-specific in talking about violence, and stressed that verbal coercion, abuse or intimidation is inflicted by some women against others as a form of "psychological violence."[55]

According to staff, prisoners and outside observers alike, the most serious form of violence at P4W is self-mutilation, specifically "slashing" of the skin with any available sharp object. (This behaviour also occurs in male institutions.)[56] The incidents of slashing are apparently frequent but a member of the health services staff observed that it is the same few women who do this to themselves on a repeated basis. This same staff member explained that after repeated slashings, the nerves are so badly damaged that subsequent pain is minimal, although considerable blood may flow and the woman is usually sent to hospital. And although self-mutilation would be appropriately diagnosed as masochism, one woman said she slashed herself often because she preferred being in hospital to being in prison. Certainly this behaviour is empowering in the negative sense that it allows the perpetrator to "own" her own body. Also, whether or not it is her intent, it causes other people to pay more attention to her. What is sometimes perceived as simple desire for attention, however, must be indicative of some deep torment. In the most dramatic instance of which I'm aware, a Native woman slashed her breast upon receiving the news that her infant child, in outside care, had died. According to the staff, in this instance the woman was not seeking attention but rather honouring a tribal custom for the expression of grief.

There is, finally, no basis for believing that the violence that does occur in P4W is of the kind depicted by John Kastner in *Turning to Stone*. No one is raped by predators or stalked by gangs of vicious madwomen. There is no social or even structural latitude within the institution for the kind of sickening attacks that Kastner portrayed so graphically, as if they were real. He claimed in the screen credits that the story was "fiction based on fact" but to the prisoners he was representing, it was a betrayal of their actual experience. By capitalizing on the hostile, media-mythologized themes of good vs. evil, masculine vs. feminine and low-class vs. middle-class, all embraced by violent fantasy, he obscures and distorts the very real problems endured by women in prison as well as those guarding over them.

No one enjoys any genuine autonomy or choice while in prison, and by and large women acquiesce to this reality simply because they want to get out. Some women protest or appeal through proper channels when there are grievances, but most go according to schedule to their jobs, school, the cafeteria, the pill line, the recreation room—and within these parameters attempt to neither cause nor get involved with any kind of trouble. Together they're stranded in a time-warped tension between loss of personal freedom and the necessity to act out daily institutional requirements. Alone they're locked in their cells several times a day to be counted, and there they watch TV (if their families are able to provide them with a set), read, write letters, worry about their kids, listen to music on the radio and, when the day is done and the lights are out, toss and turn and sometimes cry. Just like a woman.

The Good News: Film as Truth-Saying

In general, in the past decade, North American movies and television have introduced more honest and positive images of women in both traditional and contemporary roles—due in part to some excellent female writers and directors. It is now possible to turn on the television set and find female characters with whom women in the audience can realistically identify, and this is most obviously true of documentaries. In Canada three documentaries on women in prison were produced in the 1980s, two of which have been shown on national TV.

The first of these, titled *P4W*, was produced by Holly Dale and Janis Cole in 1981. The film focuses on a number of individual women serving time in Kingston, each of whom has a remarkable story to tell. Indeed, if the film has a weakness it is that the prisoners to whom the audience is introduced are so exceptional; it features, for example, the woman who was the first Canadian to receive a twenty-five-year sentence without possibility of parole even though she did not have a hand in the shoot-out in which she was implicated. The film also features a woman who in her life had killed not just one abusive husband, but two of them, and a young woman who speaks poignantly of why she slashes herself. For comic relief there is the woman for whom all the world is a stage, and who channels her energy into hilarious entertainments for her prison-mates. Another talented prisoner entertains the viewer with bizarre stories from her "kinky" life on the street; she also dances in the prison corridor and performs music she's written while in prison. All together these women convey a sense of the rich variety of personality that converges in a prison, and because most of them are so likeable and attractive they certainly dispense with stereotypes. An added value of *P4W* is the footage of the physical structure—full shots of the ranges and the interminable hallways and the suffocating sense of concrete containment in this archaic fortress, even if their cells do look like dorm rooms.

In my view, the most realistic film produced on incarcerated women to date (and, therefore, the film with the least commercial appeal) is *C'est pas*

parce que c'est un chateau qu'on est des princesses (Castle/No Princess),
directed by Lise Bonenfant and Louise Giguere at Maison Gomin in
Quebec in 1986 and produced and distributed by Video Femmes. Like
P4W, this film focuses on interviews with women locked up, but these
women and their crimes are altogether conventional and the problems they
describe are problems with which most working-class and poor women
could identify. They present an altogether realistic account of a prison experience—the intense boredom, lethargy and frustration, the arbitrariness
of rule enforcements, the paucity of resources, the loneliness and the value
of having close friends upon whom to depend for comfort and companion-
ship.

The third documentary which depicts Canadian women in prison with
accuracy as well as sensitivity was produced, ironically, by John Kastner.
This was the third film of his prison documentary trilogy, the first of which
was *The Parole Dance*, an uncanny bird's-eye view of the problems of men
seeking to gain and sustain parole status; the second, *The Lifer and the
Lady*, followed life events of a male prisoner whose girlfriend waited pa-
tiently for his release and unsuccessfully attempted to help him adjust to
life on the outside after many years in lock-up.

The third of the series, *Prison Mother, Prison Daughter* (aired on CBC
11 January 1987) focuses on two women at P4W. Darlene Baldwin is a
very pretty, blonde twenty-four-year-old middle-class woman convicted of
drug-smuggling; her parents are horrified by what they perceive to be the
injustices and double-binds of the system, and they expend great time and
devotion to ultimately obtaining her early release. Kastner claims to have
based Allison, the character in *Turning to Stone*, on Darlene.[57] However,
there is nothing in *Prison Mother, Prison Daughter* to suggest that Darlene
was ever subjected to harassment by other women, much less the horrific
tortures inflicted on the fictional character for which she was the alleged
model. As a young, sheltered middle-class person she may well have entered the prison with naive fear and trepidation but, if so, it appears in the
film as if she overcame it.

The second woman featured in this film by Kastner is Marilyn St.
Pierre, who epitomizes the social victim whose self-destructive choices—
with men, booze, dishonesty and petty crime—lock her into a system from
which she can't escape and to which she ultimately loses the one person in
the world for whom she experiences unconditional love, her infant son.
Her story is a heartbreaker, and so are the social realities from which her

tragedy is constructed. In this film Kastner surely succeeds in telling it like it is, which may or may not be enough to redeem him for the travesty of *Turning to Stone*. Throughout the segments with St. Pierre in various settings, the viewer hears the off-camera voice of Kastner as he talks with her about each new difficult development in her unsuccessful attempt to reclaim her life. It is fair to note that his presence in St. Pierre's story reveals a compassionate human being who has clearly gained the trust of his subject.

Conclusions

Film is a powerful medium with significant potential for educating the public about the social causes and consequences of imprisonment and about the women whose lives are directly affected by this anachronistic response to crime.[58] Conversely, the stigma which women carry with them from the time of their first arrest is grossly exacerbated by fictionalized film images of criminal women which defy all reasonable understanding of women's lives. Films which exploit negative female stereotypes based on class, race and/or lesbianism, and which presume with Lombroso that "the criminal woman is a monster," only serve to confirm in the public view the idea that prisons are an essential institution for separating the bad people from the good. Moreover, when women are erroneously portrayed as having a great attraction for evil as expressed through violent behaviour, all women in effect are misrepresented and the gap between knowledge and ignorance is widened.

Women's liberation depends not at all on women learning to be "more terrible than any man," as Lombroso put it. Rather, women's liberation depends on the balancing of all social relations through the elimination of arbitrary gender imperatives, class and racial hierarchies and categories of subordination. In such an ideal world, women would no longer serve as fodder for filmmakers' frightening fantasies.

Notes

1 My appreciation to the following: Della McCreary and Barbara Kuhne of Press Gang Publishers, Shelley Gavigan, who suggested the title of this chapter, Starla

Anderson, and Penny Goldsmith. I also wish to thank the many imprisoned women who have facilitated my understanding, and a number of prison staff and administrators, including George Caron, former Warden of P4W.

2 Having previously worked with male prisoners (see *Soledad Prison: University of the Poor,* ed. K. Faith [Palo Alto, CA: Science & Behavior Books, 1975]), my work with women in prison began in 1972. At this time I was teaching courses on women and criminal justice at the University of California at Santa Cruz and also teaching women's studies courses in the state prison, the California Institute for Women (CIW). During the subsequent decade, I co-ordinated a university-credit program at CIW and cultural events at other women's prisons, helped organize statewide support systems for women on parole, and produced video and radio programs for public education on women in prison. I also did research, including questionnaire surveys of the general prison population and life history interviews with one hundred women. While conducting this research, I lived at the prison for most of four months as a participant-observer.

3 There are important similarities between Canadian and American women in conflict with the law and the criminal justice apparatus that governs them. The only significant disparity is in the numbers. The state of California and Canada as a nation have almost the same total populations (approximately twenty-five million) and the female crime patterns are parallel. [See Johnson and Rodgers in this volume, and for comparative data, A. Hatch and K. Faith, "The Female Offender in Canada: A Statistical Profile," in *Crime in Canadian Society,* ed. R.A. Silverman, J.J. Teevan, Jr., and V.F. Sacco (Toronto: Butterworths, 1991), pp. 70-78.] However, at any given time, over 6,000 women are incarcerated in California state and federal prisons and in local jails, while in Canada the total number of women in federal and provincial institutions is generally less than 1,000. In both Canada and the U.S., at least half of all female prisoners are mothers of dependent children. [MacLeod estimates that during 1983–84, "the mothers of at least 5,400 children were admitted to a (Canadian) correctional facility...." (L. MacLeod, *Sentenced to Separation: An Exploration of the Needs and Problems of Mothers Who Are Offenders and Their Children* [Ottawa: Ministry of the Solicitor General of Canada, Research Division No. 1986–25, 1986], p. 12.) Baunach indicates that in the U.S., a range from 56 to 68 percent of incarcerated women have dependent children (P. Baunach, *Mothers in Prison* [New Brunswick, NJ: Transaction, Inc., 1985], p. 11, n. 1).] In both contexts, racial minorities are severely over-represented in prison: black women, who constitute 10 percent of the California female population, represent over 40 percent of the female prisoners; Native women constitute just 2.5 percent of

the total female population in Canada, but, depending on the province and the institution, Native women comprise between 13 and 100 percent of female admissions to prison. [Estimate obtained from California Dept. of Corrections for 1982. Re: Native women in Canada, see C. LaPrairie, "Selected Criminal Justice and Socio-Demographic Data on Native Women," *Canadian Journal of Criminology/Revue canadienne de criminologie* 26 (April/Avril 1984): 162–163.]

4 L. Steele, "A Capital Idea: Gendering in the Mass Media," in *Women Against Censorship*, ed. V. Burstyn (Vancouver and Toronto: Douglas & McIntyre, 1985), p. 74.

5 This is not to deny that historically women in prison have been the victims of considerable violence committed by guards and authorities as institutional punishment. There is also abundant evidence of the "widespread rape of imprisoned women" historically, by male guards as well as male inmates in mixed institutions (J. Klaits, *Servants of Satan: The Age of the Witch Hunts* [Bloomington: Indiana University Press, 1985], p. 149). See also N. Rafter, *Partial Justice: Women in State Prisons, 1800–1935* (Boston: Northeastern University Press, 1985), pp. 8, 20, 57, 73, 80, 97 and E. Freedman, *Their Sisters' Keepers: Women's Prison Reform in America, 1830–1930* (Ann Arbor: University of Michigan Press, 1981), pp. 15, 60, 99. One of the most frequently articulated reasons for nineteenth-century reformers of women's prisons advocating separate institutions for females was to save them from sexual exploitation (Freedman, op. cit., this note, pp. 40–45). Whereas anecdotal hearsay suggests that male sexual abuse of female prisoners still occurs as isolated incidents (see, for example, the story of Joan Little in J. Reston, *The Innocence of Joan Little: A Southern Mystery* [New York: Bantam Books, 1977]), it can no longer be perceived as commonplace. The preponderance of female guards in female institutions is one factor in this regard.

6 The fictionalized setting for *Caged* was modelled on the actual state prison for women in California, then located in Tehachapi. In 1952 the prison was destroyed in an earthquake. The present California Institute for Women was constructed at Frontera.

7 Examples include *Girls in Prison* (1956), in which the good chaplain takes the pretty young protagonist under his protective wing and *Reform School Girl* (1957), in which the hero, a kindly male teacher, feels he can justify his futile efforts in the prison classroom "if I can just save this one girl." The genre was dormant during the 1960s, but was revived in the 1970s with strong messages against "women's lib." The most graphic representation of this message was

Jackson County Jail (1977) starring Yvette Mimieux as a liberated woman who is wrongly jailed, and then violently raped by the deputy sheriff whom she kills in self-defence. Also released in 1977 was *Chain Gang Women*, an exceptionally misogynous film fraught with sex and violence. Tipping the scales for sheer pornographic content is the 1983 film *Chained Heat*, starring Linda Blair, in which women are raped and beaten, cut with hooks (in the neck) and razor blades and inflicted with a whole potpourri of atrocities, mayhem and death.

8 In an article in *TV Guide* ("The Dangerous World of Women behind Bars," 22 February 1986, pp. 20–23), Kastner is attributed with a remarkable statement: "We have a playwright (Judith Thompson) who's never been to prison writing dialogue that, in some cases, is more poetic than what real inmates would say. There are things that are a little more dramatic in the way the characters speak, but not in what they'd do, because what they'd do is actually *worse* than what's in the script" (emphasis in original). Presumably Kastner supplied the violent imagery on which Thompson based her script.

9 This impression was gained through personal conversation with a P4W authority following the airing of the program, and through conversation with women subsequently released from P4W.

10 The theme of moral deficiency in the female has been perpetrated by contemporary scholars, including Lawrence Kohlberg, whose theories were effectively challenged by his student Carol Gilligan in her landmark study *In a Different Voice* (Cambridge, Mass.: Harvard University Press, 1982).

11 C. Lombroso and W. Ferrero, *The Female Offender* (New York: Appleton and Company, 1899), pp. 150–152.

12 S. Freud, *New Introductory Lectures on Psychoanalysis,* trans. and ed. J. Strachey (New York: W.W. Norton & Company Inc., 1965); S. Glueck and E. Glueck, *Five Hundred Delinquent Women* (New York: Alfred A. Knopf, 1934); O. Pollak, *The Criminality of Women* (Philadelphia: University of Pennsylvania Press, 1950); K. Davis, "The Sociology of Prostitution," *American Sociological Review* II (1937): 744–755.

13 F. Adler, *Sisters in Crime: The Rise of the New Female Criminal* (New York: McGraw-Hill, 1975).

14 M. Wolfgang and F. Ferracutti, *The Subculture of Violence: Towards an Integrated Theory in Criminology* (London: Tavistock Publications, 1967), p. 259.

15 "Masculine" crime refers to offences such as burglary, robbery and auto theft. Prostitution, shoplifting and infanticide are the only crimes which are perceived as "feminine." However, prostitution involves the participation of a man and, al-

though shoplifting comprises a significant share of the offences for which females are indicted, more males than females engage in this activity. See D. Steffensmeier, "Crime and the Contemporary Woman: An Analysis of Changing Levels of Female Property Crimes, 1960–1975," in *Women and Crime in America*, ed. L. Bowker (New York: Macmillan, 1981), pp. 39–59 and Hatch and Faith, op. cit., note 3.

16 An example of how Adler's theory entered the realm of conventional wisdom came to me during a 1986 radio talk show in which I was responding to listeners' questions and comments about women in prison. One apparently middle-aged woman called to say that "women's lib" was the problem and that women in prison "should have had more spankings" when they were children. She went on to say that "If these kinds of women can't behave themselves, we should just hang them."

17 See, for example, C. Smart, *Women, Crime and Criminology: A Feminist Critique* (Boston: Routledge & Kegan Paul Ltd., 1976); S. Norland and N. Shover, "Gender Roles and Female Criminality: Some Critical Comments," *Criminology* 15 (1977): 87–104; F. Cullen, K. Golden and J. Cullen, "Sex and Delinquency: A Partial Test of the Masculinity Hypothesis," *Criminology* 17 (1979): 301–310; P. Giordano and S. Cernkovich, "On Complicating the Relationship Between Liberation and Delinquency," *Social Problems* 26 (1979): 467–481; Steffensmeier, op. cit., note 15; E. Miller, "International Trends in the Study of Female Criminality: An Essay Review," *Contemporary Crises* 7 (1983): 59–70; S. Box and C. Hale, "Liberation and Female Criminality in England and Wales Revisited," *British Journal of Criminology* 22 (1983): 35–49; N. Wolfe, F. Cullen and J. Cullen, "Describing the Female Offender: A Note on the Demographics of Arrests," *Journal of Criminal Justice* 12 (1984): 483–492; J. Messerschmidt, *Capitalism, Patriarchy and Crime: Toward a Socialist Feminist Criminology* (Totowa, New Jersey: Rowan & Littlefield, 1986).

18 Steffensmeier, op. cit., note 15, p. 54.

19 See Johnson and Rodgers in this volume, and Hatch and Faith, op. cit., note 3.

20 See Noonan in this volume; also, A. Browne and R. Flewelling, "Women as Victims or Perpetrators of Homicide," paper presented at the Annual General Meeting of the American Society of Criminology, Atlanta, GA, 29 October–1 November 1986; and A. Browne, *When Battered Women Kill* (New York: The Free Press, 1987). From my own research in 1972, sixteen women of six hundred in the California Institute for Women were imprisoned for first-degree murder; half of these women had killed a violent spouse after years of being battered.

21 Comments to this effect have been offered to me in conversations with staff at four institutions: California Institute for Women; Pleasanton Correctional Facility (federal prison, California); Purdy Treatment Center for Women (Washington state) and Prison for Women in Kingston, Ontario.

22 In my work as an organizer of prisoner support groups (1972–1982), volunteers frequently expressed disappointment that the women they met within the institutions were so traditional in their outlook and values. However contacts between feminists and women inside often resulted in some attitude change. The most striking example of this, in my experience, came through teaching women's studies in the prison in the early 1970s. The textbooks for the course included the early anthology of feminist writing by Robin Morgan, *Sisterhood is Powerful: An Anthology of Writings From the Women's Liberation Movement* (New York: Vintage Books, 1970). This was their favourite book and the fifty women taking the course would carry it around the prison "campus" with them; the book evoked curiosity among the other women and eventually we brought in a new supply to respond to the demand.

This was an anomalous situation. More commonly, women in prison randomly express the view that feminism is a movement for middle-class women who want to compete with men for straight jobs. This opinion was expressed strongly by a discussion group at the Washington state prison (October 1984); they were disgruntled because feminist volunteers who had come to the prison to help establish support services had gone away without following up on their promises because, as one woman put it, "they were too busy with their careers."

23 For a succinct and eloquent analysis of how the rule of force is manifest in male institutions, see J. Lowman, "Images of Discipline in Prison," in *The Social Dimensions of Law*, ed. N. Boyd (Scarborough, Ontario: Prentice-Hall Canada Inc., 1986), pp. 237–259. For a discussion of masculine dominance and feminine submission as a component of heterosexual eroticism, see E. Morgan, "The Eroticization of Male Dominance/Female Submission," *Papers in Women's Studies*, Vol. 11, No. 1 (Ann Arbor: University of Michigan, Women's Studies Program, September 1975), pp. 112–145.

24 Analysis of female victimization proliferated during the 1970s (and to the present). Notable examples which helped chart the course for subsequent work would include: P. Chesler, *Women and Madness* (New York: Avon Books, 1972); S. Brownmiller, *Against Our Will: Men, Women and Rape* (New York: Simon and Schuster, 1975); D. Russell, *The Politics of Rape* (New York: Stein & Day, 1975); D. Martin, *Battered Wives* (San Francisco: Glide Publications, 1976); R. Dobash and R. Dobash, "Wives: The 'Appropriate' Victims of Marital

Violence," *Victimology: An International Journal* 2 (1977): 426–442; S. Griffin, "Rape: The All-American Crime," in *Feminism and Philosophy*, ed. M. Vetterling-Braggin, F. Elliston and J. English (Totowa, New Jersey: Littlefield, Adams & Co., 1977), pp. 313–332; L. Clark and D. Lewis, *Rape: The Price of Coercive Sexuality* (Toronto: The Women's Press, 1977); E. Pizzey, *Scream Quietly or the Neighbors Will Hear* (England: Ridley Enslow, 1977); K. Barry, *Female Sexual Slavery* (New York: Avon Books, 1979); and C. MacKinnon, *Sexual Harassment of Working Women* (New Haven and London: Yale University Press, 1979). Also see L. Clark, "Boys Will Be Boys: Beyond the Badgley Report, A Critical Review," in *Regulating Sex: An Anthology of Commentaries on the Findings and Recommendations of the Badgley and Fraser Reports*, ed. J. Lowman, M. Jackson, T. Palys and S. Gavigan (Burnaby, B.C.: Simon Fraser University, School of Criminology, 1986), pp. 93–106 and N. Davis and K. Faith, "Women and the State: Changing Models of Social Control," in *Transcarceration and the Modern State of Penalty*, ed. J. Lowman, R. Menzies and T. Palys (Aldershot, England: Gower Publishers, 1987). Staff in female custodial institutions and social workers frequently speculate that girls and women in conflict with the law have a high rate of prior victimization and sexual abuse, including incest. For a review of studies concerned with this issue, see M. Chesney-Lind, "Girls' Crime and Woman's Place: Toward a Feminist Model of Female Delinquency" (University of Hawaii, Youth Development and Research Center, Report No. 334, May 1987).

25 For a criminological perspective on "masculinity" and violence as a product of culture, rather than as a behaviour determined by biological sex, see, for example, Wolfgang and Ferracutti, op. cit., note 14, pp. 147–163; 305–308.

26 S. Steinmetz, "The Battered Husband Syndrome," *Victimology* 2 (1977/78): 499–509 and M. Straus, R. Gelles and S. Steinmetz, *Behind Closed Doors* (Garden City, New York: Anchor Books, 1980) provoked controversy with the thesis that in spousal assault, women are the most frequent attackers, even though they generally lack the physical capacity to cause serious harm. For a discussion of this controversy, and a review of the literature, see M. Schwartz, "Gender and Injury in Spousal Assault," *Sociological Focus* 20 (January 1987): 61–75.

27 See *The Bem Sex Role Inventory* in S. Bem, "The Measurement of Psychological Androgyny," *Journal of Consulting and Clinical Psychology*, 1974.

28 D. Russell hypothesizes that male violence against women can be construed as over-conformity to the gender-constructed male sex role by men who feel inadequate in their masculinity (Russell, op. cit., note 24, p. 260). Also, see S. Hills,

"Rape and the Masculine Mystique," in *Gender Roles: Doing What Comes Naturally?*, ed. E. Salamon and B. Robinson (Toronto: Methuen Publications [Carswell Company Ltd.], 1987), pp. 296–307. Additional work on the causes and processes of gender construction includes: R. Stoller, *Sex and Gender: On the Development of Masculinity and Femininity* (London: Hogarth, 1968); J. Money and A. Erhardt, *Man and Woman, Boy and Girl* (Baltimore, Maryland: John Hopkins University Press, 1972); J. Money and P. Tucker, *Sexual Signatures: On Being a Man or a Woman* (Boston: Little, Brown and Company, 1975); E. Morgan, op. cit., note 23; M. Teitelbaum, *Sex Differences: Social and Biological Perspectives* (Garden City: Doubleday, 1976); N. Henley, *Body Politics: Power, Sex and Nonverbal Communication* (Englewood Cliffs: Prentice-Hall, 1977); J. Laws and P. Schwartz, *Sexual Scripts: The Social Construction of Female Sexuality* (Hinsdale, Illinois: The Dryden Press, 1977); C. Smart and B. Smart, *Women, Sexuality and Social Control* (London: Routledge & Kegan Paul Ltd., 1978); and R. Bleier, *Science and Gender: A Critique of Biology and Its Theories on Women* (New York: Pergamon Press, Inc., 1984). Salamon and Robinson argue that the interminable (and ideologically loaded) debate between biological and socialization explanations for gender behaviour is ultimately a false issue and that "one must consider both influences to understand the development of gender identity and gender behaviour" (op. cit., this note, p. 8). In an analysis of feminist politics, I. Young ("Humanism, Gynocentrism and Feminist Politics," *Women's Studies International Forum* 8 [1985]: 173–183) cites Gilligan (op. cit., note 10), N. Chodorow, *The Reproduction of Mothering* (Berkeley, California: University of California Press, 1978) and S. Griffin, *Women and Nature: The Roaring Inside Her* (New York: Harper and Row, 1978) as examples of feminist theorists who stress the positive moral valuation of feminine gender socialization, in contradistinction to the equation of femininity with victimization and inferiority, a model for which de Beauvoir's pioneering work *The Second Sex* (New York: Vintage Books, 1952) may be seen as a prototype.

29 The intake officer told me that estimates are based on a woman's appearance, whether or not she shows a "normal interest in the opposite sex," and reports of involvement with another woman during a prior incarceration.

30 In 1953, at a time when lesbianism was virtually a hidden reality, the Kinsey report shocked many people with the revelation that 28 percent of their sample had experienced a "homosexual response" with another woman and that 13 percent had been actively involved (A. Kinsey, W. Pomeroy, C. Martin and P. Gebhard, *Sexual Behavior in the Human Female* [Philadelphia: W.B. Saunders

Company, 1953], pp. 474–475). *The Hite Report: A Nationwide Study of Female Sexuality* (New York: Dell Publishing Co. Inc., 1976), pp. 389–418, indicates 8 percent as active lesbians, and an additional 9 percent who had sexual experience with both men and women. Kinsey et al., Hite, and Masters and Johnson (*Human Sexual Inadequacy* [Boston: Little, Brown and Co., 1970]) all indicate that sexuality is a continuum of response and that the world cannot be clearly divided into homosexual or heterosexual populations.

31 Two studies conducted in the 1960s, D. Ward and G. Kassebaum, *Women's Prison: Sex and Social Structure* (Chicago: Aldine Publishing Company, 1965) and R. Giallombardo, *Society of Women: A Study of a Women's Prison* (New York: John Wiley & Sons, Inc., 1966) agree that "homosexuality" in women's prisons is based not on sexuality per se, but rather on the need for affectionate relationships.

32 The attitudes of authorities toward "homosexuality" varied according to professional specialization; accordingly, the medical staff regarded it as a disease (which could be cured), the chaplain considered it a sin (which could be forgiven through repentance), and the counsellors viewed it as a deviance (from which one could be rehabilitated). The overriding priority, within the context of the custody-oriented institution, was to curtail the incidence through control and surveillance. Self-identified lesbians reported feeling persecuted in this regard but they did not suffer the indignities experienced by lesbians who are processed by the mental health system. For a remarkable account of this phenomenon, see P. Blackbridge and S. Gilhooly, *Still Sane* (Vancouver: Press Gang Publishers, 1985).

33 F. Pearce, "How to be Immoral and Ill, Pathetic and Dangerous, All at the Same Time: Mass Media and the Homosexual," in *The Manufacture of News: Social Problems, Deviance and the Mass Media,* ed. S. Cohen and J. Young (London: Constable and Company, Ltd., 1973), pp. 284–301, analyzes the impact of the media on public attitudes concerning (male) homosexuality, noting that the characterization of homosexuals as dangerous deviants who threaten the moral order provides a rationale for the persecution of homosexuals and, in that process, supports a limited view of sexuality in which heterosexuality is perceived as the only "normal" or "natural" sexual expression.

34 Indeed, lesbians and gay men are remarkably "normal," despite social, political and family pressures and hostilities. A. Barfield, "Biological Influences on Sex Differences in Behavior," in *Sex Differences: Social and Biological Perspectives,* ed. M. Teitelbaum (Garden City, New York: Anchor Books, 1976), pp. 62–121, reports on research indicating that "Almost all homosexuals have normal chro-

mosomal constitutions ... [and] There is also no known correlation between homosexuality and adult levels of sex hormones" (pp. 94–95).

E. Genders and E. Player, "Women's Imprisonment: The Effects of Youth Custody," *British Journal of Criminology* 26 (October 1986): 357–371, in their study of a youth institution in Britain, state: "Lesbian relationships, as with other forms of friendship in prison, tended to occur between consenting partners of a similar age" (p. 363). The consensual element of intimate relationships within women's prisons is also emphasized by Ward and Kassebaum (op. cit., note 31), R. Giallombardo, (op. cit., note 31) and A. Propper, *Prison Homosexuality: Myth and Reality* (Lexington, Mass.: D.C. Heath and Company [Lexington Books], 1981). Propper cites isolated self-reported incidents in youth facilities in which physical aggressions had sexual implications and she also reports on hearsay evidence that women in adult institutions in New York and California expressed fears of "lesbian" attacks (pp. 182–183). There is no indication that these alleged incidents/perceived threats were attributable to lesbian inmates.

For a thorough review of the literature concerning lesbianism, see V. Brooks, *Minority Stress and Lesbian Women* (Toronto: D.C. Heath and Company, 1981). She emphasizes the fallacies of the stereotypes of lesbians as "masculine," effectively refutes the standard mythologies regarding lesbian behaviour, and cites evidence that in general lesbians have greater self-esteem and educational/occupational achievement. See also A. Bell, M. Weinberg and S. Hammersmith, *Sexual Preference: Its Development in Men and Women* (Bloomington: Indiana University Press, 1981). For biographies and first-person accounts, see for example, B. Grier and C. Reid, *Lesbian Lives: Biographies of Women from the Ladder* (Oakland, CA: Diana Press, 1976) and R. Curb and N. Manahan, *Lesbian Nuns: Breaking Silence* (New York: Warner Books, Inc., 1985). For accounts of lesbians in academia, see M. Cruikshank, *Lesbian Studies: Present and Future* (Old Westbury, New York: The Feminist Press, 1982).

35 K. Faith, "Love Between Women in Prison," in *Lesbian Studies: Present and Future,* ed. M. Cruikshank (Old Westbury, New York: The Feminist Press, 1982), pp. 187–193.

36 Feminists in the 1960s commonly referred to themselves as "second wave" to distinguish themselves from the turn-of-the-century suffragists who fought for the vote, with the implication that considerable work remained to be done if women were to be truly emancipated.

37 The question of censorship inevitably arises and, given the exceptionally horrific violence depicted in *Turning to Stone,* one might well have expected

that it would have been withheld from prime time national broadcast on the grounds that it violated the Criminal Code (s. 159[8]), which concerns definitions of obscenity that deal with sex, crime, horror, cruelty and violence. For further discussion of the Canadian censorship debate, see *Women Against Censorship*, ed. V. Burstyn (Vancouver and Toronto: Douglas & McIntyre, 1985); D. Copp and S. Wendell, *Pornography and Censorship* (Buffalo, New York: Prometheus Books, 1983); W. Coons and P. McFarland, "Obscenity and Community Tolerance," *Canadian Psychology/Psychologie canadienne* 26 (1985): 30–38 and N. Boyd, "Pornography, Prostitution, and the Control of Gender Relations," in *The Social Dimensions of Law*, ed. N. Boyd (Scarborough, Ontario: Prentice-Hall Canada Inc., 1986), p. 130.

38 Op. cit., note 28. See especially Bleier, op. cit., note 28, pp. 182–190.

39 Apart from disciplinary abuse against children in the domestic realm, consider, for example, Margaret Thatcher's decision to invade the Falklands in 1982, female participants in what are described as "terrorist" movements, and the support among right-wing women for capital punishment.

40 One of the central arguments in opposition to the attempt in the U.S. to pass the Equal Rights Amendment was that it would result in women playing combat roles in the armed forces. This phenomenon has already occurred in numerous developing nations, and it was perceived by ERA opponents as antithetical to women's ordained functions as sustainers of the nuclear family upon which, in this view, capitalism depends. The entire debate begs the question of the appropriateness of militarism as a means of conflict resolution.

41 As reported in Clark, op. cit., note 24, p. 95, females comprise 2.8 percent of sex offenders according to the National Population Survey, and 1.1 percent of all convicted sex offenders in Canada are female. See also Clark and Lewis, op. cit., note 24; C. Shafer and M. Frye, "Rape and Respect," in *Feminism and Philosophy*, ed. M. Vetterling-Braggin, F. Elliston and J. English (Totowa, New Jersey: Littlefield, Adams & Co., 1977); Russell, op. cit., note 24 and D. Russell, *Marital Rape* (New York: Macmillan/Collier, 1982); Brownmiller, op. cit., note 24; Messerschmidt, op. cit., note 17, pp. 130–156; Bleier, op. cit., note 28; and further references cited in note 24.

42 Canadian Advisory Council on the Status of Women, Ottawa. "Sexual Assault" pamphlet, February 1985.

43 Women comprise only about 4 percent of the North American imprisoned population, even though women are more apt than men to be economically disadvantaged. Among female defendants, there is ample evidence that it is the poor, the working-class/unemployed and, by extension, women of colour, who are

most vulnerable in most U.S. constituencies in which studies have been conducted. See, for example, I. Bernstein, J. Cardascia and C. Rose, "Defendants' Sex and Criminal Court Decisions," in *Discrimination in Organizations*, ed. R. Alvarez and K. Lutterman (San Francisco: Jossey-Bass, 1979); M. Chesney-Lind, "Chivalry Reexamined: Women and the Criminal Justice System," in *Women, Crime and the Criminal Justice System*, ed. L. Bowker (Lexington, Mass.: D.C. Heath and Company, 1978), pp. 197–223; D. Lewis, "Black Women Offenders and Criminal Justice," in *Comparing Female and Male Offenders*, ed. M. Warren (Beverly Hills, CA: Sage Publications, 1981), pp. 89–105; Rafter, op. cit., note 5, p. 143; D. Bishop and C. Frazier, "The Effects of Gender on Charge Reduction," *The Sociological Quarterly* 25 (Summer 1984): 385–396; I. Nagel and J. Hagan, "Gender and Crime: Offense Patterns and Criminal Court Sanctions," in *Crime and Justice: An Annual Review of Research*, ed. N. Morris and M. Tonry (Chicago: University of Chicago Press, 1983); and C. Spohn, J. Gruhl and S. Welch, "The Impact of Ethnicity and Gender of Defendants on the Decision to Reject or Dismiss Felony Charges," *Criminology* 25 (February 1987): 175–191. J. Gruhl and S. Welch, "Women as Criminal Defendants: A Test for Paternalism," *The Western Political Quarterly*, 37 (September 1984): 456–467, suggest that women are most apt to be treated with chivalry if they can be shown to be responsible mothers. For a study of the "effects of sexism on sentencing" in the Canadian context, see C. Boyle, M.A. Bertrand, C. Lacerte-Lamontagne and R. Shamai, "Effects of Sexism on Sentencing," *A Feminist Review of Criminal Law* (Ottawa: Ministry of Supply and Services Canada, December 1985), pp. 139–147.

44 On 19 March 1976, over a thousand women rallied outside a hearing in the California state capitol to protest abuses of the human rights of women in prison. Within the chambers, legal advisers documented abuses as follows: solitary confinement without a hearing; arbitrary removal of women from the general prison population to the prison hospital for non-medical reasons; failure to provide translators for non-English-speaking prisoners, and the withholding of mail written in other languages; separation of mothers from infants; inadequate visitation programs; harassment of lesbian prisoners; the failure of foster families to facilitate communication between imprisoned mothers and their children; internal disciplinary hearings in which women are denied advocacy; reclassification procedures in which women are assigned to more restrictive custody status without due cause; inaccessibility of the prison law library to women in closed custody; improper medical procedures and inadequate health care; the arbitrary assignment of "troublesome" women to a behaviour modification unit (see K.

Faith, *Inside/Outside* [Culver City, CA: Peace Press, 1976], pp. 27–29). This and subsequent public hearings did result in some effort to improve policies and conditions in the state institution, but women inside are still vulnerable to the traditionally legal position that convicted felons lose all civil rights. See M. Haft, "Women in Prison: Discriminatory Practices and Some Legal Solutions," *Clearinghouse Review,* May 1974; D.C. Commission on the Status of Women, "Female Offenders in the District of Columbia" (Washington, D.C.: District Building, April 1972); K. Krause, "Denial of Work Release Programs to Women: A Violation of Equal Protection," *Southern California Law Review* 47 (1974): 14–18; N. Shaw, "Female Patients and the Medical Profession in Jails and Prisons: A Case of Quintuple Jeopardy," in *Judge Lawyer Victim Thief: Women , Gender Roles and Criminal Justice,* ed. N. Rafter and E. Stanko (Boston: Northeastern University Press, 1982), pp. 261–273.

45 J.Larson and J. Nelson, "Women, Friendship and Adaptation to Prison," *Journal of Criminal Justice* 12 (1984): 601–615. That men do riot is of great interest to the media, as evidenced by the voluminous attention in the past decade in Canada to major riots, incidents, and disturbances at the B.C. penitentiary, the Matsqui psychiatric centre, the Saanich, Prince Albert and Thunder Bay institutions where hostages were taken, Archambault, where in 1978 the warden was killed (resulting in the assigning of body guards to wardens in federal institutions), not to mention the highly publicized outbreaks of violence at Laval, Kingston (male), Orsainville, Dorchester, Joyceville and Millhaven. The response to these events is to provide more maximum security cells, more weapons training for guards, more searches and lock-ups and other repressive measures which, in turn, exacerbate tensions. For selected samples of scholarly analysis of violence in male institutions, see J. Fox, *Organizational and Racial Conflict in Maximum Security Prisons* (Lexington, Mass.: D.C. Heath and Company, 1982); J. Gibbs, "Violence in Prison: Its Extent, Nature and Consequences," in *Critical Issues in Corrections: Problems, Trends and Prospects,* ed. R. Roberg and V. Webb (St. Paul, Minnesota: West, 1981), pp. 110–149; J. Irwin, *Prisons in Turmoil* (Boston: Little, Brown and Company, 1980); D. Lockwood, *Prison Sexual Violence* (New York: Elsevier, 1980). Also see the following autobiographical accounts: R. Caron, *Go-Boy!* (Don Mills, Ont.: Thomas Nelson & Sons, 1979); A. Schroeder, *Shaking it Rough: A Prison Memoir* (Toronto and New York: Doubleday, 1976); J. Abbott, *In the Belly of the Beast: Letters from Prison* (New York: Vintage Books, 1982).

46 Fox, op. cit., note 45, p. 205.

47 The exception is Propper, who offers one and a half pages of discussion of pri-

marily hearsay incidents. See op. cit, note 34.

48 Hatch and Faith, op. cit., note 3, p. 2.

49 Browne and Flewelling, op. cit., note 20, p. 8. The common explanation for this phenomenon is that since women are usually unable to physically defend themselves against men by conventional means, when they do commit violence (usually against a mate) they do not want to risk retaliation and murder is committed as an absolute final resort. For such women, the murder is often their one criminal offence. We can reasonably speculate that the female homicide rate would decline significantly if women received more support, in the form of community shelters, to leave abusive relationships before they culminate in irrevocable damage.

50 In the year 1980 there were two deaths of women in all state and federal institutions in the United States (with a total of approximately 14,000 female prisoners): one suicide in Florida and one "death by injury caused by another" in Pennsylvania; it is not specified whether the perpetrator of the injury was another prisoner or a staff member. U.S. Department of Justice, *Sourcebook of Criminal Justice Statistics,* 1982, p. 567.

51 Ministry of Supply and Services Canada, *Report to Parliament: The Sub-Committee on the Penitentiary System in Canada,* 1977, p. 135.

52 B. Walford, *Lifers: The Stories of Eleven Women Serving Life Sentences for Murder* (Montreal: Eden Press, 1987), p. 15.

53 Ibid., pp. 96–98.

54 I have held conversations with approximately a dozen women who have served time at P4W and at least twice that number who have served time in provincial facilities, all since 1982. These were not formal interviews but this account seems accurate in that individuals report virtually the same experiences.

55 Private conversation, 9 July 1987. Anonymity respected.

56 Regarding male self-mutilation, see, for example, M. Jackson, *Prisoners of Isolation: Solitary Confinement in Canada* (Toronto: University of Toronto Press, 1983), p. 51. Innovative research and successful treatment programs for women who self-mutilate have been undertaken in Canada by Jan Heney. Her work is reported in J. Heney, *Report of Self-Injurious Behaviour in the Kingston Prison for Women* (Ottawa: Correctional Service of Canada, 1990).

57 *TV Guide,* 22 February 1986, p. 23.

58 It is my strong personal view that prisons are appropriate only for individuals who have demonstrated through violent actions that they are a genuine danger to society, and that the commonplace problems that result in imprisonment for some people must be resolved at the community level.

III

THEORETICAL CONSIDERATIONS ABOUT

WOMEN IN CONFLICT WITH THE LAW

Women's Crime:
New Perspectives
and Old Theories[†]

Shelley A.M. Gavigan

Until recently, it was possible to condemn criminologists both for their near silence on women and criminal law, and for their sexism when they did speak. The most recent wave of feminism has witnessed two seemingly contradictory developments in theories of women and crime. First, feminism has kindled interest in women's studies in various academic disciplines. Criminology has been no exception: the sexist treatment of women victims and offenders by police and other criminal justice officials, the sexism of traditional theories of crime, and the concept of victimless crimes have all been under attack.[1]

But, there have also been arguments that women's crime has increased as a result of the women's liberation movement. This belief has been called "the most powerful and widely held ... concerning the topic of female criminality,"[2] and its impact has been felt by women offenders being punished for their supposed acts of liberation.[3] Feminist criminologists now must do more than denounce mainstream criminology for its failure to acknowledge the significance of female crime. It is not enough simply to resurrect the neglected female offender. We must transcend the traditional

† This chapter is reprinted with minor changes from *Too Few to Count: Canadian Women in Conflict with the Law*, ed. Ellen Adelberg and Claudia Currie (Vancouver: Press Gang Publishers, 1987).

boundaries of criminology and examine the role of the state and the law in reinforcing the position of women in contemporary society.

Criminologists often assume that definitions of crime and categories of offences apply equally to all historical periods and to all cultural and social groups. However, it is important to be precise in studying crime to avoid the assumption that women's crime (or anyone else's, for that matter) is always and everywhere the same. The formal definitions of the law and the ways particular activities are criminalized, as well as the underlying social and economic structures, must be understood. For instance, the early criminologist Cesare Lombroso[4] studied prostitutes, but if prostitution had not been a crime in late nineteenth-century Italy, there would have been none in prison for him to study. Similarly, abortion in the early months of pregnancy did not become an offence in England until a statute enacted in 1803 prohibited the practice for the first time. Thus prostitution and abortion, now often considered to be women's crimes, would in other times not even have been the subject of criminological investigation.

Two criminological issues merit attention. First, women's crime has been explained in terms of sexuality and psychology, and invariably in reference to "real" (male) crime.[5] Given this, it is necessary to consider what *image* of women is reinforced by various theoretical perspectives. In other words, does criminological literature reproduce conventional wisdom about the inherent nature of women and their proper sphere?

Criminologists' images of women tend to be inconsistent and contradictory. For example, women's crime has often been explained in physiological terms, as resulting from raging female hormones (as in cases of theories that are based on premenstrual syndrome, pregnancy, postpartum depression, and menopause). Other times, the very lack of "female" qualities and the "masculinization" of women is blamed for women's involvement in crimes.

A second issue is the relationship between equality, liberation and crime. This has been a recurring theme throughout the twentieth century. It has been the focus of contentious debate[6] ever since Freda Adler[7] argued that the rise of American feminism in the late sixties and early seventies caused an increase in women's criminal activity. These are the two themes—the representation of women in criminological literature and the impact of feminism—addressed in this article.

The Biological Imperative: Lombroso's Legacy

Cesare Lombroso, a nineteenth-century Italian physician, is commonly regarded as the first criminologist. His first study of female criminality was undertaken with a colleague and "the help of 26 skulls and 5 skeletons of prostitutes."[8] It served as the basis for future work by criminologists such as Otto Pollak who will be discussed later in this article. Lombroso and his colleague Ferrero reported:

> We have seen that women have many traits in common with children; that their moral sense is deficient, that they are revengeful, jealous and inclined to vengeances of refined cruelty. In ordinary cases these defects are neutralized by piety, maternity, want of passion, sexual coldness, by neatness and an undeveloped intelligence. But when piety and maternal sentiments are wanting, and in their place are strong passions and intensely erotic tendencies, much muscular strength and a superior intelligence for the conception and execution of evil, it is clear that the innocuous semi-criminal present in the normal woman must be transformed into a born criminal more terrible than any man.[9]

For Lombroso, the "normal" woman's criminality was kept in check by fulfillment of her maternal role and by repressing her sexuality: "in the ordinary run of mothers the sexual instinct is kept in abeyance."[10] He implied that women not kept in check in this way were destined for crime.

The work of two feminists is helpful in understanding Lombroso's significance. The first is that of Susan Edwards,[11] a British criminologist, who has analyzed historical shifts in the description of women in medical and legal literature. Her central concern is the social and legal definition of female sexuality. She argues that a paradoxical image of female sexuality (i.e., both sexual passivity and sexual aggressiveness) is reflected in criminal law and medical practice.

Although protective criminal legislation is supposed to safeguard women from aggressive male sexuality, in practice women are often seen as seductresses.[12] Edwards points out that the contradictory images of women as chaste yet unchaste, good yet bad and virgin yet whore[13] have had an important impact on nineteenth- and twentieth-century English criminal law. She argues that control, not protection, of the sexual behaviour of all women was the objective of nineteenth-century criminal law.

Further, the degree and form of this control has varied according to women's social class:

> Ladies of the middle classes were as a general rule considered passive and therefore to be protected.... It was control under another guise nevertheless. The social and sexual behaviour of middle-and-upper-class wives and daughters was also controlled via the father's and husband's right to consortium, which was determined in part by the "value" of the wife or daughter with regard to her chastity. The behaviour of working-class women was regulated and rigorously controlled via the laws relating to vagrancy and prostitution.[14]

Edwards also examines definitions of femininity based on gynaecology which have been of profound significance for women in the criminal law. She argues that English legal practice in the nineteenth century:

> ... [was] increasingly influenced by medical and especially gynaecological precepts of sexuality which came to inform the various stages at each and every level of the criminal justice system. As law breakers women were rarely, if ever, recognized as criminals.... Instead, the female law breaker was defined as "sick,"and the origin of her sickness was located in her gynaecology.[15]

The historical development of criminal law concerning infanticide supports this analysis.[16] Medical and legal experts regarded all aspects of reproduction as crises for women. They claimed that menstruation and menopause, in addition to pregnancy and childbirth, contributed to female instability.[17]

The assumption that physiological factors contribute to women's involvement in crime has never been abandoned, even to this date.[18] In the 1950s, criminologist Otto Pollak[19] made the argument that "because of woman's irritability at certain times, she is often a disturber of the peace."[20]

In Canada, reference to premenstrual syndrome first appeared in the courts and the press in the early 1980s. One newspaper, under the headline "Women's crime spree linked to pregnancies," reported:

> A Mississauga woman's six-year crime career seems clearly linked to her pregnancies, a judge conceded, but she will still face a lengthy jail term as soon as she has delivered her fourth baby.

Lawyer Kenneth Anders argued his client ... had a "personality flaw" that led her to become dishonest when she became pregnant.[21]

The discussion of premenstrual syndrome and pregnancy[22] in the media and its incorporation into criminological literature[23] illustrates that attempts to understand women and crime have never lost their intimate connection to an analysis of the inherent nature of women.

Otto Pollak and the Masked Women of His Imagination

Otto Pollak, who became a major figure in criminology, distanced himself from absolute biological determinism.[24] In his attempt to be more sociological than his predecessors, he noted the importance of the family in structuring women's activities. He also noted the prevalence of a double standard of sexual conduct which was particularly harsh for women.[25] He argued, for instance, that in western culture deceit is a "socially prescribed form of behaviour" for women.[26] It follows that "many crimes which are considered highly detectable (e.g., murder) lose this quality when they are committed by women because of the way they are carried out."[27] Women, Pollak argued, compensate for lack of physical strength by devising covert and deceitful methods of crime (e.g., poisoning). Women's crime, he implied, is masked crime.

Historical research on the criminality of women in eighteenth-century England challenges, indeed contradicts, Pollak's assumption.[28] Feminist critics have also argued that Pollak did little more than reinforce prevailing myths of women's peculiar predisposition to be "strange, secretive, and sometimes dangerous," thereby giving "folklore a pseudo-scientific status."[29] And, as Australian criminologist Jocelynne A. Scutt[30] demonstrates, if one accepts Pollak's definition of masked crime, then much crime (e.g., corporate crime and sexual assault) is equally masked, because of the way it is carried out.

Pollak displayed a healthy skepticism about the reliability of official statistics to measure criminal activity. In his view, however, the primary reason for the small number of women in criminal statistics was male chivalry: "... in many instances, police, prosecution, and the courts are biased in favour of women offenders and ... criminal statistics must be analyzed with corresponding caution."[31]

Pollak did not support this suggestion with empirical data and feminist criminologists have explored and debunked the notion. American feminist criminologist Meda Chesney-Lind rejects the whole concept of chivalry. She argues that discretionary and differential treatment of women by the police is essentially harassment of women who are not "sexually monogamous and indoors at night." The police, rather than responding chivalrously to women, are "patrolling the boundaries of the female sex role."[32]

Other studies have shown that police tend to respond similarly to both men and women whose demeanour is polite and respectful, and who have not been involved in a violent crime.[33] It would appear that deference to authority is much favoured by them. Furthermore, when women are subjected to the formal processes of criminal law and justice, they are not always treated differentially and favourably by police and the courts. Chesney-Lind's characterization of the police patrol is clearly significant for women as *both* offenders and victims:

> The police force operates according to particular assumptions about gender; they are, for instance, reluctant to intervene in cases of even the most brutal marital violence because they see themselves as respecting the privacy of "the family." In rape cases the police are well known for subjecting the victim to an offensive and degrading inquisition in which her own sexual history is on trial. It is the police, too, who enjoin women not to go out alone at night when they have difficulty in tracking down a still-active rapist or murderer, thereby adding a secondary element of control to the original threat.[34]

The most disquieting aspect of Pollak's work on female criminality is his consideration of a possible correlation between formal equality and criminal behaviour:

> One of the characteristic phenomena of our time is women's progress toward reaching equality with men. This raises the interesting question whether we may assume that, in consequence of this development, female crime will change its nature, become masculinized as it were, and lose its masked character.[35]

Given that his hypotheses tended to proceed from folklore and unexamined assumptions, it is perhaps not surprising that he also assumed women's "equality" might lead to the "masculinization" of women's crime. He was aware of the adverse impact of male-dominated culture on women's lives,[36] but as Smart suggests, he was not critical of this inequitable social order: "it serves as merely another causal factor in his study."[37] He simply pondered what might happen if women ever achieved equality, without considering whether real equality would ever be possible in a society characterized by sexual, economic, and racial inequality.

Mary Eaton[38] illustrates that if one posed the question in terms of "differential treatment," one missed the subtle processes by which gender divisions are reproduced by the courts.[39] Eaton found that men and women defendants who were guilty of the same offences, and who were in the same circumstances (e.g., single, no previous criminal record) received the same sort of sentence. However, she found that men and women defendants were rarely *in the same circumstances.*[40] Both Eaton and Carol Smart[41] argue that criminologists should research the unexamined assumptions of the courts and lawmakers about women's sexuality and women's place in society.

The Women's Movement and Women's Crimes

Freda Adler's work on women and crime cautions against the achievement of equality because it will lead to more women criminals. She purports to document the changing pattern of female crime in the United States, noting that women's convictions for theft and other property offences have increased, while conviction rates for murder and aggravated assault "curiously have remained the same."[42] In her view, "Women have lost more than their chains, they have lost many of the restraints which kept them within the law."[43]

Adler implies that criminal activity is historically a male prerogative, and that the "new female criminal" is breaking with her sex role. She equates the feminist movement's struggle for formal equality and legal rights for women with the achievement of real equality, suggesting not only that women have come a long way, but that they have "made it." Adler's work has been criticized as neither theoretically nor methodologically sound.[44] She cannot, however, be ignored: her work "captured the imagination of the media and practitioners."[45]

According to a chief of police in one major American city, the women's movement triggered "a crime wave like the world has never seen before."[46] A police official in another city indicated that a "breakdown of motherhood" was the result of the feminist movement and the cause of this crime wave.[47] Morris and Gelsthorpe, using English newspapers, refer to this theme in media coverage, of which the following are but a few examples:

"Equal crimes for women!" (*Daily Mail*, 23 February 1977)

"Gangster Lib" (*Sunday Mirror*, 2 April 1978) [About an event that occurred in 1965]

"Women's Lib 'pushes up crime'" (*Daily Mail*, 1 February 1980)

"A TOUGH new breed of criminal is emerging—young women whose behaviour is increasingly masculine...." (*Daily Mail*, 12 April 1978)[48]

Similar themes have surfaced from time to time in the Canadian press:

"Lib takes the lid off the gun moll" (*Toronto Star*, 15 May 1975)

"Equality equals equal jail for pregnant woman" (*Globe and Mail*, 1 July 1975)

"Women's Lib linked to soaring crime" (*Toronto Star*, 7 August 1975)

"New female boldness is spawning more crime by women" (*Toronto Star*, 3 November 1975)

"Female crime rate soaring" (*Toronto Star*, 18 September 1983)

The argument that women's crime is rocketing ever upward rests entirely on official statistics. The Canadian figures show, however, that the headlines are misleading. A report of the Solicitor General's department observed that in 1964 there were ten times more men than women charged with Criminal Code offences, and that by 1974, the ratio was only six to one. However, the Report noted with concern:

With the exception of "rape/other sexual offences," ... the increase in the number of women charged for each criminal code offence outstripped the increase for males. The most noticeable variation occurred in fraud offences with the increase for females (306%) being five times greater than was the increase for men (59%).[49]

Fraud and other property-related offences continue to indicate higher rates of change for women than for men: the changes in the numbers of adults charged with property offences indicate a 94 percent increase for women and a 72 percent increase for men; the change in violent crime has been 68 percent and 25 percent for women and men respectively.[50]

But the actual numbers behind the percentages tell an interesting story. As Holly Johnson and Karen Rodgers note in their chapter, there is a great danger in comparing percentage increases when the base numbers are small. This is particularly true when dealing with official statistics of crime and conviction rates, because they may tell us more about enforcement than about any real increases or decreases in criminal activity. Morris and Gelsthorpe argue that it is possible for actual crime to decrease while recorded crime is increasing, because we do not know the relationship between the actual amount of crime committed and crimes traced to offenders by the police.[51] There are many factors which intervene between the commission of a criminal act and that act becoming a statistic. Such factors include decisions by victims to report or not report offences, decisions by police officers as to whether a charge should be laid and if so, how the act should be defined in order to lay the charge, and enforcement priorities of police departments.

Nevertheless, although far fewer women than men are convicted of criminal offences, the statistics from the 1960s and 1970s do indicate a real increase. We still have to ask *why* women's recorded crime is on the increase. Is this where the women's movement has had an effect?

Smart argues the existence of the women's movement affects not only the women to whom it is directed, but also "the consciousness and perceptions of the police, social workers, magistrates, judges and others, who may well interpret female behaviour in the light of the belief that women are becoming more 'liberated'."[52] Chesney-Lind suggests that any change in numbers of women charged, convicted, or incarcerated could easily be the product of an "if it's equality they want, we'll see that they get it" attitude on the part of law enforcement personnel.[53]

Morris and Gelsthorpe suggest that unemployment, low wages, and social alienation are good reasons for the jump in female crimes.[54] Along with Carol Smart[55] and Victoria Greenwood,[56] they reject simplistic explanations. However, they speculate that recorded crime has risen primarily because the women's movement has been seen as a change that threatens and challenges the social order.[57]

The notion that women offenders are influenced by feminism or "political and social beliefs and ideologies"[58] has to be addressed, although the number of "radical" women offenders is extremely small. As Weis[59] pointed out over a decade ago, the "new female criminal" was personified in the media by Bernadine Dohrn, Susan Saxe, Emily Harris, and a few others associated with American groups such as the Weather Underground and the Symbionese Liberation Army. In Canada, we can count on one hand the number of women members of the FLQ or Direct Action who were convicted or imprisoned.

Women involved in political crimes are not numerous, however notorious or celebrated they may be. Neither are they a new or universal phenomenon, as even Lombroso acknowledged in reporting on his extensive examination of the skull of Charlotte Corday, the eighteenth-century French revolutionary executed for the assassination of Marat.[60]

The assumption that feminism is a significant factor in relation to women's offences has been challenged by American criminologist Cathy Spatz Widom,[61] who (while noting a dearth of empirical research in this area) has found in her own research that female offenders tend to be "more conservative and traditional in their attitudes toward women than [comparison groups of] non-offender women."[62]

Regarding increases in women's recorded criminal activity in the area of property crime (e.g., fraud and shoplifting), British criminologist Jeanne Gregory's assessment seems accurate: "far from providing proof of liberation, these increases can be understood as a response to deteriorating economic conditions, as they occur mainly in non-occupational areas such as welfare fraud and minor property offences."[63]

Feminist Attempts to Reconstruct Criminology

Carol Smart wrote her landmark work in feminist criminology to redress the male-oriented biases integral to criminological theory.[64] Feminists were the first to challenge the marginalization and invisibility of women's crime, and to insist that it be taken seriously. They were also the first to point to the falseness of research which characterized "female crimes," such as prostitution and abortion, as "victimless."[65] As well, the oppression of women in the criminal justice apparatus by its non-treatment of sexual of-fences and wife battering was brought to the fore by feminists.[66]

But two problems in feminist theory as it relates to women and crime must be addressed. First, as Mary McIntosh has pointed out, in emphasiz-ing the sexism of criminological theory, feminist critiques of criminology do not "locate its weaknesses at a deep enough level."[67] In other words, it is not enough to say criminology has been wrong in ignoring women's in-equality. This leaves intact the notion that the criminality of *individuals* is the appropriate target of investigation and research.[68] Greenwood argues that focussing on the neglect of women's crime and criminality steers one away from the necessary analysis:

> ... whilst criminologists have undoubtedly been biased and prejudiced against the study of women's crime, they have equally shown bias and prejudice in se-lecting certain topics for scientific scrutiny. For instance, even if the rate of women's crime was very high, it might well have been neglected just as the study of corporate crime was neglected until recently by criminologists.... The scientific study of criminality has focussed on blacks and not whites, on the poor and not the rich, on men and not women. This reflects the concerns of a policy-oriented, correctionalist criminology.[69]

Greenwood argues that criminology has relied on stereotypes of men as well as women:

> ... our aim should be to develop a criminology which recognizes assumptions about gender and analytically locates crime and criminality within the sexual di-vision of labour. The particular condition of women requires a specific form of analysis which cannot be similar to that used for men.[70]

By examining late nineteenth-century British penal statistics, she dem-onstrates that prison sentences have not always been imposed on only a small number of women. She argues this raises questions about the chang-ing nature of the control of women.[71] She rejects the notion that women who have been imprisoned are inherently different from male prisoners; on the contrary, her close examination of the British statistics shows that like men, women in prison are working class, black, poor, with little or no education.[72]

Support for her analysis (and indeed the most damning challenge to the "equality, liberation, and crime" thesis in the Canadian context) emerges when one considers the position of Aboriginal women. For while all women account for only a small fraction of persons incarcerated in Canada,[73] it is clear that Aboriginal women comprise a disproportionately high percentage of the female inmate populations of Canadian penal institutions.[74] In Saskatchewan and Manitoba, Aboriginal women account for over 70 percent of women imprisoned in the provincial correctional centres; in the federal women's penitentiary, thirty-six Aboriginal women represented 21.7 percent of the women incarcerated at the prison in 1982.[75]

Aboriginal people in Canada represent only a small fraction of the total population (although admittedly this varies by province and territory), and the poverty, destitution, and racism that characterize the experience of many defy quantification. The unemployment rate for Aboriginal women is many times higher than the national average, and studies confirm what the street suggests: half the Aboriginal women in jails studied in Ontario and Manitoba had less than high school education and most had been unemployed prior to incarceration.[76] It becomes crystal clear that within criminology and criminal justice, as in social life, issues of gender cannot be considered in isolation from "the more specific factors of class, race and social position."[77]

The second problem for feminist criminology concerns the role of the state. Although some Marxists may disagree,[78] the state is not simply a coercive institution. Indeed, some feminists have insisted that the state and its law enforcement personnel provide women with social support and protection from violence at home as well as on the street.[79] But as Mary McIntosh suggests, the state is not equally concerned about the behaviour of everyone.[80]

One indication of the complex relationship between women and the state is found in the criminal law. Historically it has been indifferent to lesbian sexuality, yet punishing in its treatment of male homosexuality.[81] This is not to say that lesbianism has not been punished by the state. Although criminal codes have not been invoked as controls, the mental health system's coercion of lesbians and the incarceration of lesbians in psychiatric institutions have been well documented.[82] Lesbians have almost always had their children taken from them in custody battles in court if they live openly as lesbians.[83] Clearly, we need to look beyond the formal sanction of the criminal law to understand the oppression of women.

Conclusions

The understanding of women and crime must be broadened to include the general position of women within a given social context. This concern is not abstract or simply of academic interest. Criminology developed as a policy-oriented discipline and criminological theories find their way very directly into correctional practices. For instance, the notion that female offenders are inherently different from male offenders has long pervaded penal policy and criminological writing.[84]

In 1938, the *Report of the Royal Commission to Investigate the Penal System of Canada* (Archambault Report)[85] suggested that female delinquency was not a particularly serious problem in Canada:

... when the sick have been deducted, the number of trainable women is very small, and the women prisoners apart from young prisoners who are capable of deriving benefit from continued education would constitute a small class.[86]

In the *Report's* conclusions regarding the thirty-two prisoners of the Kingston Penitentiary for Women in 1936 it was noted:

... murder, attempted murder and manslaughter account for approximately 47 percent, or nearly half. These women are not a crime problem but are of the occasional or accidental offender class, who have been carried away by the over-mastering impulse of the moment, often the outbreak of long pent up emotion. They are not a custodial problem, and could be cared for as well in a reformatory as in a penitentiary. The same is true of the other seventeen female penitentiary inmates.[87]

Three decades later, the *Report of the Canadian Committee on Corrections* (Ouimet Report) (1969)[88] tended to echo its predecessor:

There are certain differences in the criminality of women, as compared with men, which have implications for correctional planning. The most outstanding single difference is that of numbers ... many more men than women are dealt with by the police and the courts....

There is some indication that the difference in numbers between men and women offenders tends to be lower in highly industrialized societies than in less developed ones.[89]

Addressing an apparent increase in women's crime, a more recent federal report (1977) noted:

With the pressure for equality for the sexes is coming reduced paternalism on the part of the police and the judiciary. This could lead to increased charges against women and longer sentences if convicted.[90]

Because of the way female criminality has been perceived, women prisoners have not been of great concern to correctional officials of the Canadian state. At the same time, however, the assumption that women's pressure for equality results in their apparent increased representation in crime and court statistics has gone largely unchallenged.

Until the 1990 Task Force on Federally Sentenced Women, Canadian state policy, as reflected in official reports, described the "special needs" of women offenders as largely psychological. Three of the factors cited as giving rise to special needs for women in custody are:

- low self-image, increased by society's strong condemnation of women offenders;
- weak family ties and few friends, making for a vulnerable situation of exploitation;
- tendency towards self-mutilation and self-deprecation instead of outward aggressive behaviour.[91]

Such assumptions stem largely from folklore about the inherent nature of women, rather than from scientific analysis. For instance, Widom identifies three factors (self-esteem, sex-role identity, and feminism) thought to be important to female criminality, and illustrates that all three have been based on limited empirical research.[92] She argues that research dealing with low self-esteem is methodologically weak and "limited by the fact that most of these studies are ... conducted *after* these women have been caught up in the criminal justice system." Hence, "any findings regarding self-esteem may be the *result* of a person's being labelled and incarcerated, instead of a causal factor in explaining a person's criminality" [emphasis in original].[93] Her research indicates that we cannot assume female offenders have low self-esteem prior to incarceration.

In sum, I would argue that the sexist assumptions underlying much of criminology must not give way to feminist theory that treats *only* the question of gender. In Canada, we need look no further than the position of Aboriginal women to illustrate that issues of race and class are of equal significance.

As well, feminist criminology must avoid general, ahistorical explanations of women's crime. In our struggle to understand the intricate weave of law and crime into women's lives, the change over time in definitions and positions of law must be examined.

Notes

1 See, among others, Dorie Klein, "The Etiology of Women's Crime: A Review of the Literature," *Issues in Criminology* 8 (Fall 1973): 3–30; Carol Smart, *Women, Crime and Criminology: A Feminist Critique* (London: Routledge & Kegan Paul, 1976); Susan Brownmiller, *Against Our Will: Men, Women and Rape* (New York: Bantam, 1975); Dorie Klein and June Kress, "Any Woman's Blues: A Critical Overview of Women, Crime and the Criminal Justice System," *Crime and Social Justice* 5 (Spring-Summer 1976): 34–39; Joseph G. Weis, "Liberation and Crime: The Invention of the New Female Criminal," *Crime and Social Justice* 6 (Fall-Winter 1976): 17–27; Jocelynne A. Scutt, "Debunking the Theory of the Female 'Masked Criminal'," *Aust. & N.Z. Journal of Criminology* 11 (March 1978): 23–42; Jocelynne A. Scutt, "Sexism in Criminal Law," in *Women and Crime*, ed. S.K. Mukherjee and Jocelynne A. Scutt (Sydney: Aust. Inst. of Criminology/George Allen & Unwin, 1981), pp. 1–21; Carol Smart and Barry Smart, *Women, Sexuality and Social Control* (London: Routledge & Kegan Paul, 1978); Clarice Feinman, *Women in the Criminal Justice System* (New York: Praeger, 1980); Ann Jones, *Women Who Kill* (New York: Holt, Rinehart & Winston, 1980); and Susan Edwards, *Female Sexuality and the Law* (Oxford: Martin Robertson, 1981).

2 Meda Chesney-Lind, "Women and Crime: The Female Offender," *Signs* 12 (Autumn 1986): 78–96.

3 Ibid.

4 Cesare Lombroso and Enrico Ferrero, *The Female Offender* (New York: D. Appleton, 1900).

5 Weis, "Liberation and Crime," pp. 17–27.

6 Klein and Kress, "Any Woman's Blues," pp. 34–49; Weis, "Liberation and Crime," pp. 17–27; Carol Smart, "The New Female Criminal: Reality or Myth?" *British Journal of Criminology* 19 (January 1979): 50–59; Meda Chesney-Lind, "Re-discovering Lilith: Misogyny and the New Female Criminal," in *The Female Offender: Selected Papers from an International Symposium,* ed. Curt Taylor Griffiths and Margit Nance (Vancouver: Criminology Research Centre, Simon Fraser Univ., 1980), pp. 1–37; and Allison Morris and Loraine Gelsthorpe, "False Clues and Female Crime," in *Women and Crime* (Cropwood Conf. Series No. 13), ed. Allison Morris and Loraine Gelsthorpe (Cambridge: Inst. of Criminology, 1981), pp. 49–70.

7 Freda Adler, *Sisters in Crime: The Rise of the New Female Criminal* (New York: McGraw-Hill, 1975).

8 Lombroso and Ferrero, *The Female Offender,* pp. 2–3.

9 Ibid., p. 151. I am indebted to Meda Chesney-Lind, whose "Re-discovering Lilith: Misogyny and the New Female Criminal," drew this passage to my attention.

10 Lombroso and Ferrero, *The Female Offender,* p. 153.

11 Edwards, *Female Sexuality and the Law.*

12 Ibid., p. 50.

13 Ibid., p. 49. Others have noted similar images which have long pervaded the criminal law's theory and practice; see Feinman, for reference to the madonna/ whore distinction; for discussion of the Lilith/Eve image, see Chesney-Lind, "Re-discovering Lilith."

14 Edwards, *Female Sexuality and the Law,* p. 55.

15 Ibid., p. 74.

16 See also Nigel Walker, *Crime and Insanity in England,* vol. 1: The Historical Perspective (Edinburgh: Edinburgh Univ. Press, 1968); and Scutt, "Sexism in Criminal Law."

17 Edwards, *Female Sexuality and the Law,* pp. 75–80.

18 Herschel Prins, *Offenders, Deviants, or Patients?* (London: Tavistock, 1980), pp. 316–317.

19 Otto Pollak, *The Criminality of Women* (New York: A.S. Barnes, 1961).

20 Ibid., p. 2.

21 *Toronto Star,* 14 April 1981. This article was followed by "Female hormones head for the courts," *Toronto Star,* 18 April 1981. For other articles dealing with premenstrual syndrome, see "Women's violence blamed on period," *Tor-*

onto Star, 25 August 1978 and "Menstrual stress a factor in crime?" *Toronto Star,* 14 April 1981.

22 Katharina Dalton, *Once a Month* (Glasgow: Fontana, 1978).

23 Prins, *Offenders, Deviants, or Patients?*

24 Pollak, *The Criminality of Women.*

25 Ibid., p. 161.

26 Ibid., p. 111.

27 Ibid., p. 3.

28 John M. Beattie, "The Criminality of Women in Eighteenth-Century England," *Journal of Social History* 8 (Summer 1974–75): 80–116.

29 Smart, *Women, Crime and Criminology.*

30 Scutt, "Debunking the Theory of the Female 'Masked Criminal'," pp. 23–42.

31 Pollak, *The Criminality of Women,* p. 5.

32 Meda Chesney-Lind, "Chivalry Reexamined: Women and the Criminal Justice System," in *Women, Crime and the Criminal Justice System,* ed. Lee H. Bowker with contributions by Meda Chesney-Lind and Joy Pollack (Lexington: D.C. Heath, 1978), p. 207.

33 Feinman, p. 23.

34 Michele Barrett, *Women's Oppression Today: Problems in Marxist Feminist Analysis* (London: Verso & NLB, 1978), pp. 236–237.

35 Pollak, p. 154.

36 Ibid., p. 149.

37 Smart, *Women, Crime and Criminology,* p. 50.

38 Mary Eaton, "Mitigating Circumstances: Familiar Rhetoric," *International Journal of the Sociology of Law* 11 (November 1983): 385–400; "Documenting the Defendant: Placing Women in Social Inquiry Reports," in *Women in Law: Explorations in Law, Family and Sexuality,* ed. Julia Brophy and Carol Smart (London: Routledge & Kegan Paul, 1985).

39 Eaton, "Documenting the Defendant," p. 138.

40 Eaton, "Mitigating Circumstances," pp. 385–400.

41 Carol Smart, "Legal Subjects and Sexual Objects: Ideology, Law and Female Sexuality," in *Women in Law: Explorations in Law, Family and Sexuality,* ed. Julia Brophy and Carol Smart (London: Routledge & Kegan Paul, 1985).

42 Adler, p. 16.

43 Ibid., p. 24.

44 Smart, "The New Female Criminal," pp. 50–59; Morris and Gelsthorpe, pp. 49–70.

45 Morris and Gelsthorpe, p. 53.

46 Quoted in Weis, p. 17 and in Chesney-Lind, "Re-discovering Lilith," p. 3.

47 Quoted in Chesney-Lind, "Re-discovering Lilith," p. 3.

48 Morris and Gelsthorpe, pp. 63–66, fn. 5.

49 *The Female Offender—Selected Statistics: Report of the National Advisory Committee on the Female Offender* (Ottawa: Solicitor General Canada, 1977), p. 7.

50 See Alison Hatch and Karlene Faith, "The Female Offender in Canada," paper presented at the Annual General Meeting of the American Society of Criminology, San Diego, CA, 13–17 November 1985, p. 9, table 3.

51 Morris and Gelsthorpe, p. 56.

52 Smart, "The New Female Criminal," p. 57.

53 Chesney-Lind, "Re-discovering Lilith," pp. 14–15.

54 Morris and Gelsthorpe, p. 57.

55 Smart, "The New Female Criminal," pp. 50–59.

56 Victoria Greenwood, "The Myths of Female Crime," in *Women and Crime* (Cropwood Conf. Series No. 13), ed. Allison Morris and Lorraine Gelsthorpe (Cambridge: Inst. of Criminology, 1981), pp. 73–84.

57 Morris and Gelsthorpe, "False Clues and Female Crime," pp. 49–70.

58 *Report of the National Advisory Committee on the Female Offender* (Ottawa: Solicitor General Canada, 1977), p. 16.

59 Weis, pp. 17–27.

60 Lombroso and Ferrero, pp. 3–35.

61 Cathy Spatz Widom, "Perspectives of Female Criminality: A Critical Examination of Assumptions," in *Women and Crime* (Cropwood Conf. Series No. 13), ed. Allison Morris and Loraine Gelsthorpe (Cambridge: Inst. of Criminology, 1981), pp. 33–44.

62 Ibid., p. 38.

63 Jeanne Gregory, "Sex, Class and Crime: Towards a Non-Sexist Criminology," in *The Political Economy of Crime: Readings for a Critical Criminology*, ed. Brian D. Maclean (Scarborough: Prentice-Hall, 1986), p. 320.

64 Smart, *Women, Crime and Criminology*.

65 Klein and Kress, p. 37.

66 Smart, *Women, Crime and Criminology*, pp. 77–107; Klein and Kress, pp. 38–42; and Nicole H. Rafter and Elena M. Natalizia, "Marxist Feminism: Implications for Criminal Justice," *Crime and Delinquency* 27 (January 1981): 83–87.

67 Mary McIntosh, "Review Symposium: 'Women, Crime and Criminology',"

British Journal of Criminology 17 (October 1977): 396.

68 Ibid., p. 396; Mark Cousins, "Mens Rea: Sexual Difference and the Criminal Law," in *Radical Issues in Criminology,* ed. Pat Carlen and Mike Collison (Oxford: Martin Robertson, 1980), p. 111; and Greenwood, pp. 73–74.

69 Greenwood, pp. 75–76.

70 Ibid.

71 Ibid., p. 79.

72 Ibid., p. 81.

73 Hatch and Faith, op. cit.

74 Carol P. LaPrairie, "Selected Criminal Justice and Socio-Demographic Data on Native Women," *Canadian Journal of Criminology* 26 (April 1984).

75 Ibid., p. 162.

76 Ibid., p. 166.

77 Greenwood, p. 82.

78 Rafter and Natalizia, pp. 81–98.

79 See Linda MacLeod, *Wife Battering in Canada: The Vicious Circle* (Ottawa: Canadian Advisory Council on the Status of Women, 1980); and Ian Taylor, *Law and Order: Arguments for Socialism* (London: Macmillan, 1981).

80 McIntosh, p. 396.

81 Barrett, p. 240.

82 Persimmon Blackbridge and Sheila Gilhooly, *Still Sane* (Vancouver: Press Gang Publishers, 1986); P. Susan Penfold and Gillian Walker, *Women and the Psychiatric Paradox* (Montreal: Eden Press, 1983); Dorothy Smith and Sara David, eds., *Women Look at Psychiatry* (Vancouver: Press Gang Publishers, 1976).

83 In a recent Canadian case dealing with the law's attitude towards lesbian mothers, the judge decided custody in favour of the father when the mother resumed living with her lover in contradiction to her original custody order. In the original order, the mother got custody after telling the court that she had ceased living with her lesbian lover (*Elliott vs. Elliott* (1987) B.C.D. Civ. 1528-01—unreported).

84 Prins, op. cit.

85 *Report of the Royal Commission to Investigate the Penal System of Canada (Archambault Report)* (Ottawa: King's Printer, 1938).

86 Ibid., p. 145.

87 Ibid., p. 147.

88 *Report of the Canadian Committee on Corrections (Ouimet Report)* (Ottawa: Queen's Printer, 1969).

89 Ibid., p. 389.

90 *Report of the National Advisory Committee on the Female Offender* (Ottawa: Solicitor General Canada, 1977), p. 15.

91 Ibid., p. 14.

92 Widom, op. cit.

93 Ibid., p. 34.

Aboriginal Women
and Crime in Canada:
Identifying the Issues[1]

Carol LaPrairie

The 1992 constitutional discussions and other events in Canada, particularly in the last decade, revealed the enormous political gains made by Aboriginal people on a number of fronts. Unfortunately, these gains have not translated into a reduction in the proportion of Aboriginal women serving time in Canadian correctional institutions. This chapter explores the broader historical context of Aboriginal women's conflict with the law. It links the present marginalization of Aboriginal women to a number of social and economic factors.

An Overview of the Issues

Data show that Aboriginal people are heavily over-represented in jails and prisons across the country. Far fewer women than men go to prison, but Aboriginal women are still disproportionately involved in conflict with the law compared both to non-Aboriginal women and to their representation in the general population.[2] In British Columbia in the early 1980s, self-identified Aboriginal women comprised 20 percent of all women incarcerated, yet Aboriginal people comprise only about 5 percent of the total British Columbia population. In Ontario, the figures are 17 percent and about 2 percent, respectively.[3] Data from the Whitehorse Correctional

Centre in the Yukon Territory from 1988 to 1991 revealed that three-quarters of all women sentenced and 43 percent of all women remanded for trial were Aboriginal, even though Aboriginal women in the Yukon comprise only 11 percent of the population.[4] In 1991, Aboriginal women accounted for nearly a quarter of the inmate population of Kingston Prison for Women (P4W), the federal women's prison, although Aboriginal women comprise less than 2 percent of the Canadian population.[5]

Since data have been collected on comparative offences of incarcerated Aboriginal and non-Aboriginal women, they have consistently revealed that Aboriginal women are incarcerated for more violent crimes than are non-Aboriginal women.[6] Research findings from a study for the Task Force on Federally Sentenced Women revealed that of thirty-nine Aboriginal women interviewed, 26 percent had been charged with murder, 38 percent had served time for manslaughter, and nearly half had served time for assault.[7] Moyer, in examining twenty-two years of homicide data, found an increase in the proportion of Aboriginal women involved as offenders in homicide, and a rate that was nearly twice that for non-Aboriginal women. She also found that 55 percent of all juvenile female homicide suspects were Aboriginal.[8]

Aboriginal women are also more likely than non-Aboriginal women to be arrested and serve time for defaulting on payment of fines, because they have lower incomes due to a lack of skills, education, and employment.[9] Compared to Aboriginal men, available data indicate that Aboriginal women in prison are twice as likely to have had alcohol play a role in their offences.[10] Alcohol also plays a role in offences against Aboriginal women.[11] Recent research in Cree communities in James Bay, Quebec revealed that women were the primary victims in interpersonal offences, and that alcohol was a factor in virtually all the sexual assaults and a major factor in all other interpersonal offences.[12]

A socio-demographic profile of Aboriginal women in prison suggests that their disadvantaged position is a result of various abuses and other circumstances. After reviewing data on the background experiences of Aboriginal female inmates, Grossman concluded that this group was particularly disadvantaged in the areas of education, employment, and family history, compared to their non-Aboriginal counterparts. The Aboriginal group suffers "from a variety of disadvantaged conditions and life experiences, including poverty, unemployment, abusive family situations, poor education, criminal victimization and prejudice."[13]

Earlier work by the Ontario Native Women's Association found that over a third of the Aboriginal women interviewed in Ontario provincial correctional institutions were twenty years of age or younger; slightly over half were first arrested in their middle teenage years (ages fourteen to seventeen) and an additional 18 percent were even younger when first arrested. Forty percent had been arrested fifteen times or more and 55 percent had been incarcerated one to three times previously; over one-fifth had seventeen prior incarcerations.[14] Shaw found more recently that 41 percent of women (Aboriginal and non-Aboriginal) serving federal sentences were first charged with offences in their teens, 36 percent had no previous convictions, and 51 percent had no previous incarcerations.[15]

Studies during the past few years have provided more complete information about the disproportionate involvement of Aboriginal women with the criminal justice system. Research on family violence, violence against women, and the way the criminal justice system responds to certain groups of offenders has provided a much better context within which to understand the nature of the problem.[16] The importance of the links between the victimization of Aboriginal women as children, youth, or young women due to sexual assault or family violence and future conflict with the law cannot be overemphasized.[17]

Macro Forces

The historical processes that have shaped contemporary Aboriginal society and relations between men and women help us to understand the present situation of Aboriginal women in Canadian society, and in prison. The colonization of Aboriginal people and the marginalization of Aboriginal society, in conjunction with modernization, relocation, and the unification of small groups into larger sedentary communities (compounded by the effects of mass communication), have dramatically altered traditional Aboriginal life. As a result of these changes there have been ruptures in Aboriginal people's social relations, and the traditional mechanisms of social control have deteriorated.[18]

The history of European settlement of Canada provides the context for understanding contemporary Aboriginal reserve communities. Many Indian communities were moved off highly productive land onto that which was marginally productive. As a result, Indians' local economies were underdeveloped, and they became economically subordinate to the new Canadians. Many Indian communities were able to continue subsistence-level activities such as hunting, fishing, trapping, and crop cultivation until the 1950s. But during the post-war period, those economies in community after community declined as the corrosive influence of the welfare state and the dominant group's economic system reached into their lives. Dependence upon welfare payments led to loss of self-esteem, alcohol abuse, and greater poverty; many Aboriginal women were forced to leave their home communities and migrate to cities.

Prior to the 1985 amendments to the *Indian Act,* this problem was compounded for those women who lost their Indian status due to marrying a non-Indian, as they lost all rights on reserves. Ineligible for band housing, if they were allowed to live on the reserve at all, they usually had to share crowded accommodation with relatives. When that proved unsatisfactory, they often had little choice but to migrate to urban areas. The ruptures this policy created continue today, even with the amendment to the *Indian Act* (whereby Aboriginal women who lost their Indian status, through marriage to a non-Indian or a non-status Aboriginal, and their descendants are reinstated). Many women who regained status after 1985 were met with resentment and rejection on their home reserves. Upon re-entering their home communities they were faced with limited housing and other resources, and long-standing tensions.

The social problems evidenced in contemporary communities are directly related to the loss of traditional economic activities. Today, a reliance on external institutions for economic subsistence and on internal ones for the distribution of these resources, in the form of jobs and housing, has created divisions between individuals and families. This is exacerbated by a lack of employment and reliance on social assistance. It is within this context that the involvement of Aboriginal women as offenders in the criminal justice system must be considered.

Micro Forces

The contemporary situation of Aboriginal women and their involvement with the criminal justice system, especially their incarceration for violent crimes, must also be understood from the perspective of the family. In particular, it is important to consider the breakdown of traditional Aboriginal roles, responsibilities, and values, and the loss of power and personal status experienced by Aboriginal people, especially Aboriginal men. The social disorganization seen in communities today is related to broader social and economic forces, but it is played out at the level of families and individuals.

Within the traditional Aboriginal economy, the household was the basic unit of production and consumption. Men and women maintained distinct roles and skills, although these differed from one cultural group to another. These roles were important because they defined social relations and individual responsibilities. The extended family, sharing, a sense of place and community, stability, tradition, co-operation, and avoidance of in-group conflict were the overriding values and characteristics of life.[19]

With the coming of the Europeans, Indian people were encouraged to abandon traditional economic activities, such as hunting, in favour of trapping and barter—the prevalent economic activities requested by the transnational fur-trading companies.[20] Not only did this shift set in motion a series of changes in the power relations between various groups, but it also fundamentally altered the reliance of Indian people on traditional economic activities. With the decline of traditional economies came profound changes in, and the blurring of, family and gender roles.

The residential school system, which took Indian children out of their home communities, also had an adverse impact. Parental values were denigrated, parental options were discounted, and children lost parents as role models by being removed from them at a young age. The teaching of European skills and knowledge was probably less destructive for girls than for boys, as the disparity between the traditional and the Euro-Canadian lifestyles was greater for male roles than for female roles. Thus, women were able to retain many of their traditional roles while male roles were greatly diminished and men were forced to resort to welfare or other western economic options, or to depend on women for support.

As traditional economies failed, forcing more families into the cycle of welfare, the system itself assisted in the confusion of roles and resulting frictions between Aboriginal men and women. Women became primary breadwinners under the welfare system because they received more funds than men by virtue of raising children. As a result, men lost their status as providers in the family. This role reversal led to a growing sense of impotence and frustration on the part of Aboriginal men.

The eventual outcome of these attempts at assimilation and the relentless effects of modernization (particularly in relation to waged labour and mass communication) was to distort traditional relations between Indian men and women. Men came to lose their sense of purpose in their community and to feel increasingly useless. This sense of loss continues to plague contemporary communities. Men still rely on seasonal employment and occasional hunting and trapping activities, with little hope of full-time employment, while women now frequently have dual roles, in their families and with full-time jobs, usually in band offices. Disparity in employment is a source of modern male-female friction.[21]

With the loss of traditional male roles and as a result of being reduced to a state of powerlessness and vulnerability which their own culture deemed highly inappropriate, Indian men came to experience severe role strain. The disparity between the desired traditional roles and the available or achievable roles was so great as to produce tension, anxiety, frustration, and anger, to which different men reacted in different ways. Psychological literature identifies aggression, regression, withdrawal, and accommodative behaviour as common reactions to frustration. The following description of the aggression reaction captures many of the behaviours exhibited by Indian men:

> Aggression may be expressed in overt behaviour or verbally. It may be directed at the source of frustration or at a substitute target. The substitute target may bear a symbolic relationship to the source of frustration, or it may simply serve as a convenient scapegoat on which to displace aggression. If no scapegoat is available, aggression may be directed toward the members of one's own group.[22]

The loss of status and roles is a particular problem for Aboriginal men living on reserve. Unlike life in off-reserve areas, where employment opportunities may be greater, reserve life has traditionally been plagued with high unemployment and survival on social assistance.[23] There is competition for the few available jobs and resentments often result over the distribution of scarce jobs. The fact that women are more employable in the local waged labour economy because of the clerical nature of the available jobs and the women's skill levels, makes the unemployment and economic alienation of men even more visible.[24]

Opportunities to satisfy power needs (lost to Indian men in their own society and denied by the dominant society) may be found in exercising control over others who are more vulnerable. In Indian communities in recent years, rape, child sexual abuse, and wife battering are reported with increasing frequency. A 1990 study of twenty-four Aboriginal communities in Georgian Bay revealed that

> family violence is a serious, self-perpetuating problem plaguing native life in Northern Ontario ... the study estimates that as many as half the households experience some family violence ... and that almost one-third of the victims are children whose first experience of violence occurs before they are ten.

Estimates of the proportion of female victims ranged from 60 to 72 percent.[25] A survey of 300 Micmac women found more than 75 percent were subjected to abuse.[26] Recent research with the James Bay Cree revealed that nearly two-thirds of all victims of interpersonal offences were women.[27] A 1991 joint publication of the Canadian Council on Social Development and the Native Women's Association of Canada stated that "It is an exception rather than the rule to know of an Aboriginal woman who has not experienced some form of family violence throughout her life."[28]

The role of alcohol in the commission of Aboriginal offences of violence is also widely documented. Heather Robertson describes the consequences of alcohol in this process:

> ... [I]nternal tensions become explosive, and alcohol provides a release by destroying inhibitions.... Intoxicated, an Indian's repressed hate comes to the surface and is expressed physically and verbally. He hits out at his wife, his children, his friends. This violence, like the drinking itself, is strongly suicidal, and the victims are those persons nearest to the drunk man. He is hitting, indirectly, at himself.[29]

Jim Harding provides another perspective on the relationship between underdevelopment and alcohol abuse. He concludes that:

> ... underdevelopment created enormous stresses and contradictions and alcohol is used as a means of managing alienation by assisting people to modify their moods and thereby escape their real life situations.[30]

Although research in this area is still limited, mounting evidence suggests a direct causal relationship between the role strain of Aboriginal men, violence against women, and subsequent criminal activity by Aboriginal women. In the survey by Sugar and Fox, nearly 70 percent of the thirty-nine Aboriginal women who had involvement with the criminal justice system had suffered violence during adolescence.[31]

Sociological literature provides support for the linkage between victimization and subsequent criminality. The notion that "violence breeds violence" is supported in the literature on battered children and juvenile delinquents. For instance, emotional or physical maltreatment during childhood is a common feature in the background of child-abusing parents and other violent offenders. Research has indicated clearly that certain types of child-rearing are more conducive to the adoption of deviant behaviours than are others. Early childhood victimization appears to increase the probability of a person committing a criminal act in the first instance and at a young age, and early antisocial behaviour is one of the best predictors of later antisocial behaviour. A recent examination of the effects of child abuse and neglect on later behaviour concluded that "Generally, abused and neglected children were significantly more likely than their counterparts in the control group to be arrested for delinquency, adult criminality and violent criminal behaviour."[32] Family stress, marital discord, unemployment and poverty, and various types of physical and sexual abuse are also linked to higher rates of delinquency.[33] The generational aspects of family violence and child abuse have also garnered considerable research attention in the past decade. Family violence and sexual abuse are often generational and "institutionalized" in families.[34]

Aboriginal women's conflict with the law may be linked to the role strain experienced by Aboriginal men and the subsequent gender role tensions. Some Aboriginal women may retaliate in kind against physically abusive Aboriginal men; others may escape a violent or otherwise abusive situation at home and migrate to an urban area where discrimination by the larger society, combined with their own usually low level of skills and education, may relegate them to the ranks of the unemployed or unemployable. That in turn increases the probability that they will resort to alcohol or drug abuse or to prostitution, all of which increase the potential for conflict with the law. Even without engaging in any of these activities, being in an urban area increases exposure to criminal justice officials. Recent research reveals that most Aboriginal inmates in correctional institutions are drawn from urban settings, and particularly the inner cores of Western cities.[35]

Conclusions

A broad range of economic, socio-cultural, and legal factors associated with being Aboriginal and female in a male-dominated, non-Aboriginal society, contribute to Aboriginal women coming into conflict with the law. The violent behaviour often demonstrated by Aboriginal women offenders is a product of historical socio-economic forces and background factors. The undermining of traditional Aboriginal roles and values, the acceptance of violence in society, discriminatory provisions of the *Indian Act,* and tensions in male-female relationships have conspired to relegate many Aboriginal women to a marginalized status.

The reader should not, however, infer from the above discussion that family violence and interpersonal abuse are accepted behaviours in Aboriginal society, even though they may be commonplace in contemporary families and communities. Findings from research in Canada and other countries with indigenous populations suggest that violence and alcoholism are often the result of long-standing oppression and marginalization.[36] Indeed, the dominant non-Aboriginal cultures could profit from traditional Aboriginal practices where roles and responsibilities, and age and gender dictated the ways in which people related to and treated one another. Unfortunately, many of the social and economic forces that have shaped contemporary non-Aboriginal society have affected Aboriginal society even more profoundly, with the result that customary practices and respect between the sexes and age groups have declined.[37]

In spite of the limitations of the information available, it is obvious that many Aboriginal women are alienated from the mainstream of Canadian life and, as recently indicated on the national political scene (when the Native Women's Association of Canada was excluded from the constitutional negotiating table), from the mainstream of Aboriginal political life. Alienation is not so much a product of an individual's inability to cope as it is a product of social inequality, in both society as a whole and on a personal level. Social science research needs to take account of this fact, and of the fundamental disparities structured into the Canadian social system and along gender lines. Perhaps most importantly, we must find ways and means to tackle structural inequality and violence in Canada and in Aboriginal communities, to better address the issue of Aboriginal women in conflict with the law.

Notes

1 This is an updated version of an article by Carol LaPrairie, "Native Women and Crime in Canada: A Theoretical Model," in *Too Few to Count: Canadian Women in Conflict with the Law*, ed. Ellen Adelberg and Claudia Currie (Vancouver: Press Gang Publishers, 1987).

2 The term "Aboriginal" is used throughout the text to denote all women of Aboriginal descent, whether status, non-status, or Métis. The term "Indian" usually refers to individuals with status under the *Indian Act*.

3 Carol Pitcher LaPrairie, "Selected Criminal Justice and Socio-Demographic Data on Native Women," *Canadian Journal of Criminology* 26 (April 1984): 162.

4 Carol Pitcher LaPrairie, "Exploring the Boundaries of Justice: Aboriginal Justice in the Yukon" (unpublished report to the Department of Justice, Yukon Territorial Government; First Nations, Yukon Territory; and Justice Canada, Ottawa, 1992).

5 Margaret Shaw, with Karen Rodgers, Johanne Blanchette, Tina Hattem, Lee Seto Thomas, and Lada Tamarack, *Paying the Price: Federally Sentenced Women in Context* (Ottawa: Ministry of the Solicitor General, 1991), p. 59.

6 This conclusion is drawn from an analysis of the offences for which women were incarcerated at the Prison for Women in 1982 and in 1991. Canada, Correctional Service of Canada, "Non-Native Population Profile Report and Native Population Profile Report" (Ottawa: Solicitor General of Canada, Information Services Branch, March 1982); see also Shaw et al., *Paying the Price.*

7 Fran Sugar and Lana Fox, *Survey of Federally Sentenced Aboriginal Women in the Community* (Ottawa: Native Women's Association of Canada, 1990).

8 Sharon Moyer, *Homicides Involving Adult Suspects, 1962–1984: A Comparison of Natives and Non-Natives,* User Report No. 1987-29 (Ottawa: Ministry of the Solicitor General, 1987).

9 Canada, Department of Indian and Northern Affairs, *Highlights of Aboriginal Conditions, 1981–2001, Part II: Social Conditions* (Ottawa: Supply and Services, 1989); Canada, Health and Welfare, Medical Services Branch, *Statistics and Demographics* (Ottawa: Supply and Services, 1990); P.M. White,

Native Women: A Statistical Review (Ottawa: Secretary of State, 1985).

10 Sugar and Fox, *Survey*.

11 Moyer, *Homicides*. Moyer found that homicides involving Aboriginal people were more likely to involve alcohol than were those involving non-Aboriginals. She also found Aboriginal women to be homicide victims in numbers disproportionate to the number of non-Aboriginal women victims.

12 Carol LaPrairie, with the assistance of Yves Leguerrier, *Justice for the Cree: Communities, Crime and Order* (Cree Regional Authority, Nemaska, Quebec, 1991), chapter 3.

13 Michelle G. Grossman, "Two Perspectives on Aboriginal Female Suicides," *Canadian Journal of Criminology* 34, nos. 3–4 (1992).

14 Bernice Dubec, "Native Women and the Criminal Justice System: An Increasing Minority" (Ontario Native Women's Association, Thunder Bay, 1982).

15 Shaw et al., *Paying the Price,* Executive Summary, p. iv.

16 For references to this literature, see Grossman, "Two Perspectives on Aboriginal Female Suicides"; Shaw et al., *Paying the Price;* Sugar and Fox, *Survey*; and Michelle Grossman, "Aboriginal Women in Canada: Socio-Economic, Cultural and Demographic Review" (Department of Justice, Ottawa, 1991).

17 Sugar and Fox, *Survey*; Grossman, "Two Perspectives on Aboriginal Female Suicides."

18 Roger McDonnell, *Customary Beliefs and Practices* (Cree Regional Authority, Nemaska, Quebec, 1992), chapter 6. For a good analysis of the impact of colonization see Gail Kellough, "From Colonialism to Imperialism: The Experience of Canadian Indians," in *Structured Inequality in Canada,* ed. John Harp and John R. Hofley (Scarborough, Ont.: Prentice-Hall, 1980).

19 Peter J. Usher, "A Northern Perspective on the Informal Economy," *Perspectives* (1980). See also McDonnell, *Customary Beliefs and Practices*.

20 Victor Valentine, "Native People and Canadian Society: A Profile of Issues and Trends," in *Cultural Boundaries and the Cohesion of Canada,* ed. R. Breton, J. Reitz, and V. Valentine (Montreal: Institute of Research on Public Policy, 1980), pp. 35–136.

21 McDonnell, *Customary Beliefs and Practices*.

22 Walter I. Wardell, "The Reduction of Strain in a Marginal Social Role," in *Problems in Social Psychology,* ed. Carl W. Backman and Paul S. Secord (New York: McGraw-Hill, 1966), p. 331.

23 According to 1986 Census employment data, two-and-one-half times more people receive social assistance on reserves than elsewhere in Canada.

24 McDonnell, *Customary Beliefs and Practices,* chapter 7.

25 Rudy Platiel, "Violence Plaguing Native Life in Ontario," *The Globe and Mail,* Friday, 14 December 1990.

26 Kathleen Whip, "Wife Battering on Indian Reserves: Application of Germain's Ecological Perspective" (Carleton University, Ottawa, 1985), p. 1.

27 LaPrairie, *Justice for the Cree,* p. 83.

28 Canadian Council on Social Development and Native Women's Association of Canada, *Voices of Aboriginal Women: Aboriginal Women Speak Out* (Ottawa, 1991).

29 Heather Robertson, *Reservations are for Indians* (Toronto: James Lewis and Samuel, 1970), p. 283.

30 Jim Harding, "Unemployment, Racial Discrimination and Public Drunkenness in Regina" (Faculty of Social Work, University of Regina, Regina, 1984), pp. 13–14.

31 Sugar and Fox, *Survey,* p. 7.

32 Cathy Spatz Widom, "Early indicators: How Early, and What Indicators?" *Forum* 3, no. 3 (1991): 5–6.

33 Clem Henricson, "Tackling the Causes of Crime: Labour's Crime Management Policy for the 1990's" (Labour Party, London, U.K., April 1991).

34 Jeffrey Fagan and Sandra Wexler, "Family Origins of Violent Delinquents," *Criminology* 25, no. 3 (1987): 643–49; Anthony Bottoms, "Crime Prevention Facing the 1990's," *Policing and Society* 1, no. 1 (1990): 1–22; Wesley Skogan, "Recent Research on Urban Safety, Drugs and Crime Prevention in the United States: A Report Submitted to the Scientific Committee of the Second International Conference on Urban Safety, Drugs and Crime Prevention" (sponsored by the Forum of Local and Regional Authorities of Europe, the U.S. Conferences of Mayors, and the Federation of Canadian Municipalities; Paris, France, November 1991); Henricson, "Tackling the Causes of Crime"; LaPrairie, *Justice for the Cree.*

35 Carol LaPrairie, *Dimensions of Aboriginal Over-representation in Correctional Institutions and Implications for Crime Prevention* (Aboriginal Peoples Collection, Ottawa: Ministry of the Solicitor General, Corrections Branch, 1993).

36 Kayleen M. Hazelhurst,"Passion and Policy: Aboriginal Deaths in Custody in Australia, 1980–1989," in *Crimes by the Capitalist State,* ed. Gregg Barak (New York: State University of New York Press, 1991); Jean-Paul Brodeur with Yves Leguerrier, *Justice for the Cree: Policing and Alternate Dispute Resolution* (Cree Regional Authority, Nemaska, Quebec, 1991); *Report of the Aboriginal Justice Inquiry: Justice on Trial* (Winnipeg: Queen's Press, 1991).

37 McDonnell, *Customary Beliefs and Practices.*

Strategies of Survival: Moving Beyond the Battered Woman Syndrome[1]

Sheila Noonan

To the degree that institutions and social practices encourage, tolerate, or enable the perpetration of violence against members of specific groups, those institutions and practices are unjust and should be reformed. Such reform may require the redistribution of resources and positions, but in large part can come only through a change in relations of dominance and aversion in the gestures of everyday life.[2]

Introduction

This chapter emerged from political work seeking the release of Canadian women currently incarcerated for having killed their abusive partners. This work was inspired by efforts which led to the release of women with similar legal status in a number of jurisdictions in the United States. The mechanisms used to secure this outcome have varied: in some states Governors or parole board equivalents granted clemency to individual women;[3] in other states reviews granted *"en bloc"* resulted in the early release of groups of women.[4] Elsewhere applications for clemency, pardon, or commutation are currently underway.[5]

The Canadian Association of Elizabeth Fry Societies (CAEFS) is engaged in a similar undertaking in Canada. As a member of that organization, I have conducted interviews with women who have killed their abusive partners. We hope to secure freedom for approximately twelve women, some of whom are currently serving life sentences.

I begin this chapter by addressing the law of self-defence as it existed in Canada before 1990, and discussing the formal acceptance of the "battered woman syndrome" by the Supreme Court in *R. v. Lavallee.* Next, I focus on the limitations of the battered woman syndrome due to the way it has been constructed. This is followed by a statistical and sociological overview of women who kill their abusive partners, based in part on interviews with women at the Prison for Women in Kingston, Ontario. I then review a variety of legal strategies for securing release. In conclusion, I consider possible legal strategies for altering the terrain of self-defence.

The Law of Self-Defence

Until the Canadian judiciary accepted the battered wife syndrome in 1990, both statutory and common law dealt harshly with women forced to defend themselves against abusive male spouses or partners. The statutory requirements, together with judicial interpretations of the relevant sections of the Criminal Code, offered very little protection for women whose actions were motivated by self-preservation.

Although the common law has changed due to *R. v. Lavallee* (1990), the Code still specifies that where a woman responds to an unprovoked assault intending to kill the assailant, she must show that she acted under reasonable apprehension of death or grievous bodily harm.[6] Moreover, she must establish that she reasonably believed that she had no other means of preventing this harm. However, where the woman does not intend to inflict death or grievous bodily harm, proof that no more force was used than necessary to repel the attack will suffice.

The difficulty with the Code requirements often consists in the proof. Generally, under s.34(2), where death is intended, a successful plea of self-defence requires a close scrutiny of the circumstances under which the killing transpired. As mentioned above, the accused woman must demonstrate that at the time of her actions, she believed she was about to suffer death or grievous bodily harm and that such harm could only be averted by resorting to deadly force.[7] The difficulty is that her subjective apprehensions alone are necessary but insufficient; a demonstration that these beliefs were objectively reasonable is also required.[8]

Prior to 1990, the standard for assessing the objective reasonableness of a given woman's actions was whether an "ordinary man" in similar circumstances would have believed himself under threat of death or grievous bodily harm, and whether he further believed that self-preservation required him to deploy the amount of force he did.[9] The highly gendered construction of this test revealed a notion of violence such as might unfold within the context of a "bar room brawl," or a sudden attack (with no prior history of violence between the two parties) by a stranger, or a fight between persons of similar size, weight, and strength.[10] This notion failed to acknowledge the seamless web of violence which characterizes a battering relationship. Prolonged abuse was never considered in analyzing single incidents of violence culminating in death. The potential size and strength differentials between male and female partners and the cumulative psychic and emotional effects of an abusive relationship were discounted, resulting in the incarceration of women who killed their partners after they had already been severely victimized within battering relationships. The above difficulties were compounded by the ruling imposed by judges requiring an "imminent attack"; effectively, this doctrine held that a woman could only take defensive action in the face of immediate danger in order for her actions to be adjudged non-culpable. The requirement of imminence (again "objectively" assessed) meant that a battered woman was required to wait until a potentially fatal attack was underway before she could defend herself.

The most controversial application of the above principles arose in a 1983 case decided in Nova Scotia. In *R. v. Whynot*[11] the court convicted a woman who shot her husband while he was asleep. Evidence was presented at trial that the deceased had physically abused Jane Stafford and other members of her family on a number of occasions. On the night in question, the deceased threatened to kill her son. The deceased had been drinking heavily and as he lay passed out in his truck, Ms. Stafford shot him. The Nova Scotia Court of Appeal ruled that s.37, which pertains to the prevention of an assault or the repetition of it, could not be applied: "In my opinion, no person has the right in anticipation of an assault that may or may not happen, to apply force to prevent the imaginary assault."

The doctrinal requirements articulated in *Whynot* of imminence of attack and proportionality of force imposed significant barriers to the availability of self-defence for women in situations of ongoing or threatened attacks.

The first critical examination and substantive reworking of these principles occurred in *R. v. Lavallee*.[12] While the decision largely focussed on issues pertaining to the admissibility of expert evidence,[13] it was the first Canadian Supreme Court decision to recognize the significance of battering within the context of a domestic homicide. During the course of the relationship, Ms. Lavallee had frequently been a victim of physical abuse, at times requiring medical attention. At a party on the night of the killing, Ms. Lavallee was assaulted by the deceased. In a statement later given to the police, Ms. Lavallee indicated that he had assaulted her and had threatened to kill her when the rest of the guests departed. As he exited from the bedroom having levelled the attack and this threat against her, Ms. Lavallee shot him in the back of the head. Given that the fatal shot was imparted at a moment when such a life-threatening attack was not imminent, a self-defence plea would not have been successful on the principles articulated in *Whynot*. However, the defence sought to introduce expert testimony to establish that Ms. Lavallee was suffering from the "battered woman syndrome" and accordingly American precedent, which would allow for a reformulation of self-defence rules, should be followed.

Such evidence was advanced at trial by a psychiatrist, who testified that Ms. Lavallee felt worthless, and trapped within her relationship. In his opinion her act had unfolded under circumstances where she believed "unless she defended herself, unless she reacted in a violent way, that she would die."[14] The jury acquitted Ms. Lavallee, but the Crown appealed to the Manitoba Court of Appeal, challenging the introduction of expert evidence on the issue of the "battered woman syndrome." As the evidence given consisted partially of hearsay,[15] the Crown stated that inadequate instructions had been given to the jury as to the weight to be attached to the expert testimony. Moreover, there was no established precedent in Canadian jurisprudence which would permit the introduction of evidence on the consequences and effects of domestic assault. The appeal succeeded and a new trial was ordered. Ms. Lavallee then appealed this decision to the Supreme Court of Canada, who unanimously restored the acquittal.

Madame Justice Wilson delivered an opinion for the Court which fundamentally altered the traditional bounds of self-defence doctrine. In particular, she stressed that the masculine standard of reasonableness "must be adapted to circumstances which are, by and large, foreign to the world inhabited by the hypothetical 'reasonable man'."[16] Directly calling into question the requirement of imminent attack, Madame Justice Wilson endorsed an American case[17] which argued that requiring "a battered woman wait until the physical attack is 'underway' before her apprehensions can be validated by law would ... be tantamount to sentencing her to 'murder by installment'." In her view, expert evidence of the effect of battering on women in domestic relationships with the batterer was necessary to assess the individual woman's state of mind. Otherwise the jury might not be able to appreciate questions such as why she would continue to live in an abusive situation, or why, given the treatment to which she was subjected, she didn't simply leave. Such evidence could assist the jury in determining if the woman's subjective fear "may have been reasonable within the context of the relationship."[18]

The Supreme Court relied upon Dr. Lenore Walker's cycle theory of violence, which posits three distinct phases within a recurring battering cycle: "(1) tension building, (2) the acute battering incident, and (3) loving contrition."[19] In the Court's view, the cyclical nature of abuse is relevant to understanding the accused's state of mind at the moment at which the killing occurs. The woman's mental state must be understood in light of the "cumulative effect of months or years of brutality."[20] Another pertinent aspect is that a battered woman may have a heightened sensitivity to her partner's violence, so that she can more readily predict the onset of an attack before a blow is ever struck. Finally, expert evidence may shed light on the "learned helplessness" and/or "traumatic bonding" which may characterize the relationship between abuser and abused. The court stressed, however, that even where the introduction of such evidence relating to the battered women syndrome is permitted, it remains for the judge or jury to establish whether the perceptions and actions of the accused were reasonable, and therefore constitute a defence in law.

As currently structured in Canadian law, the outcome which turns on these questions is stark. If a judge or jury finds that an individual woman reasonably apprehended death or grievous bodily harm (given the context of the battering relationship), and deployed an appropriate amount of force in responding to this threat, she is entitled to an acquittal. For women who fail to meet this criterion, the conviction can be murder, dictating a lengthy period of incarceration. And this is where American experience warns us of significant dangers.

Problems with Self-Defence

Under the current construction of the battered woman syndrome, an abused woman who kills her male partner in self-defence is at best acting in a manner that can be excused. And like other categories of excuse, it functions by way of explaining her behaviour rather than sanctioning it as appropriate. Elizabeth Schneider articulates this distinction as follows:

> Self-defence as justification focuses on the act of defending oneself; it rests on a determination that the act was right because of its circumstances. In contrast, a finding of excuse, like insanity or heat of passion, focuses on the actor; it is a finding that the act, although wrong, should be tolerated because of the actor's characteristics or state of mind.[21]

While for men self-defence is regarded as a legal justification, evidence that an abused woman suffers from the battered wife syndrome appears to function in law largely as an excuse.

This is true in the United States, where evidence of battering has been admissible in heterosexual couple killings for over a decade.[22] The psychological profile of a battered woman was largely formulated in response to erroneous beliefs as to why an abused woman would remain in an abusive situation.[23] In seeking to explain this phenomenon, however, the battered woman syndrome stresses the woman's victimization and paralysis within the abusive relationship: it cannot therefore simultaneously assert her act of self-preservation is reasonable.

A paradox ensues. In broadening assessments of reasonableness to include the situation of battered women, the focus shifts away from the reasonableness of the act of self-defence. Victimization is invoked to explain the otherwise unintelligible actions of the battered woman. But it is precisely the assertion that her actions are unreasonable which assists in casting the battered woman as suffering from a form of mental incapacity. In this way, the battered woman syndrome "is in tension with the notion of reasonableness necessary to self-defence since it emphasizes the woman's defects and incapacity."[24]

There are many dangers in the legal adoption of the battered wife syndrome, including reliance on its dubious definition, and the constitution of "expertise" within this domain.[25] The introduction of expert psychological evidence of the battered woman syndrome makes the woman's actions appear to be pathological. While the syndrome was designed to describe a "terrified human being's response to an abnormal and dangerous situation," many clinicians and judges diagnose the symptoms of sustained brutality as signs of mental illness:

> Battered women have been viewed as masochistic, provocative and passive/aggressive. Because many health professionals do not understand why a battered woman stays in an abusive situation, they assume that battered women either like the violence or are "crazy." The practitioners often confuse symptoms of mental illness and the effects of battering, frequently leading to misdiagnosis of battered women as suffering from schizophrenic disorders or borderline personality disorders.[26]

Given that historically the argument has been that women are more often mad than bad,[27] battered women facing serious criminal charges are at least doubly pathologized. They are regarded as deviant for not having left an abusive relationship and also for having resorted to violence rather than becoming self-destructive.

Another problem with the battered woman syndrome defence is that the individual woman's account of her relationship and the reason for her actions are only relevant to the degree to which they successfully converge with medical and legal accounts of the syndrome. In this respect, the battered woman syndrome fails to allow a woman to reveal the particular context in which her action was taken.

In practice, the battered woman syndrome sanctions very few accounts of abuse. It requires that a woman have suffered physical abuse.[28] Further, a woman has to have been through the "cycle of violence" twice to qualify.[29] In American jurisdictions, actions and behaviours must conform with diagnostic criteria (such as passivity in the face of abuse) to qualify for consideration.

Even where the accepted symptoms are demonstrated, the legal availability of self-defence requires an examination of a discrete incident at a particular moment in time. This analysis fits uncomfortably with the contextualization of abuse that the battered woman syndrome seeks to inject into the process. The conflict between these approaches is often resolved by closely scrutinizing the actions of the battered woman.

Women whose actions fail to conform to stereotypically passive behaviour are seen to calculatedly plot their own revenge, and they are frequently convicted of murder:

> The courts seem to treat the battered woman syndrome as a standard to which all battered women must conform rather than as evidence that illuminates the defendant's behaviour and perceptions. As a result, a defendant may be considered a battered woman only if she never fought back....[30]

Jurisprudence and commentary in the United States suggest that incarceration is likely in circumstances in which a woman leaves, fights back,[31] attacks the abuser when he is asleep,[32] seeks outside assistance in ending the violence,[33] or otherwise fails to display characteristically passive behaviour.[34] Yet women often act outside of situations of imminent violence in the hope of ending the abuse without risking themselves being killed.[35] Many women have felt compelled to resort to the intervention of third parties because strength differentials led them to believe that they might die first if an effort to repel an attack were required.

Finally, the very notion of syndrome suggests that the abused woman is suffering from an individual defect. It fails to locate particular incidents within the culturally sanctioned practice of violence against women.[36] The degree to which male rage against women is sanctioned tends to be disguised. Furthermore, male rage receives protection within existing categories of criminal defence, such as provocation.[37] The net effect of relying on the "syndrome" as defence is that female deviation from passivity is pathologized, systematized, and penalized, while the social factors that lead to violence against women remain unaddressed.

Statistical Overview and Interviews with Women

Given the extent of woman-battering in Canada, the attempt in homicide cases to portray women's failure to leave the home as deviant seems ironic.[38] The limited prescriptions for appropriate gender roles, constrained job opportunities, low-wage ghettos, and the lack of women's political representation are but a few facets of women's inequality. As Elizabeth Comack states, the fundamental problem faced by battered women is a lack of control over their own lives that "is rooted in social and economic—not psychological—determinants."[39] In short, it is women's subordination to and dependency upon male partners that is problematic.

Unquestionably this dependency is fraught with danger. A 1992 report on the murder of women in Ontario[40] graphically underscores the danger to women of involvement in violent heterosexual unions. This detailed analysis of coroners' data reveals that intimate femicide[41] accounted for 61 percent to 78 percent of all killings of women between 1974 and 1990 where an assailant was identified. The comparable rate of women killing male partners during this same period was approximately 8 percent of male homicide victims. This study confirms other data indicating that in spousal homicide, male partners kill female partners at a rate of approximately three to one.[42]

Equally significant is the finding that women who are separated from their spouses remain at great risk of death.[43] While the majority of women killed were married to and living with their killers, one-third were separated.[44] The authors of the report inferred that anger and rage precipitated by estrangement resulted in women's deaths. This supports earlier conclusions drawn in the Barnard Study which suggest that men and women accused of spousal homicide kill for different reasons.

The data collected by Barnard et al. suggest that men most often commit "sex-role threat homicide." Men who killed were inappropriately and violently expressing the pain of withdrawal, whereby "a walkout, a demand, a threat of separation were taken by the men to represent intolerable desertion, rejection, and abandonment."[45] Homicide was an expression of control over their spouses. In contrast, the study found that women tend to commit "victim precipitated homicide." This implies that the victim had in some way engaged in activity which contributed to the killing. Most often, women who killed did so in response to physical attacks and threats. This is consistent with an earlier Canadian study of spousal homicide by Peter Chimbos in which 75 percent of the women interviewed had either just been assaulted or were being assaulted when the killing transpired.[46]

Given current levels of violence against women, it remains unclear why some women feel compelled to kill their spouses while others do not. In comparing abused women who did not take lethal action with those who did, Angela Browne concluded that the most significant differences between the two groups consisted in the behaviour of the men. She identified seven key dynamics which distinguished the two groups, namely: "the frequency with which abusive incidents occurred; the severity of the women's injuries; the frequency of forced or threatened sexual acts by the man; the man's drug use; the frequency of his intoxication; the man's threats to kill; and the woman's threats to commit suicide."[47]

As Holly Johnson's and Karen Rodgers' chapter in this book indicates, relatively few women, compared to men, are charged with violent crimes. Police data for 1991 indicated that of the 534 adults charged with homicide, only 9 percent were women. This figure fails to disclose that homicide committed by women largely transpires within domestic situations.[48]

The number of Canadian women admitted to prison each year for homicide offences has remained fairly stable. In 1991, fourteen women were serving time for first degree murder, forty for second degree murder, five for attempted murder, and forty-two for manslaughter. Similarly, in 1990 there were fifteen on register for first degree murder, thirty-eight for second degree murder, two for attempted murder, and fifty for manslaughter. Virtually the same pattern emerges for 1989, during which there were twelve women serving time for first degree, thirty-nine for second degree, three for attempted, and forty-eight for manslaughter. The collected data do not reveal the average length of sentence for a woman who kills an intimate partner.

Unfortunately, there are no Canadian data pertaining to the sentences women receive when they kill their spouses or partners. Data collected in the United States suggest that women convicted of homicide serve longer periods of incarceration than men. This is remarkable given that women who kill generally have less serious pre-conviction records than men.[49] While women who kill their partners have the least extensive criminal records of any category of female offenders, they tend to face harsher penalties than men who kill their mates. FBI statistics indicate that men who kill people they know face fewer first and second degree murder charges than women who kill men in such situations.[50] In a study by Ewing, almost half of those women convicted in the death of their partners faced sentences of more than ten years, and one-fifth were sentenced to life imprisonment.[51] In contrast, it has been reported that abusive men in the United States who kill their partners are incarcerated for terms averaging two to six years.[52] Women who killed intimates, even though the killings often occurred in the course of protecting themselves, received an average sentence of fifteen years.[53]

In 1991 and 1992 I spoke with nine women at the Prison for Women who were incarcerated for having killed their abusive partners. (I also spoke with at least ten other women whose abusive histories and relationships had contributed significantly to the crimes with which they were charged.) My colleague, lawyer Felicity Hawthorn, conducted in-depth interviews with the women who seemed most closely to approximate the type of case scenario in *R. v. Lavallee.* The purpose of these interviews was to assess which cases might form the basis for an *en bloc* review of the type that has occurred in the United States.

The majority of these women were convicted of first degree murder and were serving life sentences with no parole eligibility for twenty-five years. All of these women were sentenced before the emergence of the so-called battered wife syndrome. Virtually none had been permitted to tell the stories of their abuse in court.

In discussing with the women what prompted their action to kill their husbands, the most typical answer was "I just couldn't take it any more." All of the women felt under threat; one in fact always slept with a weapon near her to protect against assaults which ensued whenever her partner returned home drunk. Because of her actions in defending herself in the past, when police assistance was sought she was seen to be the aggressor. Most existed in a state of extreme isolation. Those who were mothers were concerned not only for their own safety, but also for that of their children.

All of the women disclosed a lengthy history of sexual abuse within their original families. Many had subsequently suffered at least one instance of rape during their adulthood. One woman had been so severely victimized from the time of infancy that there was no point at which the torture of physical and sexual abuse had ceased; rather, the faces of perpetrators had simply changed over time. Sometimes drug-dependent themselves, a number of the women entered relationships with men who had severe drug problems, relationships in which they were emotionally, physically, and sexually abused. In descriptions of their relationships, the physical abuse featured less centrally; to them it was only one of the kinds of abuse to which they were subjected which ultimately culminated in their action.

Unquestionably, the women saw their actions as linked directly to the preservation of their life and integrity. Some had left their partners but lived in fear of being discovered. Others took defensive action outside the context of an attack by their partner. Still others sought the assistance of third parties in ending the reign of terror to which they had been subjected.

The overall picture calls into question the notion that if women leave abusive relationships they will eliminate the risk of death. For many, the threat from abusive male partners did not appear to dissipate when they left. As Cynthia Gillespie notes:

> There is seldom any place of refuge in a house or apartment from someone in determined pursuit; and even if she does manage to lock herself in the bathroom, she will eventually have to come out, and he will still be there. Fleeing out the door is seldom an option either. He can easily prevent her from leaving and can or will come after her if she does. Most of these serious assaults take place late at night when the woman has no place to go; and even if she can get away, she will often be reluctant to leave her children behind.[54]

Representations of battered women which characterize their actions as unusual or deviant forms of self-defence must be challenged. Strategies of survival are as varied as the abuse which gives rise to them:

> Like other victims, battered women's affective, cognitive, and behavioural responses are likely to be distorted by their intense focus on survival. They may have developed a whole range of responses such as controlling their breathing or not crying out when in pain, in an effort to mitigate the severity of abuse during violent episodes.[55]

A shift away from the rigidity of former doctrinal requirements of self-defence was begun in the Lavallee case. However, there remain serious questions about whether the use of the battered woman syndrome will only legitimate legal and psychological discourses that disempower women, and disguise the broader social and economic conditions under which such actions unfold.

Strategies to Free Battered Women Who Kill

One of the most hopeful events that has transpired in the United States in seeking to remedy the injustice of incarcerating battered women who kill has been the granting of clemency, pardon, or sentence commutation. This has largely been the product of a grass-roots effort by women who have advocated on behalf of others in prison. In some cases, women in prison have organized their own campaigns.

More than one strategy has emerged from the various efforts to secure release.[56] For Canadian women who were prevented from telling of their abuse in court, these strategies are vital in seeking access to justice. They are also essential for women who cannot use the battered woman syndrome because of its rigid medical formulation and legal application.

Lawyers representing women incarcerated for murdering an abusive partner should assess whether a change in plea is possible; whether an appeal could be launched on the basis of new evidence; whether a sentence appeal might be appropriate; or whether to make application for parole. Advocacy groups might consider other options, namely clemency, commutation, or pardons, which have led to both individual and *en bloc* reviews in the United States.[57]

Information from the National Clearinghouse for the Defense of Battered Women in the United States indicates that although the numbers of cases in which post-conviction relief has been sought and obtained are not high, the effort to secure the release of those incarcerated is gaining momentum.[58] Two major *en bloc* reviews have resulted in the extension of clemency. In 1990 Governor Celeste in Ohio granted clemency to twenty-six women. A further ten women in Maryland were released by Governor Schaefer in 1991. Individual petitions for commutation have been successful in New Jersey, Washington, Florida, Iowa, and Illinois. In Virginia, a pardon was extended to one prisoner, while in California and Michigan two others were released early due to illness. Colorado and Kansas each allowed one woman to be paroled; Nevada granted clemency to another to seek parole. In Nebraska a woman was pardoned some time after her release. Further efforts are currently in progress, such as a campaign begun in 1989 to secure the release of women in Massachusetts prisons. In California, thirty-four women have written to the governor requesting review, and in Texas a resolution was passed in April 1991 commanding review of the cases of all women who killed in abusive situations. In Louisiana an effort to organize petitions for release is underway.

Not all of these strategies are necessarily available in Canada, given the differences between Canadian and American jurisdictions with respect to the procedural rules and government structures relevant to these issues. In this jurisdiction, the following procedural strategies are all worth review-

ing: the Royal Prerogative of Mercy, pardons, and lobbying for new structures to review such cases.

The Royal Prerogative of Mercy[59] may be invoked to obtain clemency,
to rectify a "miscarriage of justice," or to alleviate situations in which punishment may be unduly harsh.[60] It is an exceptional remedy, available only
when all other avenues of reprieve have been exhausted. Power to grant
the pardon rests with the Governor General; in practice, pardon applications are granted on the recommendation of the Solicitor General.[61]
Pardon may take either a free or conditional form.[62] While it is unclear
whether a free pardon is available only if innocence has been clearly established, in practice it has been restricted to those types of cases. The conditional pardon, which secures early release, is available when consideration
for any form of parole is not legally possible. It can be obtained on grounds
of undue hardship, for health reasons, or where an accomplice agrees to
give testimony that leads to conviction of another party to the offence.
Persons released by way of conditional pardon are supervised as if they
were on parole.

The Royal Prerogative can also be used to remit a sentence. Remission
of a sentence in whole or part is available where the sentence imposed cre-
ates undue hardship or is based upon an error of law, or where inequity has
been created on the basis of a change in legislation. A remission of sentence has the effect of ending the sentence. In its *Policy and Procedures
Manual,* the National Parole Board suggests that remission is typically considered on the basis of "pure compassion on the existence of some inequality."[63]

The major obstacle with Royal Prerogative is that to date very few instances of reprieve have been granted.[64]

The Minister of Justice also possesses statutory power in respect of applications for mercy,[65] also known as pardons.

Under s.690 of the Criminal Code, the Minister may ask the judiciary to
review legal and evidentiary issues. Effectively, this option permits the case
to be returned to the Court. Given that this power has been invoked to review sentences imposed prior to new psychiatric understandings of insanity, it could prove a satisfactory vehicle for raising issues pertaining to the
exclusion of women's history of abuse within battering relationships.[66] The
Minister of Justice is reported to receive approximately thirty requests for
reviews annually, and it is still exceptional for a case to be referred back for
the court's reconsideration.[67]

Nonetheless, the three recent reviews of Marshall, Milgaard, and Nepoose resulted in the ultimate release of all the applicants.[68] While these were exceptional cases, the incarceration of women under circumstances where they were unable to give evidence relating to their history of abuse within the relationship presents an equally compelling situation, bearing as it does upon the issue of self-defence.

Successful applications for the Royal Prerogative of Mercy are rare, and mounting an application under s.690 requires legal assistance and formal court processes. Both approaches provide relief only on an individual basis; therefore the Canadian Association of Elizabeth Fry Societies is exploring other options to secure the release of women in the federal prison. Lobbying efforts are likely to be directed toward two options. The first would involve requesting Parliament to authorize an independent committee such as a citizens' inquiry, charged with reviewing the cases of all battered women who have killed abusive spouses, and empowered to make recommendations for release. A further option would be to push for the establishment of new criteria for review which would expressly refer to history of abuse in assessing whether release was warranted. However, this would need to be accompanied by changes to existing bureaucratic and regulatory structures, to permit *en bloc* reviews to be accommodated.[69] Finally, legislative change to the gender-neutral construction of self-defence should be sought to prevent future incarceration of women who do not conform to the representation of battered women accepted in *Lavallee*.

Conclusion: Thoughts for Reform

How might current understandings of self-defence be reformulated to respond to the dilemmas battered women face? Elizabeth Sheehy has proposed replacing the current Criminal Code provisions on self-defence with a new gender-neutral defence of "self-preservation."[70] It would apply where the accused acted out of desperation, believing that the action represented her only option. Under such a defence the trier-of-fact would be required to assess whether the accused sought assistance in any form of protection from the state, or whether she feared retaliation.[71]

In addressing similar concerns, Christine Boyle has suggested that the trier-of-fact consider the following factors in assessing whether self-defence would be available:

(1) Were there realistic alternative means which the accused could have used to protect herself or other persons?

(2) (if relevant) With respect to (1), had the accused attempted alternatives in the past?

(3) Was she afraid of retaliation if she attempted any alternative?

(4) What was the accused's economic and psychological state?

(5) How did the accused and the person she killed or assaulted compare in size and strength?

(6) Was the accused's action reasonable, given her socialization?[72]

Both these proposals, like *Lavallee,* require a subjective belief that the woman felt under threat of death or grievous bodily harm, but provide for an objective assessment of this apprehension. However, reliance on objective criteria still runs the risk of attaching insufficient weight to the individual woman's situation and her perception of danger. Moreover, these suggestions seem to place importance on whether or not the woman has attempted to leave the dwelling. Nonetheless, balancing the objectives of protecting women and restricting cases of self-defence to those where lethal action is necessary is an incredibly difficult task. The advantage these proposals share is that they eliminate the pathologizing of women's actions.

Some recent legislative reforms in the United States have involved deeper substantive changes. California recently proposed legislation that significantly affects the range of circumstances and behaviours in which evidence relating to abuse is admissible. Included among these changes is a concept of abuse which extends beyond battery to include both sexual and psychological abuse; however, expert witnesses are still relied upon for proof.[73] Even where the evidence of abuse falls short of providing an absolute defence, such information can be considered in arriving at an appropriate sentence. However, California has already incorporated one of the changes to the process that we would advocate: namely, it has adopted legislation which specifically permits evidence of abuse to be considered in applications for commutation and clemency.

Each of these reform proposals has advantages and drawbacks. Perhaps the most satisfactory resolution would be to insist upon a contextual analysis of the homicide from the perspective of the abused woman. This could include an examination of the factors suggested by Boyle and Sheehy, as long as the analysis does not presuppose that all behaviour by abused women can be neatly charted and categorized. However, this would need to be combined with a broadened understanding of abuse to include sexual and emotional abuse by spouses. Special consideration should also be given to histories of childhood abuse that may influence events leading to homicide. Above all, any proposed Criminal Code amendment should expressly reject the premise of imminence, namely that a woman's act of self-defence can only be legitimately deployed during an attack. Nor should any criteria be adopted which would impose a duty to retreat, requiring a woman under attack to withdraw from the home rather than defend herself.[74] In particular, the articulated criteria should not import an established understanding, psychological or otherwise, of how battered women typically behave. Finally, the role of expert witnesses insofar as it is currently occupied by medical and psychological professionals needs to be displaced. Shelter workers could bring a breadth of understanding to bear on these issues.

To render intelligible the drastic measures to which some women must resort to survive violence, we need to re-analyze their circumstances and de-pathologize their behaviour. Demanding rigid adherence to symptoms which stereotype battered women must end. Moreover, legal inquiries which attempt to establish retreat or imminence of attack are counterproductive. To free abused women who have killed partners and are serving sentences, we must stop demanding strict conformity with these two principles.

Contrary to popular fears, the introduction of expert testimony on the battered woman syndrome has not produced an "open season" on men. When women feel compelled to resort to such drastic measures, society, and in particular the justice system, must take some responsibility for our collective failure to respond to calls for help and to provide a safe environment for women and children.

Notes

1 I would like to acknowledge all the assistance I have received from all the women who have been working on behalf of this project, namely: Bonnie Diamond, Kim Pate, Pam Mayhew, Lucie LaLiberte, Dawn Fleming, and Shelley Belhumeur. Special appreciation must go to Felicity Hawthorn, who conducted in-depth interviews with a number of the women, and to Joanne Connolly, who assisted invaluably with research. I would also like to thank Allan Manson for his helpful

comments on an earlier draft. Finally, I wish to thank the women in P4W who shared so much of their pain. This especially was a precious gift.

2 Iris Young, *Justice and the Politics of Difference* (Princeton: Princeton University Press, 1990), p. 63.

3 Clemency or pardon extended to individual women has now been granted in Illinois, Washington, Florida, New Jersey, Virginia, Nevada, Iowa, and Kansas.

4 Clemency was granted to twenty-six women in Ohio in December 1990 by Governor Celeste. In Maryland during February 1991, Governor Schaefer granted release to eight women who had killed abusive spouses.

5 Clemency is presently being sought for groups of women in Massachusetts, where a campaign to secure their release has been underway since 1989. In California, thirty-four women have written to the governor requesting review. In Texas, a resolution was passed in April 1991 commanding review of all women who killed in abusive situations.

6 It is worth noting here that there are a number of specific scenarios which the Criminal Code contemplates in the three sections relating to self-defence. The various self-defence provisions are reasonably complex given that the different sections establish disparate criteria as the basis for non-culpability. For an excellent discussion of the intricacies of these sections see Martha Shaffer, "*R. v. Lavallee*: A Review Essay," *Ottawa Law Review* 22 (1990): 607–624.

7 *Reilly v. R.* [1984] 2 S.C.R. 396, p. 404.

8 Ibid.

9 Ibid.

10 Susan Edwards, "Gender 'Justice'? Defendants and Mitigating Sentence," in *Gender, Sex and the Law*, ed. S. Edwards (Kent: Croom Helm, 1985), p. 144.

11 *R. v. Whynot* (1983), 37 C.R. (3d) 198 (N.S.C.A.).

12 *R. v. Lavallee* (1990), 76 C.R. (3d) 329 (S.C.C.).

13 One of the evidentiary issues was whether or not expert evidence was admissible to support the view that the accused suffered from the battered woman syndrome. The Court held that such evidence was necessary to assist a layperson of the jury in dispelling various myths about battery. Another crucial issue was whether such evidence could be introduced, as it was partially based on out-of-court interviews with the accused, yet she did not give evidence and was not subject to cross-examination at trial.

14 *R. v. Lavallee*, p. 335.

15 Specifically, the psychiatrist was relying on out-of-court interviews held with Ms. Lavallee and conversations held with her mother.

16 *R. v. Lavallee*, p. 347.

17 *State vs. Gallegos*, 719 P.2d. 1268, p. 1271 (N.M. App. 1986).

18 *R. v. Lavallee*, p. 352.

19 Ibid., p. 350.

20 Ibid., pp. 350–51.

21 Elizabeth Schneider, "Describing and Changing: Women's Self-Defense Work and the Problem of Expert Testimony on Battering," *Women's Rights Law Reporter* 9 (1986): 215.

22 Here, it must be noted that there is a systematic refusal at both the legal and the social level to explore lesbian battering and to extend legal relief to lesbians who have undergone abuse. For a thorough discussion of this issue see Ellen Faulkner, "Lesbian Abuse: The Social and Legal Realities," *Queen's Law Journal* 16 (1991): 261–86.

23 Examples of such beliefs include the following: "that battered women are masochistic, that they stay with their mates because they like beatings, that the violence fulfills a deep-seated need within each partner, or that they are free to leave such relationships if that is what they really want" (Lenore Walker, Roberta Thyfault, and Angela Browne, "Beyond the Jurors' Ken: Battered Women," *Vermont Law Review* 7 [1982]: 1–2.

24 Schneider, "Describing and Changing," p. 216.

25 For an excellent overview of these concerns see Shaffer, "*R. v. Lavallee*: A Review Essay"; Elizabeth Comack, "Women Defendants and the 'Battered Wife Syndrome': A Plea for the Sociological Imagination," *Crown Counsel Rev.* 5 (1987): 6–10; and Schneider, "Describing and Changing."

26 For discussion of the clinical issues, see Lynne Rosewater, "The Clinical and Courtroom Application of Battered Women's Personality Assessments," in *Domestic Violence on Trial: Psychological and Legal Dimensions of Family Violence*, ed. D. Sonkin (New York: Springer Publishing Co., 1987).

27 See Pat Carlen, *Women's Imprisonment* (London: Routledge & Kegan Paul, 1983); Carol Smart, *Women, Crime and Criminology: A Feminist Critique* (London: Routledge & Kegan Paul, 1977).

28 It should be noted, however, that in *R. v. Pappin* (unreported), Lavallee principles were applied in respect of a woman who had previously been sexually abused who believed she was about to be sexually assaulted by the victim.

29 In the introduction to her book, Dr. Lenore Walker states, "[a]ny woman may find herself in an abusive relationship with a man once. If it occurs a second time, and she remains in the situation, she is defined as a battered woman" (*The Battered Woman* [New York: Harper and Row, 1979], p. xv). This definition was cited with apparent approval in *R. v. Lavallee*.

30 Phyllis Crocker, "The Meaning of Equality for Battered Women Who Kill Men in Self Defense," *Harvard Women's Law Journal* 8 (1985): 122.

31 For example, in *Mullis v. State* 282 S.E.2d 334 (Ga.S.Ct, 1981), the exclusion of testimony on the battered woman syndrome was upheld where there was evidence establishing the accused's ability to fight back. While the Court did not rule directly on this issue it is noteworthy that evidence was held admissible by the same court four months earlier where the woman in question had never fought back. See *Smith v. State* 274 S.E.2d 703 (Ga.S.Ct. 1980) Ga., p. 613.

32 See *State v. Stewart* 763 P.2d 572 (Ka.S.Ct. 1988). For a discussion of this case, see Comment, "Rendering Each Woman Her Due: Can a Battered Woman Claim Self-Defense When She Kills Her Sleeping Batterer?" *University of Kansas Law Review* 38 (1989): 169–92.

33 See *State v. Martin,* 666 S.W.2d 895 (Mo.App. 1984), where a wife hired a man to kill her husband; and *Commonwealth v. Grove,* 526 A.2d 369 (Pa.Super. 1987). In the latter case, the defendant was convicted both of murder and conspiracy because her daughter had participated in the killing.

34 See, for example, *State v. Kelly* 655 P.2d 1202 at 1203 (Wash.Ct. App. 1982), where a defendant pounding on her abuser's car was taken as an indication that she was not a battered woman in spite of having sustained years of physical abuse.

35 Susan Podebradsky and Mary Triggiano-Hunt, "An Overview of Defense of Battered Women From a Post-Conviction Perspective," *Wisconsin Women's Law Journal* 4 (1988): 98.

36 For an excellent discussion of the de-politicizing force of the battered woman syndrome and other concerns, see Comack, "Women Defendants and the 'Battered Wife Syndrome'."

37 See Susan Edwards, "Battered Women Who Kill," *New Law Journal* 140 (October 1990): 1380–81; and Sue Bandalli, "Battered Wives and Provocation," *New Law Journal* 142 (February 1992): 212–13.

38 Recent figures suggest that one in six Canadian women is physically or sexually abused by her husband, ex-husband, or common-law spouse. Of these women, one in ten is abused severely. See Eugen Lupri, "Male Violence in the Home," *Canadian Social Trends* 14 (Autumn 1989): 19–21.

39 Comack, "Women Defendants and the 'Battered Wife Syndrome'," p. 9.

40 Maria Crawford and Rosemary Gartner, *Woman Killing: Intimate Femicide in Ontario, 1974–1990* (Toronto: Women We Honour Action Committee, 1992).

41 Ibid., p. 3. Intimate femicide is defined as "the killing of women by intimate

male partners." Unlike the data on homicide compiled by Statistics Canada, this includes killings of women by legal spouses, common-law partners, and boyfriends, whether current or estranged.

42 The conclusion of the Ontario study was that women killed by intimate male partners (see note 41) accounted for roughly 61 percent of adult female homicide victims, while men killed by spouses represented approximately 8 percent of adult male homicide victims. Statistics compiled by the Canadian Centre for Justice Statistics in 1991 revealed a similar pattern in Canada. In 1990, seventy-four wives (either married or living common-law) were killed by their husbands, while twenty-six husbands were killed by their wives (*Juristat* 15 [1991]: 10).

43 Crawford and Gartner, p. 52. This finding is in keeping with national data compiled by the 1982 Canadian Urban Victimization Survey, which found that separated women were much more likely to be abused than married or divorced women. See Holly Johnson, "Wife Abuse," *Canadian Social Trends* 8 (Spring 1988): 17–20.

44 Crawford and Gartner conclude that women who are separated are approximately five times more likely than other women to be the victims of intimate femicide (p. 52).

45 See George Barnard, Herman Vera, Maria Vera, and Gustav Newman, "Till Death Do Us Part: A Study of Spouse Murder," *Bulletin of the American Academy of Psychiatry and the Law* 10 (1982): 278.

46 Peter Chimbos, *Marital Violence: A Study of Interspousal Homicide* (Toronto: Holt, Rinehart and Winston Associates, 1978), p. 55.

47 Angela Browne, *When Battered Women Kill* (New York: The Free Press, 1987), p. 128.

48 Robert Silverman and S.K. Mukherjee, "Intimate Homicide: An Analysis of Violent Social Relationships," *Behavioural Sciences and the Law* 5 (1987): 38–39.

49 Elizabeth Bochnak, ed., *Women's Self Defense Cases: Theory and Practice* (Charlottesville, Virginia: The Michie Company, 1981).

50 Browne, *When Battered Women Kill*, p. 11.

51 Charles Ewing, *Battered Women Who Kill: Psychological Self-Defense as Legal Justification* (Lexington: Lexington Books, 1987).

52 *National Estimates and Facts About Domestic Violence (1989)* (Philadelphia: National Clearinghouse for the Defense of Battered Women, 1991).

53 *Battered Women and Criminal Justice: The Unjust Treatment of Battered Wom-*

en in a System Controlled By Men—A Report of the Committee on Domestic Violence and Incarcerated Women (1987) (Philadelphia: National Clearinghouse for the Defense of Battered Women, 1991).

54 Cynthia Gillespie, *Justifiable Homicide* (Columbus: Ohio State University Press, 1989), p. 186.

55 Browne, *When Battered Women Kill*, p. 126.

56 In a document prepared to assist those undertaking this effort, the following possible strategies have been suggested:

> submitting an individual petition with individually-oriented advocacy; submitting multiple individual petitions simultaneously, with joint lobbying and advocacy; requesting the governor to direct the appropriate board of pardons to review an entire class of cases which meet particular criteria; lobbying the state Legislature to request the governor to direct such a review; or other approaches. Another option could be to seek commutation for groups of individuals organized in waves at a time.... The approaches that simultaneously seek relief for a whole class of women may be especially practical in states with a large number of potentially eligible women, or where there are too few advocates to work individually, in teams with the women, or where the governor is especially receptive.

See Lisa Sheehy, Melissa Reinberg, and Deborah Kirchwey, "Commutation for Women Who Defended Themselves Against Abusive Partners: An Advocacy Manual and Guide to Legal Issues" (unpublished report available through the National Clearinghouse for the Defense of Battered Women, Philadelphia, 1991), p. 38.

57 Basically, the distinctions among these can be articulated as follows: Clemency is granted by the chief executive (e.g., a governor) in either conditional or unconditional form and typically implies forgiveness. The related pardoning power is also a manifestation of the discretion vested in the Executive. Commutation refers to the process of seeking sentence reduction for those already serving time.

58 The National Clearinghouse for the Defense of Battered Women collects information from activists and lawyers and distributes it to groups interested in mounting petitions to secure the release of battered women. The information which follows was given verbally to me from their records updated in May 1992.

59 See s.751 of the Criminal Code, which states that "[n]othing in this Act in any manner limits or affects Her Majesty's royal prerogative of mercy."

60 Allan Manson, "Answering Claims of Injustice," *Criminal Reports (4th)* 12 (1992): 305–24.

61 Ibid.

62 Section 749 of the Code acknowledges that the Governor in Council may grant a free or conditional pardon.

63 National Parole Board of Canada, *Policy and Procedures Manual* (Revised January 1988). For an overview of the Royal Prerogative of Mercy, see David Cole and Allan Manson, *Release From Imprisonment* (Toronto: Carswell, 1990).

64 In essence, successful applications for a free pardon have only been permitted where a claim was established that the convicted person was innocent in respect of the crime charged. So while it is available in theory, in practice this would be very difficult to argue because the law has changed from the time of conviction. Although grounds of undue hardship might be alleged, the case law does not appear to suggest that a free pardon is available where a sentence is unduly harsh under the circumstances. In short, to render this a truly viable option, statutory revisions should be undertaken to expressly deal with the pertinence of a history of abuse at the hands of an assailant.

65 Section 690 provides:

> The Minister of Justice may, upon an application for mercy of the Crown by or on behalf of a person who has been convicted in proceedings under indictment or who has been sentenced to preventive detention under Part XXI,
>
> (a) direct, by order in writing, a new trial or, in the case of a person under sentence or preventive detention, a new hearing, before any court that he thinks proper, if after inquiry he is satisfied that in the circumstances a new trial or hearing, as the case may be, should be directed;
>
> (b) refer the matter at any time to the court of appeal for hearing and determination by that court as if it were an appeal by the convicted person or the person under sentence of preventive detention, as the case may be; or
>
> (c) refer to the court of appeal at any time, for its opinion, any question upon which he desires the assistance of that court, and the court shall furnish its opinion accordingly.

66 See *R. v. Roberts* (1962), 39 C.R.1 (Ont. C.A.); Reference Re *R. v. Gorecki* (No. 2) (1976), 32 C.C.C.(2d) 135 (Ont. C.A.).

67 Manson, "Answering Claims of Injustice," p. 307.

68 For a very thorough discussion of these cases, and some of the difficulties with the present structure of decision-making in this area, see Manson, "Answering Claims of Injustice," p. 307. It should be noted for clarity that although Milgaard applied for a remedy pursuant to s.690, the case was not referred to the Saskatchewan Court of Appeal, but rather to the Supreme Court of Canada under s.53 of the Supreme Court Act, R.S.C. 1985, c. S-26.

69 Generally, the difficulty has been that review processes under s.690 and the

Royal Prerogative of Mercy occur on an individualized basis. Much remains unclear about the precise form of review mandated and the manner in which discretion is to be exercised; see Manson, p. 307. A further problem is that the existing post-conviction parole processes would not permit introduction of evidence pertaining to the offence for which an accused person has served time.

In short, it would be best to empower a body specifically charged with reviewing only the cases of battered women. Such a body would hopefully be more attentive to the parallel circumstances presented in individual women's cases. An attempt to pass legislation of this nature was recently vetoed by the Governor of California (1991 CA A.B. 2373). Instead, legislation was adopted which provides that:

> The Board of Prison Terms may report to the Governor, from time to time, the names of any and all persons imprisoned who, in its judgment, ought to have a commutation of sentence or be pardoned and set at liberty on account of good conduct, or unusual term of sentence, or any other cause including evidence of battered women syndrome, which, in its opinion, should entitle the prisoner to a pardon or commutation of sentence. (1991 CA A.B. 3436)

70 Elizabeth Sheehy, *Personal Autonomy and the Criminal Law: Emerging Issues For Women* (Ottawa: Canadian Advisory Council on the Status of Women, 1987) p. 40.

71 Ibid.

72 Christine Boyle et al., *A Feminist Review of Criminal Law,* ed. J. Russell (Ottawa: Minister of Supply and Services, 1985), p. 41.

73 The Bill provides that in a criminal action, expert testimony is admissible in respect of the "experiences of victims of domestic violence, battered, abused, or molested children's experiences, battered woman syndrome ... from the sequelae of the physical, emotional or sexual abuse of a child, whether or not the sequelae are labelled a syndrome, including the effects of physical, emotional or sexual abuse upon the beliefs, perceptions, or behaviour of victims of domestic violence, or child abuse..." (1993 CA A.B. 947).

74 Above all, any enactment must ensure that the central questions are not whether a woman was in immediate peril, or whether she had a suitable opportunity to leave the home.

Bibliography

Abbott, J. *In the Belly of the Beast: Letters from Prison.* New York: Vintage Books, 1982.

Aboriginal Justice Inquiry. *Justice on Trial: Report of the Aboriginal Justice Inquiry.* Winnipeg: Queen's Press, 1991.

Adelberg, Ellen. *A Forgotten Minority: Women in Conflict with the Law.* Ottawa: Canadian Association of Elizabeth Fry Societies, 1985.

Adelberg, E. and Currie, C., eds. *Too Few To Count: Canadian Women in Conflict with the Law.* Vancouver: Press Gang Publishers, 1987.

Adler, Freda. *Sisters in Crime: The Rise of the New Female Criminal.* New York: McGraw-Hill, 1975.

Akers, R. *Deviant Behavior: A Social Learning Approach.* Belmont, Cal.: Wadsworth, 1977.

Alder, P. "On Becoming a Prostitute." In *Criminal Life: Views from the Inside,* ed. David M. Peterson and Marcello Truzzi. Englewood Cliffs, N.J.: Prentice-Hall, 1972.

Axon, Lee. *Model and Exemplary Programs for Female Inmates: An International Review.* Ottawa: Solicitor General of Canada, 1989.

Backhouse, Connie. "Canadian Prostitution Law 1939–1972." In *Prostitution in Canada.* Ottawa: Canadian Advisory Council on the Status of Women, 1984.

———. "Nineteenth Century Canadian Prostitution Law: Reflection of a Discriminatory Society." *Social History* 53 (1985): 387–423.

Bandalli, Sue. "Battered Wives and Provocation." *New Law Journal* 142 (12 February 1992): 212–13.

Barfield, A. "Biological Influences on Sex Differences in Behavior." In *Sex Differences: Social and Biological Perspectives,* ed. M. Teitelbaum. Garden City, N.Y.: Anchor Books, 1976.

Barnard, George; Vera, Herman; Vera, Maria; and Newman, Gustav. "Till Death Do Us Part: A Study of Spouse Murder." *Bulletin of the American Academy of Psychiatry and the Law* 10 (1982): 271–90.

Barrett, Michele. *Women's Oppression Today: Problems in Marxist Feminist Analysis.* London: Verso & NLB, 1978.

Barry, K. *Female Sexual Slavery.* New York: Avon Books, 1979.

Battered Women and Criminal Justice: The Unjust Treatment of Battered Women in a System Controlled By Men—A Report of the Committee on Domestic Violence and Incarcerated Women (1987). Philadelphia: National Clearinghouse for the Defense of Battered Women, 1991.

Baunach, P. *Mothers in Prison.* New Brunswick, N.J.: Transaction, Inc., 1985.

Beattie, John M. "The Criminality of Women in Eighteenth-Century England." *Journal of Social History* 8 (Summer 1975): 80–116.

Beauvoir, Simone de. *The Second Sex.* Trans. H.M. Parshley. New York: Vintage Books, 1974 (original 1952).

Bell, A.; Weinberg, M.; and Hammersmith, S. *Sexual Preference: Its Development in Men and Women.* Bloomington: Indiana University Press, 1981.

Bell, Laurie. *Good Girls/Bad Girls: Sex Trade Workers and Feminists Face to Face.* Toronto: The Women's Press, 1987.

Bem, S. "The Measurement of Psychological Androgyny." *Journal of Consulting and Clinical Psychology* 42, no. 2 (1974): 155–62.

Bernstein, I.; Cardascia, J.; and Rose, C. "Defendants' Sex and Criminal Court Decisions." In *Discrimination in Organizations,* ed. R. Alvarez and K. Lutterman. San Francisco: Jossey-Bass, 1979.

Berzins, Lorraine and Cooper, Sheelagh. "The Political Economy of Correctional Planning for Women: The Case of the Bankrupt Bureaucracy." *Canadian Journal of Criminology* 24 (October 1982).

Berzins, L. and Hayes, B. "The Diaries of Two Change Agents." In *Too Few To Count: Canadian Women in Conflict with the Law,* ed. E. Adelberg and C. Currie. Vancouver: Press Gang Publishers, 1987.

Biron, L.L. "Les femmes et l'incarceration. Le temps n'arrange rien." *Criminologie* 25, no. 1 (1992): 119–34.

Bishop, D. and Frazier, C. "The Effects of Gender on Charge Reduction." *Sociologi-*

cal Quarterly 25 (Summer 1984): 385–96.

Blackbridge, Persimmon and Gilhooly, Sheila. *Still Sane.* Vancouver: Press Gang Publishers, 1985.

Bleier, R. *Science and Gender: A Critique of Biology and Its Theories on Women.* New York: Pergamon Press, 1984.

Blumstein, A. "The Influence of Capacity on Prison Population: A Critical Review of Some Recent Evidence." *Crime and Deliquency* 19 (1983): 1–51.

Bochnak, Elizabeth, ed. *Women's Self Defense Cases: Theory and Practice.* Charlottesville: The Michie Company, 1981.

Bottoms, Anthony. "Crime Prevention Facing the 1990's." *Policing and Society* 1, no. 1 (1990).

Box, S. and Hale, C. "Liberation and Female Criminality in England and Wales Revisited." *British Journal of Criminology* 22 (1983): 35–49.

Boyd, N. "Pornography, Prostitution, and the Control of Gender Relations." In *The Social Dimensions of Law,* ed. N. Boyd. Scarborough, Ont.: Prentice-Hall Canada, 1986.

Boyle, C.; Bertrand, M.-A.; Lacerte-Lamontagne, C.; and Shamai, R. "Effects of Sexism on Sentencing." In *A Feminist Review of Criminal Law,* ed. J. Russell. Ottawa: Ministry of Supply and Services Canada, 1985.

Brannigan, Augustine; Knafla, L.; and Levy, C. *Street Prostitution: Assessing the Impact of the Law—Calgary, Regina, Winnipeg.* Ottawa: Department of Justice Canada, 1989.

Brock, Debbi. "Feminist Perspectives on Prostitution: Addressing the Canadian Dilemma." Master's thesis, Sociology and Anthropology, Carleton University, Ottawa, 1984.

Brodeur, Jean Paul, with Leguerrier, Yves. *Justice for the Cree: Policing and Alternate Dispute Resolution.* Nemaska, Que.: Cree Regional Authority, 1991.

Brooks, V. *Minority Stress and Lesbian Women.* Toronto: D.C. Heath and Co., 1981.

Brown, D. and Quinn, M. "Women in Prison: Review of the New South Wales Task Force Report." *Legal Service Bulletin* (December 1985).

Browne, A. *When Battered Women Kill.* New York: The Free Press, 1987.

Browne, A. and Flewelling, R. "Women as Victims and Perpetrators of Homicide." Paper presented at the Annual General Meeting of the American Society of Criminology, Atlanta, Georgia, 29 October–1 November 1986.

Brownmiller, Susan. *Against Our Will: Men, Women and Rape.* New York: Bantam Books, 1975.

Bryant, Clifton D. and Kenneth B. Perkins. "Containing Work Disaffection: The

Poultry Processing Worker." In *Varieties of Work,* ed. P.L. Stewart and M.G. Cantor. Beverly Hills: Sage Publications, 1982.

Bureau of Municipal Research. *Civic Affairs: Street Prostitution in Our Cities.* Toronto: Author, 1983.

Burstyn, Varda, ed. *Women Against Censorship.* Vancouver: Douglas & McIntyre, 1985.

Canada. *Annual Reports of the Directors of Penitentiaries in the Dominion of Canada.* 1868–1874.

Canada. *Annual Reports of the Inspectors of Penitentiaries.* 1914–1918.

Canada. *Annual Reports of the Minister of Justice as to Penitentiaries in Canada.* 1875–1913.

Canada. *Annual Reports of the Superintendent of Penitentiaries.* 1864–1867; 1919–1938.

Canada. *Canadian Human Rights Commission. Annual Report.* Ottawa: Canadian Human Rights Commission, 1988.

Canada. *Childhood Experiences as Causes of Criminal Behaviour.* Ottawa: Proceedings of the Senate of Canada, no. 7, 1978.

Canada. *The Female Offender: Selected Statistics. Report of the National Advisory Committee on the Female Offender.* Ottawa: Solicitor General of Canada, 1977.

Canada [Upper]. *Journals of the House of Assembly.* 1833–1839.

Canada. *Journals of the Legislative Assembly.* 1840–1849.

Canada [Province of]. *Journals of the Legislative Assembly.* 1849, Appendix BBB-BB.

Canada. *Report of the Canadian Committee on Corrections* (Ouimet Report). Ottawa: Queen's Printer, 1969.

Canada. *Report of the Commission on Equality in Employment.* Ottawa: Supply and Services, 1985.

Canada. *Report of the Committee Appointed to Inquire into the Principles and Procedures Followed in the Remission Service of the Department of Justice of Canada* (Fauteux Report). Ottawa: Supply and Services, 1956.

Canada. *Report of the Committee on Sexual Offences Against Children and Youths* (Badgely Report). Ottawa: Supply and Services, 1984.

Canada. *Report of the National Advisory Committee on the Female Offender.* Ottawa: Solicitor General of Canada, 1977.

Canada. *Report of the Royal Commission on Penitentiaries.* Sessional paper no. 252, 1914.

Canada. *Report of the Royal Commission on the Status of Women in Canada.* Ottawa: Supply and Services, 1970.

Canada. *Report of the Royal Commission to Inquire and then Report upon the Conduct, Economy, Discipline and Management of the Provincial Penitentiary* (Brown Report). 1849.

Canada. *Report of the Royal Commission to Investigate the Penal System of Canada* (Archambault Report). Ottawa: King's Printer, 1938.

Canada. *Report of the Special Committee on Pornography and Prostitution.* Ottawa: Supply and Services, 1985.

Canada. *Report of the Standing Committee on Justice and Solicitor General on Its Review of Sentencing, Conditional Release and Related Aspects of Corrections* (Daubney Report). Ottawa: Supply and Services, 1988.

Canada. *Report on the State and Management of the Female Prison.* 1921.

Canada. *Report to Parliament by the Sub-Committee on the Penitentiary System in Canada* (MacGuigan Report). Ottawa: Supply and Services, 1977.

Canada. *Standing Committee on Justice and the Solicitor General. Crime Prevention in Canada: Toward a National Strategy.* Ottawa: House of Commons, no. 87, 23 February 1993.

Canada, Correctional Service of Canada. *Basic Facts About Corrections in Canada.* Ottawa: Author, 1986.

Canada, Correctional Service of Canada. "History of Crime and Punishment in Canada." *Crime and Punishment Journal* 10 (15 August 1985): 6–7.

Canada, Correctional Service of Canada. "Non-Native Population Profile Report and Native Population Profile Report." Ottawa: Solicitor General of Canada, Information Services Branch, March 1982.

Canada, Correctional Service of Canada. *Progress Report on the Federal Female Offender Program.* Ottawa: Solicitor General of Canada, 1978.

Canada, Department of Indian and Northern Affairs. *Health of Indian Women.* Ottawa: Author, 1990.

Canada, Department of Indian and Northern Affairs. *Highlights of Aboriginal Conditions, 1981–2001. Part II: Social Conditions.* Ottawa: Supply and Services, 1989.

Canada, Department of Justice. *Street Prostitution: Assessing the Impact of the Law—Synthesis Report.* Ottawa: Supply and Services, 1989.

Canada, Health and Welfare, Medical Services Branch. *Statistics and Demographics.* Ottawa. Supply and Services, 1990.

Canada, House of Commons. *Minutes of Proceedings and Evidence of the Standing Committee on Justice and Legal Affairs.* Issues no. 86, 90, and 91 (May and June 1982).

Canada, Statistics Canada. *Women in Canada: A Statistical Report.* Ottawa: Supply and Services, 1990.

Canada, Statistics Canada, Canadian Centre for Justice Statistics. *Canadian Crime Statistics* (catalogue no. 85–205). Ottawa: Author.

Canadian Advisory Council on the Status of Women. *Evaluating Child Support Policy: A Brief to the Federal/Provincial/Territorial Family Law Committee.* Ottawa: Author, 1992.

Canadian Advisory Council on the Status of Women. *On Pornography and Prostitution: A Brief Presented to the Special Committee on Pornography and Prostitution.* Ottawa: Author, 1984.

Canadian Advisory Council on the Status of Women. *Ten Years Later.* Ottawa: Author, 1979.

Canadian Council on Social Development and the Native Women's Association of Canada. *Voices of Aboriginal Women: Aboriginal Women Speak Out.* Ottawa: Canadian Council on Social Development, 1991.

Carlen, Pat. *Alternatives to Women's Imprisonment.* Philadelphia: Open University Press, 1990.

———, ed. *Criminal Women.* Cambridge, U.K.: Polity Press, 1985.

———. *Women's Imprisonment: A Study in Social Control.* London: Routledge & Kegan Paul, 1983.

Carlen, Pat and Worrall, Anne, eds. *Gender, Crime and Justice.* Philadelphia: Open University Press, 1987.

Caron, R. *Go-Boy!* Don Mills, Ont.: Thomas Nelson & Sons, 1979.

Carrington, Peter J. and Moyer, Sharon. "A Comparison of the Treatment of Prostitutes and Their Customers by the Police and Courts in Toronto, 1986–87." Paper presented at the Canadian Sociology and Anthropology Association Annual Meeting, June 1991.

Chesler, Phyllis. *Women and Madness.* New York: Doubleday & Co., 1972.

Chesney-Lind, Meda. "Chivalry Re-examined: Women and the Criminal Justice System." In *Women, Crime and the Criminal Justice System,* ed. Lee H. Bowker. Lexington: D.C. Heath, 1978.

———. "Girls' Crime and Woman's Place: Towards a Feminist Model of Female Delinquency." University of Hawaii: Youth Development and Research Center, Report no. 334, May 1987.

———. "Is Sexism a Dead Issue?" Paper presented at the Annual General Meeting of the American Society of Criminology, San Diego, California, 13–16 November 1985.

———. "Judicial Enforcement of the Female Sex Role, the Family Court and the Female Delinquent." *Issues in Criminology* 8 (Fall 1973).

——. "Re-discovering Lilith: Misogyny and the New Female Criminal." In *The Female Offender: Selected Papers from an International Symposium,* ed. Curt Taylor Griffiths and Margit Nance. Vancouver: Simon Fraser University, Criminology Research Centre, 1980.

——. "Sexist Juvenile Justice: A Continuing International Problem." *Resources for Feminist Research* 13 (December 1985–January 1986).

——. "Women and Crime: The Female Offender." *Signs* 12 (Autumn 1986): 78–96.

Chimbos, Peter. *Marital Violence: A Study of Interspousal Homicide.* Toronto: Holt, Rinehart and Winston Associates, 1978.

Chodorow, N. *The Reproduction of Mothering.* Berkeley, Cal.: University of California Press, 1978.

Clark, Lorenne. "Boys Will Be Boys: Beyond the Badgley Report, A Critical Review." In *Regulating Sex: An Anthology of Commentaries on the Findings and Recommendations of the Badgley and Fraser Reports,* ed. J. Lowman et al. Burnaby, B.C.: Simon Fraser University, School of Criminology, 1986.

Clark, Lorenne and Lewis, Debra. *Rape: The Price of Coercive Sexuality.* Toronto: The Women's Press, 1977.

Clark, L.M.G. "Feminist Perspectives on Violence Against Women and Children: Psychological, Social Service, and Criminal Justice Concerns." *Canadian Journal of Women and the Law* 3 (1989–90): 420–31.

Cohen, S. "Taking Decentralization Seriously." In his *Against Criminology.* Oxford: Transaction Books, 1988.

——. *Visions of Social Control.* Cambridge, U.K.: Polity Press, 1983.

Cole, David and Manson, Allan. *Release From Imprisonment.* Toronto: Carswell, 1990.

Cole, Susan. "Child Battery." In *No Safe Place,* ed. Connie Guberman and Margie Wolfe. Toronto: The Women's Press, 1985.

Comack, E. "Legal Recognition of the 'Battered Wife Syndrome': A Victory for Women?" Paper presented to the American Society of Criminology, San Francisco, November 1991.

Comack, Elizabeth. "Women Defendants and the 'Battered Wife Syndrome': A Plea for the Sociological Imagination." *Crown Counsel Rev.* 5 (1987): 6–10.

Comack, E. and Brickley, S., eds. *The Social Basis of Law: Critical Readings in the Sociology of Law* (2d ed.). Halifax: Garamond, 1991.

Coons, W. and McFarland, P. "Obscenity and Community Tolerance." *Canadian Psychology/Psychologie canadienne* 26, no. 1 (1985): 30–38.

Copp, D. and Wendell, S. *Pornography and Censorship.* Buffalo, N.Y.: Prometheus

Books, 1983.

Cousins, Mark. "Mens Rea: Sexual Difference and the Criminal Law." In *Radical Issues in Criminology*, ed. Pat Carlen and Mike Collison. Oxford: Martin Robertson, 1980.

Crawford, Maria and Gartner, Rosemary. *Woman Killing: Intimate Femicide in Ontario 1974–1990*. Toronto: Women We Honour Action Committee, 1992.

Crites, Laura. "Women Offenders: Myth vs. Reality." In *The Female Offender*, ed. L. Crites. Lexington: Lexington Books, 1976.

Crocker, Phyllis. "The Meaning of Equality for Battered Women Who Kill Men in Self Defense." *Harvard Women's Law Journal* 8 (1985): 121–53.

Crook, Nikita. *A Report on Prostitution in the Atlantic Provinces*. Ottawa: Department of Justice Canada, 1984.

Cruikshank, M. *Lesbian Studies: Present and Future*. Old Westbury, N.Y.: The Feminist Press, 1982.

Cullen, F.; Golden, K.; and Cullen, J. "Sex and Delinquency: A Partial Test of the Masculinity Hypothesis." *Criminology* 17 (1979): 301–10.

Curb, R. and Manahan, N. *Lesbian Nuns: Breaking Silence*. New York: Warner Books, 1985.

Currie, D. and Kline, M. "Challenging Privilege: Women, Knowledge and Feminist Struggles." *Journal of Human Justice* 2, no. 2 (1991): 1–26.

Dalton, Katharina. *Once A Month*. Glasgow: Fontana, 1978.

Daly, K. and Chesney-Lind, M. "Feminism and Criminology." *Justice Quarterly* 5, no. 4 (1988): 101–43.

Davis, K. "The Sociology of Prostitution." *American Sociological Review* 2, no. 5 (1937): 744–55.

Davis, N. and Faith, K. "Women and the State: Changing Models of Social Control." In *Transcarceration and the Modern State of Penalty*, ed. J. Lowman, R. Menzies and T. Palys. Aldershot, U.K.: Gower Publishers, 1987.

D.C. Commission on the Status of Women. "Female Offenders in the District of Columbia." Washington, D.C.: District Building, April 1972.

Dobash, R. and Dobash, R. "Wives: The 'Appropriate' Victims of Marital Violence." *Victimology: An International Journal* 2, nos. 3–4 (1977): 426–42.

Drew, D. and Drake, J. *Boys for Sale*. New York: Brown, 1969.

Dubec, Bernice. "Native Women and the Criminal Justice System: An Increasing Minority." Mimeographed. Thunder Bay: Ontario Native Women's Association, 1982.

Eaton, Mary. "Documenting the Defendant: Placing Women in Social Inquiry Reports." In *Women in Law: Explorations in Law, Family and Sexuality*, ed. Julia Brophy and Carol Smart. London: Routledge & Kegan Paul, 1985.

———. "Mitigating Circumstances: Familiar Rhetoric." *International Journal of the Sociology of Law* 11 (November 1983): 385–400.

Edwards, Susan. "Battered Women Who Kill." *New Law Journal* 140 (5 October 1990): 1380–81.

———. *Female Sexuality and the Law.* Oxford: Martin Robertson, 1981.

———. "Gender 'Justice'? Defendants and Mitigating Sentence." In *Gender, Sex and the Law,* ed. S. Edwards. Kent: Croom Helm, 1985.

Ekstedt, John W. and Griffiths, Curt T. *Corrections in Canada: Policy and Practice.* Toronto: Butterworths, 1984.

Evans, M. *A Survey of Institutional Programmes Available to Federally Sentenced Women.* Ottawa: Correctional Service of Canada, 1989.

Ewing, Charles. *Battered Women Who Kill: Psychological Self-Defense as Legal Justification.* Lexington: Lexington Books, 1987.

Fagan, Jeffrey and Wexler, Sandra. "Family Origins of Violent Delinquents." *Criminology* 25, no. 3 (1987): 643–49.

Faith, Karlene. *Inside/Outside.* Culver City, Cal.: Peace Press, 1976.

———. "Love Between Women in Prison." In *Lesbian Studies: Present and Future,* ed. M. Cruikshank. Old Westbury, N.Y.: The Feminist Press, 1982.

———, ed. *Soledad Prison: University of the Poor.* Palo Alto, Cal.: Science & Behavior Books, 1975.

———. *Unruly Women: The Politics of Confinement and Resistance.* Vancouver: Press Gang Publishers, 1993 (in press).

Faulkner, Ellen. "Lesbian Abuse: The Social and Legal Realities." *Queen's Law Journal* 16 (1991): 261–86.

Feinman, Clarice. *Women in the Criminal Justice System.* New York: Praeger, 1980.

Finnie, Ross. "Women, Men, and the Economic Consequences of Divorce: Evidence from Canadian Longitudinal Data." *Canadian Review of Sociology and Anthropology* 30, no. 2 (1993): 205–41.

Firestone, Shulamith. *The Dialectic of Sex.* New York: Bantam Books, 1970.

Fleishman, John. *A Report on Prostitution in Ontario.* Ottawa: Department of Justice Canada, 1984.

Flowers, Ronald B. *Women and Criminality: The Woman as Victim, Offender and Practitioner.* New York: Greenwood Press, 1987.

Forbes, G. *Street Prostitution in Vancouver's West End.* Vancouver: Vancouver Police Department, 1977.

Fraser, Paul et al. *Pornography and Prostitution in Canada. Report of the Special Committee on Pornography and Prostitution, vol. 2.* Ottawa: Supply and Services Canada, 1985.

Fox, J. *Organizational and Racial Conflict in Maximum Security Prisons.* Lexington, Mass.: D.C. Heath and Co., 1982.

Freedman, Estelle. *Their Sisters' Keepers: Women's Prison Reform in America, 1830–1930.* Ann Arbor: University of Michigan Press, 1981.

Freedman, Lisa. "Wife Assault." In *No Safe Place,* ed. Connie Guberman and Margie Wolfe. Toronto: The Women's Press, 1985.

Freud, Sigmund. *New Introductory Lectures on Psychoanalysis.* Trans. and ed. J. Strachney. New York: W.W. Norton & Co., 1933.

Gannagé, Charlene. *Double Day, Double Bind: Women Garment Workers.* Toronto: The Women's Press, 1986.

Geller, Gloria. "Young Women in Conflict with the Law." In *Too Few To Count: Canadian Women in Conflict with the Law,* ed. E. Adelberg and C. Currie. Vancouver: Press Gang Publishers, 1987.

Gelsthorpe, Loraine and Morris, Allison, eds. *Feminist Perspectives in Criminology.* Philadelphia: Open University Press, 1990.

Gemme, R.; Murphy, A.; Bourque, M.; Nemeh, M.-R.; and Payment, N. *A Report on Prostitution in Quebec.* Ottawa: Department of Justice Canada, 1984.

Gemme, Robert; Payment, N.; and Malenfant, L. *Street Prostitution: Assessing the Impact of the Law—Montreal.* Ottawa: Department of Justice Canada, 1989.

Genders, E. and Player, E. "Women's Imprisonment: The Effects of Youth Custody." *British Journal of Criminology* 26 (October 1986): 357–71.

Giallombardo, R. *Society of Women: A Study of a Women's Prison.* New York: John Wiley & Sons, 1966.

Gibbs, J. "Violence in Prison: Its Extent, Nature and Consequences." In *Critical Issues in Corrections: Problems, Trends and Prospects,* ed. R. Roberg and V. Webb. St. Paul, Minn.: West, 1981.

Gillespie, Cynthia. *Justifiable Homicide.* Columbus: Ohio State University Press, 1989.

Gilligan, C. *In a Different Voice.* Cambridge: Harvard University Press, 1982.

Giordano, P. and Cernkovich, S. "On Complicating the Relationship Between Liberation and Delinquency." *Social Problems* 26 (1979): 467–81.

Glueck, S. and Glueck, E. *Five Hundred Delinquent Women.* New York: Alfred A. Knopf, 1934.

Gomme, Ian M. et al. "Rates, Types and Patterns of Male and Female Delinquency in an Ontario County." *Canadian Journal of Criminology* 26 (July 1984): 313–24.

Graves, F. *Street Prostitution: Assessing the Impact of the Law—Halifax.* Ottawa: Department of Justice Canada, 1989.

Gray, D. "Turning Out: A Study of Teenage Prostitution." *Urban Life and Culture* 1, no. 4 (1973): 401–26.

Greenwald, H. *The Elegant Prostitute.* New York: Ballantine, 1970.

Greenwood, Victoria. "The Myths of Female Crime." In *Women and Crime* (Cropwood Conference Series No. 13), ed. A. Morris and L. Gelsthorpe. Cambridge: Institute of Criminology, 1981.

Gregory, Jean. "Sex, Class and Crime: Towards a Non-Sexist Criminology." In *The Political Economy of Crime: Readings for a Critical Criminology,* ed. Brian D. Maclean. Scarborough, Ont.: Prentice-Hall, 1986.

Grier, Barbara and Reid, C. *Lesbian Lives: Biographies of Women from The Ladder.* Oakland, Cal.: Diana Press, 1976.

Griffin, Susan. "Rape: The All American Crime." In *Feminism and Philosophy,* ed. M. Vetterling-Braggin, F. Elliston and J. English. Totowa, N.J.: Littlefield, Adams & Co., 1977.

———. *Women and Nature: The Roaring Inside Her.* New York: Harper & Row, 1978.

Griffiths, C.T. and Verdun-Jones, S. *Canadian Criminal Justice.* Toronto: Butterworths, 1989.

Grossman, Michelle G. "Aboriginal Female Suicides in Custody." Unpublished paper, July 1992.

———. "Aboriginal Women in Canada: Socio-Economic, Cultural and Demographic Review." Unpublished paper, Department of Justice, Ottawa, 1991.

Gruhl, J. and Welch, S. "Women as Criminal Defendants: A Test for Paternalism." *Western Political Quarterly* 37 (September 1984): 456–67.

Haft, M. "Women in Prison: Discriminatory Practices and Some Legal Solutions." *Clearinghouse Review* (May 1974).

Hann, R. and Harman, W. "Full Parole Release: An Historical Descriptive Analysis." Ottawa: Ministry of the Solicitor General, 1986.

Harding, Jim. "Unemployment, Racial Discrimination and Public Drunkenness in Regina." Unpublished paper, Faculty of Social Work, University of Regina, 1984.

Hatch, Alison and Faith, Karlene. "The Female Offender in Canada." Paper presented at the Annual Meeting of the American Society of Criminology, San Diego, California, 13–17 November 1985.

———. "The Female Offender in Canada: A Statistical Profile." *Canadian Journal of Women and the Law* 3 (1989–90): 432–56.

———. "The Female Offender in Canada: A Statistical Profile." In *Crime in Canadian Society* (4th ed.), ed. R.A. Silverman, J.J. Teevan, Jr., and V.F. Sacco. Toronto: Butterworths, 1991.

Hattem, T. "L'Histoire se poursuit..." *Femmes et Justice* (Organe d'information de la Societé Elizabeth Fry de Montréal) 5, no. 5 (June 1990).

Hazelhurst, Kayleen M. "Passion and Policy: Aboriginal Deaths in Custody in Australia 1980–1989." In *Crimes by the Capitalist State,* ed. Gregg Barak. New York: State University of New York Press, 1991.

Heney, Jan. *Report on Self-Injurious Behaviour in the Kingston Prison for Women.* Ottawa: Correctional Service of Canada, 1990.

Henley, N. *Body Politics: Power, Sex and Nonverbal Communication.* Englewood Cliffs, N.J.: Prentice-Hall, 1977.

Henricson, Clem. *Tackling the Causes of Crime: Labour's Crime Management Policy for the 1990's.* London: British Labour Party, 1991.

Henriques, Z.W. *Imprisoned Mothers and Their Children.* New York: University Press of America, 1982.

Hill, Christina M. "Women in the Canadian Economy." In *The Political Economy of Dependency,* ed. Robert Laxer. Toronto: McClelland and Stewart, 1973.

Hills, S. "Rape and the Masculine Mystique." In *Gender Roles: Doing What Comes Naturally?* ed. E. Salamon and B. Robinson. Toronto: Methuen Publications (Carswell Co. Ltd.), 1987.

Hirshi, T. "The Professional Prostitute." *Berkeley Journal of Sociology* 7 (1969): 37–41.

Hite, S. *The Hite Report: A Nationwide Study of Female Sexuality.* New York: Dell Publishing Co., 1976.

Irwin, J. *Prisons in Turmoil.* Boston: Little, Brown and Co., 1980.

Jackson, M. *Justice Behind the Walls.* Ottawa: Canadian Bar Association, 1988.

———. *Prisoners of Isolation: Solitary Confinement in Canada.* Toronto: University of Toronto Press, 1983.

James, Jennifer et al. *The Politics of Prostitution.* Seattle, Wash.: Social Research Associates, 1975.

Jefferson, Christie. "The Female Offender: A Status of Women Issue." *Canadian Association of Elizabeth Fry Societies Newsletter* 10 (March 1984).

Jennes, Valerie. "From Sex as Sin to Sex as Work." *Social Problems* 37, no. 3 (1990): 403–20.

Johnson, Brian. "Women Behind Bars." *Equinox* (March/April 1984).

Johnson, Holly. "Wife Abuse." *Canadian Social Trends* 8 (Spring 1988): 17–20.

———. *Women and Crime in Canada.* Ottawa: Solicitor General of Canada, 1986.

Jones, Ann. *Women Who Kill.* New York: Holt, Rinehart & Winston, 1980.

Kellough, Gail. "From Colonialism to Imperialism: The Experience of Canadian Indians." In *Structured Inequality in Canada,* ed. John Harp and John R. Hofley.

Scarborough, Ont.: Prentice-Hall, 1980.

Kershaw, Anne and Lasovich, Mary. *Rock-A-Bye-Baby: A Death Behind Bars.* Toronto: McClelland and Stewart, 1991.

Kinsey, A.: Pomeroy, C.; Martin, C.; and Gebhard, P. *Sexual Behavior in the Human Female.* Philadelphia: W.B. Saunders Co., 1953.

Klaits, J. *Servants of Satan: The Age of the Witch Hunt.* Bloomington: Indiana University Press, 1985.

Klein, Dorie. "The Etiology of Women's Crime: A Review of the Literature." *Issues in Criminology* 8 (Fall 1973): 3–30.

Klein, Dorie and Kress, June. "Any Woman's Blues: A Critical Overview of Women, Crime and the Criminal Justice System." *Crime and Social Justice* 5 (Spring/Summer 1976): 34–49.

Krause, K. "Denial of Work Release Programs to Women: A Violation of Equal Protection." *Southern California Law Review* 47 (1974): 14–18.

Landau, B. "The Adolescent Female Offender: Our Dilemma." *Canadian Journal of Criminology and Corrections* 17 (1975): 146–53.

LaPrairie, Carol. *Dimensions of Aboriginal Over-representation in Correctional Institutions and Implications for Crime Prevention* (Aboriginal Peoples Collection). Ottawa: Ministry of the Solicitor General, Corrections Branch, 1993.

———. *Exploring the Boundaries of Justice: Aboriginal Justice in the Yukon. Report to the Department of Justice, Yukon Territorial Government.* Ottawa: First Nations, Yukon Territory and Justice Canada, 1992.

———. "Selected Criminal Justice and Socio-Demographic Data on Native Women." *Canadian Journal of Criminology* 26 (April 1984): 161–69.

LaPrairie, Carol Pitcher, with the assistance of Leguerrier, Yves. *Justice for the Cree: Communities, Crime and Order.* Nemaska, Que.: Cree Regional Authority, 1991.

Larson, J. and Nelson, J. "Women, Friendship, and Adaptation to Prison." *Journal of Criminal Justice* 12 (1984): 601–15.

Larson, N. "Canadian Prostitution Control between 1914 and 1970: An Exercise in Chauvinist Reasoning." *Canadian Journal of Law and Society* 7, no. 2 (1992): 137–56.

Lavell, Alfred. "The History of Prisons of Upper Canada." Mimeographed. Kingston: Queen's University, 1948.

Laws, J. and Schwartz, P. *Sexual Scripts: The Social Construction of Female Sexuality.* Hinsdale, Ill.: Dryden Press, 1977.

Leonard, Eileen. *Women, Crime and Society: A Critique of Theoretical Criminology.* New York: Longman Inc., 1982.

Lewis, D. "Black Women Offenders and Criminal Justice." In *Comparing Female and Male Offenders,* ed. M. Warren. Beverly Hills, Cal.: Sage Publications, 1981.

Lloyd, R. *For Money or Love: Boy Prostitution in America.* New York: Ballantine, 1972.

Lockwood, D. *Prison Sexual Violence.* New York: Elsevier, 1980.

Lombroso, Cesare and Ferrero, Enrico. *The Female Offender.* New York: D. Appleton, 1900.

Lowman, J. "Images of Discipline in Prison." In *The Social Dimensions of Law,* ed. N. Boyd. Scarborough, Ont.: Prentice-Hall Canada, 1986.

Lowman, J.; Jackson, M.; Palys, T.; and Gavigan, S., eds. *Regulating Sex: An Anthology of Commentaries on the Findings and Recommendations of the Badgley and Fraser Reports.* Burnaby, B.C.: Simon Fraser University, School of Criminology, 1986.

Lowman, John. "Street Prostitution." In *Deviance: Conformity and Control in Canadian Society,* ed. V.F. Sacco. Scarborough, Ont.: Prentice-Hall, 1989.

———. *Street Prostitution: Assessing the Impact of the Law—Vancouver.* Ottawa: Department of Justice Canada, 1989.

———. *Vancouver Field Study of Prostitution: Research Notes.* Ottawa: Department of Justice Canada, 1984.

Lupri, Eugen. "Male Violence in the Home." *Canadian Social Trends* 14 (Autumn 1989): 19–21.

MacDonald, Maggie with Gould, Allan. *The Violent Years of Maggie MacDonald: An Autobiography.* Scarborough, Ont.: Prentice-Hall Canada, 1987.

MacKinnon, Catherine. *Sexual Harassment of Working Women.* New Haven: Yale University Press, 1979.

———. *Toward a Feminist Theory of the State.* Cambridge: Harvard University Press, 1989.

MacLeod, Linda. *Battered But Not Beaten: Preventing Wife Battering in Canada.* Ottawa: Canadian Advisory Council on the Status of Women, 1987.

———. *Sentenced to Separation: An Exploration of the Needs and Problems of Mothers Who are Offenders and their Children* (User Report No. 1986–25). Ottawa: Solicitor General of Canada, 1986.

———. *Wife Battering in Canada. The Vicious Circle.* Ottawa: Canadian Advisory Council on the Status of Women, 1980.

Manson, Allan. "Answering Claims of Injustice." *Criminal Reports* (4th) 12 (1992): 305–24.

Martin, Del. *Battered Wives.* San Francisco: Glide Publications, 1976.

Masters, W. and Johnson, V. *Human Sexual Inadequacy.* Boston: Little, Brown and

Co., 1970.

McDonnell, Roger. *Customary Beliefs and Practices.* Nemaska, Que.: Cree Regional Authority, 1992.

McIntosh, Mary. "Review Symposium: Women, Crime and Criminology." *British Journal of Criminology* 17 (October 1977).

McKillop, Barry and Clarke, Michelle. *Safer Tomorrow Begins Today.* Ottawa: Canadian Council on Children and Youth, 1989.

McLaren, John P.S. "Chasing the Social Evil: Moral Fervour and the Evolution of Canada's Prostitution Laws, 1867–1917." *Canadian Journal of Law and Society* 1 (1986): 125–65.

McLeod, Eileen. *Working Women: Prostitution Now.* London: Cromm Ltd., 1982.

McNeil, Gerard and Vance, Sharon. *Cruel and Unusual.* Toronto: Deneau & Greenberg, 1978.

Mendelsohn, Robert S. *Mal(e) practice: How Doctors Manipulate Women.* Chicago: Contemporary Books, 1981.

Messerchmidt, J. *Capitalism, Patriarchy and Crime: Toward a Socialist Feminist Criminology.* Totowa, N.J.: Rowman & Littlefield, 1986.

Miller, E. "International Trends in the Study of Female Criminality: An Essay Review." *Contemporary Crises* 7 (1983): 59–70.

Moffat, K.H. "Creating Choices or Repeating History: Canadian Female Offenders and Correctional Reform." *Social Justice* 18, no. 3 (1991): 184–203.

Mohr, Renate M. "Sentencing as a Gendered Process: Results of a Consultation." *Canadian Journal of Criminology* 32 (1990): 479–85.

———. *Sentencing in Context: Revealing the Realities of Women in Conflict with the Law.* Ottawa: Canadian Association of Elizabeth Fry Societies, 1988.

Money, J. and Erhardt, A. *Man and Woman, Boy and Girl.* Baltimore, Maryland: Johns Hopkins University Press, 1972.

Money, J. and Tucker, P. *Sexual Signatures: On Being a Man or a Woman.* Boston: Little, Brown and Co., 1975.

Morgan, E. "The Eroticization of Male Dominance/Female Submission." In *Papers in Women's Studies 11.* Ann Arbor: University of Michigan, Women's Studies Program, 1975.

Morgan, Robin. *Sisterhood is Powerful: An Anthology of Writings From the Women's Liberation Movement.* New York: Vintage Books, 1970.

Morris, Allison. *Women, Crime and Criminal Justice.* New York: B. Blackwell, 1987.

Morris, Allison and Gelsthorpe, Loraine. "False Clues and Female Crime." In *Women and Crime* (Cropwood Conference Series No. 13), ed. Allison Morris and

Loraine Gelsthorpe. Cambridge: Institute of Criminology, 1981.

Moyer, Sharon. *Homicides Involving Adult Suspects, 1962–1984: A Comparison of Natives and Non-Natives* (User Report No. 1987–29). Ottawa: Ministry of the Solicitor General, 1987.

Moyer, Sharon and Carrington, Peter J. *Street Prostitution: Assessing the Impact of the Law—Toronto.* Ottawa: Department of Justice Canada, 1989.

Naffine, Ngaire. *Female Crime: The Construction of Women in Criminology.* Boston: Allen & Unwin, 1987.

Nagel, I. and Hagan, J. "Gender and Crime: Offense Patterns and Criminal Court Sanctions." In *Crime and Justice: An Annual Review of Research,* ed. N. Morris and M. Tonry. Chicago: University of Chicago Press, 1983.

National Action Committee on the Status of Women. *Prostitution: A Brief presented to the Special Committee on Pornography and Prostitution.* Ottawa: Author, 1984.

National Council of Welfare. *Poverty Profile Update for 1991.* Ottawa: Author, Winter 1993.

National Estimates and Facts About Domestic Violence (1989) Philadelphia: National Clearinghouse for the Defense of Battered Women, 1991.

Norland, S. and Shover, N. "Gender Roles and Female Criminality: Some Critical Comments." *Criminology* 15 (1977): 87–104:

Nova Scotia. *Blueprint for Change. Report of the Solicitor General's Special Committee on Provincially Incarcerated Women.* Halifax: Province of Nova Scotia, 1992.

Overall, Christine. "What's Wrong with Prostitution? Evaluating Sex Work." *Signs: Journal of Women in Culture and Society* 17, no. 4 (1992): 705–24.

Pateman, Carole. *The Sexual Contract.* Stanford: Stanford University Press, 1988.

Pearce, F. "How to be Immoral and Ill, Pathetic and Dangerous, All at the Same Time: Mass Media and the Homosexual." In *Manufacture of News: Social Problems, Deviance and the Mass Media,* ed. S. Cohen and J. Young. London: Constable and Co., 1973.

Penfold, P. Susan and Walker, Gillian. *Women and the Psychiatric Paradox.* Montreal: Eden Press, 1983.

Pheterson, Gail. *A Vindication of the Rights of Whores.* Seattle, Wash.: The Seal Press, 1989.

Pizzey, Erin. *Scream Quietly or the Neighbors Will Hear.* Harmondsworth, Middlesex: Penguin Books, 1974.

Podebradsky, Susan and Triggiano-Hunt, Mary. "An Overview of Battered Women From a Post-Conviction Perspective." *Wisconsin Women's Law Journal* 4

(1988): 95–115.

Poff, Deborah C. "Feminism and Canadian Justice: How Far Have We Come?" *Journal of Human Justice* 2 (Autumn 1990): 93–104.

Pollak, Otto. *The Criminality of Women.* Philadelphia: University of Pennsylvania Press, 1950.

Pollock-Byrne, Jocelyn M. *Women, Prison and Crime.* Pacific Grove, Cal.: Brooks/ Cole Publishing, 1990.

Prins, Herschel. *Offenders: Deviants or Patients?* London: Tavistock Publications, 1980.

Propper, A. *Prison Homosexuality: Myth and Reality.* Lexington, Mass.: D.C. Heath and Co. (Lexington Books), 1981.

Rafter, Nicole H. *Partial Justice: Women in State Prisons, 1800–1935.* Boston: Northeastern University Press, 1985.

Rafter, Nicole H. and Natalizia, Elena. "Marxist Feminism: Implications for Criminal Justice." *Crime and Delinquency* 27 (January 1981).

Razack, Sherene. *Canadian Feminism and the Law.* Toronto: Second Story Press, 1991.

Reston, J. *The Innocence of Joan Little: A Southern Mystery.* New York: Bantam Books, 1977.

Robertson, Heather. *Reservations are for Indians.* Toronto: James Lewis and Samuel, 1970.

Rock, P. *A View from the Shadows: The Ministry of the Solicitor General of Canada and the Justice for Victims of Crime Initiative.* Oxford: Clarendon Press, 1966.

Rosenblatt, E. and Greenland, C. "Female Crimes of Violence." *Canadian Journal of Criminology and Corrections* 16 (1974): 173–80.

Rosewater, Lynne. "The Clinical and Courtroom Application of Battered Women's Personality Assessment." In *Domestic Violence on Trial: Psychological and Legal Dimensions of Family Violence,* ed. D. Sonkin. New York: Springer Publishing, 1987.

Ross, Robert R. and Fabiano, E.A. *Correctional Afterthoughts: Programs for Female Offenders.* Ottawa: Solicitor General of Canada, 1985.

Rubin, Gayle. "Thinking Sex: Notes for a Radical Theory of the Politics of Sexuality." In *Pleasure and Danger: Exploring Female Sexuality,* ed. C.S. Vance. Boston: Routledge & Kegan Paul, 1984.

Russell, D. *Marital Rape.* New York: Macmillan/Collier, 1982.

——. *The Politics of Rape.* New York: Stein & Day, 1975.

Salamon, E. and Robinson, B., eds. *Gender Roles: Doing What Comes Naturally?* Toronto: Methuen Publications (Carswell Co. Ltd.), 1987.

Sansfaçon, Daniel. *Prostitution in Canada: A Research Review Report.* Ottawa: Department of Justice Canada, 1984.

Schneider, Elizabeth. "Describing and Changing: Women's Self-Defense Work and the Problem of Expert Testimony on Battering." *Women's Rights Law Reporter* 9 (1986): 195–222.

Schroeder, Andreas. *Shaking It Rough: A Prison Memoir.* Toronto: Doubleday, 1976.

Schur, Edwin. *Labeling Women Deviant.* Philadelphia: Temple University Press, 1984.

Schwartz, M. "Gender and Injury in Spousal Assault." *Sociological Focus* 20 (January 1987): 61–75.

Scutt, Jocelynne A. "Debunking the Theory of the Female 'Masked Criminal'." *Australia and New Zealand Journal of Criminology* 11 (March 1978): 23–42.

———. "Sexism in Criminal Law." In *Women and Crime,* ed. S.K. Mukerjee and Jocelynne A. Scutt. Sydney: Australia Institute of Criminology/George Allen and Unwin, 1981.

Shafer, C. and Frye, M. "Rape and Respect." In *Women and Crime,* ed. M. Vetterling-Braggin, F. Elliston and J. English. Totowa, N.J.: Littlefield, Adams & Co., 1977.

Shaffer, Martha. "*R. v. Lavallee*: A Review Essay." *Ottawa Law Review* 22 (1990): 607–24.

Shaver, Frances M. "A Critique of the Feminist Charges Against Prostitution." *Atlantis* 4, no. 1 (1988): 82–89.

———. "Prostitution: A Critical Analysis of Three Policy Approaches." *Canadian Public Policy* 11, no. 3 (1985): 493–503.

———. "The Regulation of Prostitution: Avoiding the Morality Traps." *Canadian Journal of Law and Society,* forthcoming.

Shaw, Margaret. *The Federal Female Offender: Report on a Preliminary Study.* Ottawa: Solicitor General of Canada, 1990.

———. "Issues of Power and Control: Women In Prison and Their Defenders." *British Journal of Criminology* 32, no. 4 (1992): 438–52.

———. *Ontario Women in Conflict with the Law: A Survey of Women in Institutions and Under Community Supervision in Ontario.* Toronto: Ontario Ministry of Correctional Services, 1993.

Shaw, Margaret et al. *Paying the Price: Federally Sentenced Women in Context.* Ottawa: Solicitor General of Canada, 1991.

———. *The Release Study: Survey of Federally Sentenced Women in the Community.* Ottawa: Solicitor General of Canada, 1990.

———. *Survey of Federally Sentenced Women.* Ottawa: Solicitor General of Canada, 1990.

Shaw, Nancy. "The Female Offender." In *Judge, Lawyer, Victim, Thief: Women, Gender Roles and Criminal Justice,* ed. Nicole H. Rafter and Elizabeth A. Stanko. Boston: Northeastern University Press, 1982.

———. "Female Patients and the Medical Profession in Jails and Prisons: A Case of Quintuple Jeopardy." In *Judge, Lawyer, Victim, Thief: Women, Gender Roles and Criminal Justice,* ed. Nicole H. Rafter and Elizabeth A. Stanko. Boston: Northeastern University Press, 1982.

Sheehy, Elizabeth. *Personal Autonomy and the Criminal Law: Emerging Issues for Women.* Ottawa: Canadian Advisory Council on the Status of Women, 1987.

Sheehy, Lisa; Reinberg, Melissa; and Kirchwey, Deborah. "Commutation for Women Who Defended Themselves Against Abusive Partners: An Advocacy Manual and Guide to Legal Issues." Unpublished paper, available through the National Clearinghouse for the Defense of Battered Women, Philadelphia, 1991.

Silverman, Robert and Mukherjee, S.K. "Intimate Homicide: An Analysis of Violent Social Relationships." *Behavioural Sciences and the Law* 5 (1987): 37–47.

Simon, Rita. *Women and Crime.* Toronto: Lexington Books, 1975.

Simpson, S. "Feminist Theory, Crime and Justice." *Criminology* 27, no. 4 (1989): 605–31.

Skogan, Wesley. *Recent Research on Urban Safety, Drugs and Crime Prevention in the United States: A Report Submitted to the Scientific Committee of the Second International Conference on Urban Safety, Drugs and Crime Prevention.* Ottawa: Federation of Canadian Municipalities, 1988.

Smart, Carol. *Feminism and the Power of Law.* London: Routledge, 1989.

———. "Legal Subjects and Sexual Objects: Ideology, Law and Female Sexuality." In *Women in Law: Explorations in Law, Family and Sexuality,* ed. Julia Brophy and Carol Smart. London: Routledge & Kegan Paul, 1985.

———. "The New Female Criminal: Reality or Myth?" *British Journal of Criminology* 19 (January 1979): 40–59.

———. *Women, Crime and Criminology: A Feminist Critique.* London: Routledge & Kegan Paul, 1976.

Smart, Carol and Smart, Barry. *Women, Sexuality and Social Control.* London: Routledge & Kegan Paul, 1978.

Smith, Dorothy and David, Sara, eds. *Women Look at Psychiatry.* Vancouver: Press Gang Publishers, 1975.

Snider, L. "The Potential of the Criminal Justice System to Promote Feminist Concerns." In the *Social Basis of Law: Critical Readings in the Sociology of Law,* ed.

E. Comack and S. Brickley. Halifax: Garamond, 1991.

Spohn, C.; Gruhl, J.; and Welch, S. "The Impact of the Ethnicity and Gender of Defendants on the Decision to Reject or Dismiss Felony Charges." *Criminology* 25 (February 1987): 175–91.

Steele, Lisa. "A Capital Idea: Gendering in the Mass Media." In *Women Against Censorship,* ed. Varda Burstyn. Vancouver: Douglas & McIntyre, 1985.

Steffensmeier, D. "Crime and the Contemporary Woman: An Analysis of Changing Levels of Female Property Crimes, 1960–1975." In *Women and Crime in America,* ed. L. Bowker. New York: Macmillan, 1981.

Steinmetz, S. "The Battered Husband Syndrome." *Victimology* 2 (1977/78): 499–509.

Stoller, R. *Sex and Gender: On the Development of Masculinity and Femininity.* London: Hogarth Press, 1968.

Straus, M.; Gelles, R.; and Steinmetz, S. *Behind Closed Doors.* Garden City, N.Y.: Anchor Books, 1980.

Sugar, Fran and Fox, Lana. *Survey of Federally Sentenced Aboriginal Women in the Community.* Ottawa: Native Women's Association of Canada, 1990.

Task Force on Federally Sentenced Women. *Creating Choices: The Report of the Task Force on Federally Sentenced Women.* Ottawa: Correctional Service of Canada, 1990.

Taylor, Ian. *Law and Order: Arguments for Socialism.* London: Macmillan, 1981.

Teitelbaum, M. *Sex Differences: Social and Biological Perspectives.* Garden City, N.Y.: Doubleday, 1976.

Tightwire. Magazine published by women at Prison for Women, Kingston: July 1989 and Summer 1992.

Toronto Rape Crisis Centre. "Rape." In *No Safe Place,* ed. Connie Guberman and Margie Wolfe. Toronto: The Women's Press, 1985.

Trevethan, Shelley. *Aboriginal Crime in Urban Centres.* Ottawa: Canadian Centre for Justice Statistics, 1992.

Usher, Peter J. "A Northern Perspective on the Informal Economy." *Perspectives* (1980).

Valentine, Victor. "Native People and Canadian Society: A Profile of Issues and Trends." In *Cultural Boundaries and the Cohesion of Canada,* ed. R. Breton, J. Reitz and V. Valentine. Montreal: Institute of Research on Public Policy, 1980.

Valverde, Mariana. "Feminist Perspectives on Criminology." In *Criminology: A Reader's Guide,* ed. J. Gladstone, R. Ericson and C. Shearing. Toronto: University of Toronto, Centre of Criminology, 1991.

Walford, Bonnie. *Lifers: The Stories of Eleven Women Serving Life Sentences for Murder.* Montreal: Eden Press, 1987.

Walker, Lenore. *The Battered Woman.* New York: Harper & Row, 1979.

———. *Terrifying Love: Why Battered Women Kill and How Society Responds.* New York: Harper & Row, 1989.

Walker, Lenore; Thyfault, Roberta; and Browne, Angela. "Beyond the Jurors' Ken: Battered Women." *Vermont Law Review* 7 (1982): 1–14.

Walker, Nigel. *Crime and Insanity in England. Vol. 1: The Historical Perspective.* Edinburgh: Edinburgh University Press, 1968.

Ward, D. and Kassebaum, G. *Women's Prison: Sex and Social Structure.* Chicago: Aldine Publishing Co., 1965.

Wardell, Walter I. "The Reduction of Strain in a Marginal Social Role." In *Problems in Social Psychology,* ed. Carl W. Backman and Paul S. Secord. New York: McGraw-Hill, 1966.

Webber, Marlene. *Street Kids: The Tragedy of Canada's Runaways.* Toronto: University of Toronto Press, 1991.

Weis, Joseph G. "Liberation and Crime: The Invention of the New Female Criminal." *Crime and Social Justice* 6 (Fall–Winter 1976): 17–27.

Weisheit, Ralph and Mahan, Sue. *Women, Crime and Criminal Justice.* Cincinnati, Ohio: Anderson Publishing Co., 1988.

West, Gordon. *Young Offenders and the State: A Canadian Perspective on Delinquency.* Toronto: Butterworths, 1984.

Whip, Kathleen. "Wife Battering on Indian Reserves: Application of Germain's Ecological Perspective." Unpublished paper, Carleton University, 1985.

White, P.M. *Native Women: A Statistical Review.* Ottawa: Secretary of State, 1985.

Widom, Cathy Spatz. "Early Indicators: How Early, and What Indicators?" *Forum* 3, no. 3 (1991): 5–6.

———. "Perspectives of Female Criminality: A Critical Examination of Assumptions." In *Women and Crime* (Cropwood Conference Series No. 13), ed. Allison Morris and Loraine Gelsthorpe. Cambridge: Institute of Criminology, 1981.

Winslow, R. and Winslow, V. *Deviant Reality.* Boston: Allyn and Bacon, 1974.

Wolfe, N.; Cullen, F.; and Cullen, J. "Describing the Female Offender: A Note on the Demographics of Arrests." *Journal of Criminal Justice* 12 (1984): 483–92.

Wolfgang, M. and Ferracutti, F. *The Subculture of Violence: Towards an Integrated Theory in Criminology.* London: Tavistock Publications, 1967.

Women for Justice. "Brief to the Canadian Human Rights Commission." Ottawa: Author, 1980.

Worrall, Anne. *Offending Women: Female Lawbreakers and the Criminal Justice System.* New York: Routledge, 1990.

Young, I. "Humanism, Gynocentrism and Feminist Politics." *Women's Studies International Forum* 8 (1985): 173–83.

Young, Iris. *Justice and the Politics of Difference.* Princeton: Princeton University Press, 1990.

Index

Contributors

(*left to right*) Claudia Currie and Ellen Adelberg

ELLEN ADELBERG is the public affairs coordinator for the Canadian Advisory Council on the Status of Women. She has an Honours B.A. in Journalism and a master's degree in Social Work from Carleton University, has done research and written articles on women offenders, and worked for two years as a halfway house director for the Elizabeth Fry Society of Ottawa.

CLAUDIA CURRIE has a master's degree in Applied Criminology. During her work of more than a decade in the field of corrections and criminology, she directed residential and community programs for offenders, and worked as a research consultant specializing in the area of women in conflict with the law. She currently teaches at Algonquin College in Ottawa.

SHEELAGH COOPER, B.A., M.C.A., is a former coordinator of Female Offender Programs for the Correctional Service of Canada. She now lives in Bermuda, is chair of the Coalition for the Protection of Children, and recently authored the book *Child Maltreatment in Bermuda*.

KARLENE FAITH has been doing research and working with women in prison since the early 1970s in the United States and Canada. She has a Ph.D. in History of Consciousness from the University of California at Santa Cruz and is now on the faculty of the School of Criminology at Simon Fraser University. Her book *Unruly Women: The Politics of Confinement and Resistance* is forthcoming from Press Gang Publishers in 1993.

SHELLEY A.M. GAVIGAN is an associate professor of Law at Osgoode Hall Law School, York University. Her research centres on women, law, and the state, and she has written a number of journal articles in this area. With Jane Jenson and Janine Brodie she recently published *The Politics of Abortion in Canada* (Oxford University Press, 1992).

HOLLY JOHNSON is a senior analyst with the Canadian Centre for Justice Statistics. The focus of her work is the statistical analysis of criminal justice data. She has a special interest in violence against women and in women offenders, and is the author of several publications in these areas.

CAROL LAPRAIRIE is with the Aboriginal Justice Directorate, Department of Justice. She has a Ph.D. in Sociology and an M.A. in Criminology, and has worked in the area of Aboriginal criminal justice for the past thirteen years.

THE NATIVE WOMEN'S ASSOCIATION OF CANADA (NWCA) is a non-profit organization founded with the collective goal to enhance, promote, and foster the social, economic, cultural, and political well-being of First Nations and Métis women within First Nations and Canadian societies.

SHEILA NOONAN is an assistant professor of Law at Queen's University. She is currently vice-president of the Canadian Association of Elizabeth Fry Societies and has been involved for many years in issues relating to women and criminal justice.

KAREN RODGERS has worked and been a volunteer with the Canadian and Ottawa Elizabeth Fry societies. For the Task Force on Federally Sentenced Women, she interviewed women in P4W and women on release across Canada. Currently, she is an analyst for the Canadian Centre for Justice Statistics, where her work centres on violence against women.

FRANCES M. SHAVER is an assistant professor in the Department of Sociology and Anthropology at Concordia University. She teaches courses in criminology, the social construction of sexuality, and research methods. She has been working on issues related to prostitution and sex work since 1983 and is currently involved in a project comparing sex work to other forms of service work.

MARGARET SHAW has worked as a criminologist and social policy advisor since 1964 in England and Canada. As an independent research consultant, she has a particular interest in women in conflict with the law, and has undertaken a number of studies of women's imprisonment in Canada. She teaches at Concordia University and is a research associate at the Simone de Beauvoir Institute in Montreal.

PRESS GANG PUBLISHERS FEMINIST CO-OPERATIVE is committed to producing quality books with social and literary merit. We priorize Canadian women's work and include writing by lesbians and by women from diverse cultural and class backgrounds. Our list features vital and provocative fiction, poetry and non-fiction. A free catalogue is available from Press Gang Publishers, 101 – 225 East 17th, Vancouver, B.C. V5V 1A6 Canada.